Bumbling Through the Hindu Kush

A Memoir of Fear and Kindness in Afghanistan

Chris Woolf

ISBN-13: 978-1-7375303-5-0

Library of Congress Control Number: 2021914644

A portion of the proceeds from this book is being donated to help Afghan children with disabilities (EnabledChildren.org), and to help clear landmines (HALOTrust.org).

All photos are by the author, unless otherwise noted.

Set in Palatino and Optima
Maps hand-drawn by Ellen J Keiter
Designed and edited by Ellen's Arts,
Wrentham, Massachusetts 02093

This book is dedicated to my daughter, Ellen,
who asked for it;

to my wife, Lynn, whose support made it possible;

to my Afghan friends,
and to the Afghan people more broadly.
Your kindness, generosity and hospitality know no bounds.

And to the memory of Muhammad Masum (1958-1993)
and to the Afghanistan he loved.

To finally put pen to paper creates a knot in my stomach.
Is it fear? Excitement? A tear of happiness wells in my eye.
How can a short story from so long ago
still create so much emotion?
Instantly.

Franklin, Massachusetts.
July 1st 2020

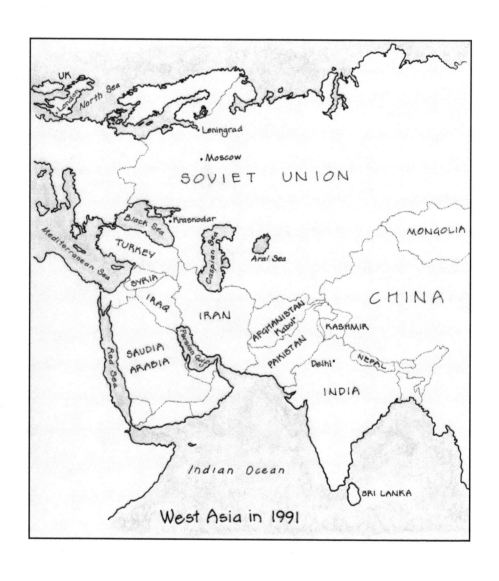

West Asia in 1991

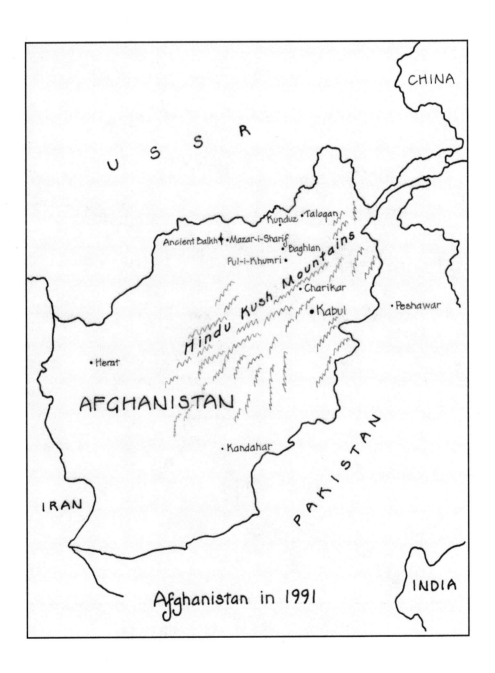

CHINA

U S S R

Kunduz •Taloqan
Ancient Balkh⚑ •Mazar-i-Sharif
•Baghlan
Pul-i-Khumri •

Hindu Kush Mountains

•Charikar

• Peshawar

•Kabul

• Herat

AFGHANISTAN

• Kandahar

PAKISTAN

IRAN

INDIA

Afghanistan in 1991

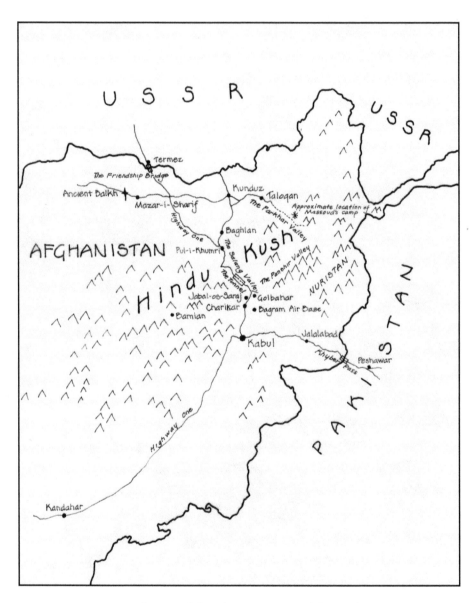

Northeast Afghanistan, 1991, with roads

Contents

Contents

Author's Note

Afghanistan has seen many epic battles. The Macedonian King, Alexander the Great, conquered Bactriana and occupied its already ancient and splendid capital, Balkh, in 329 BCE, before passing over the rugged Hindu Kush mountains[1] on his way to invade India. An entire British army brigade was defeated and routed in a single day at Maiwand in 1880[2], a major humiliation for Queen Victoria's Empire. More recently, in the 1980s, the legendary Afghan warrior, Ahmed Shah Massoud and his rag-tag rebel army, withstood no less than nine assaults by the Red Army of the Soviet Union[3] into his home turf in the Panjshir Valley.

No such epic historical episodes took place during my short visit to Afghanistan in November 1991. Indeed, Balkh was far less splendid by the time that I bumbled through the Hindu Kush, 2,320 years after Alexander, and to much less purpose. But it was an epic historical episode for me personally. Those ten days changed my life.

I was there to see if I would like the life of a foreign correspondent. I had been a journalist with the BBC World Service for a couple of years, and it was time to try something a little different. One of my peers, a friend called Chris Bowers, had got the job of Kabul

---

[1]South of the Hindu Kush, Alexander founded the city of Kandahar, named after him, in 330BC. He was known as Sekander or Iskander in this part of the world.

[2]The Afghan heroine of Maiwand, 27th July 1880, was a woman called Malala, who inspired Afghan troops to persist during a setback in the battle. The women's rights activist Malala Yousafzai is named after her.

[3]For an example of Western coverage of Massoud's resistance in the Panjshir, see: "Guerrillas survive biggest attack yet as Soviets roar into Panjshir Valley," June 22, 1982, by Edward Girardet, special correspondent of The Christian Science Monitor. [csmonitor.com/1982/0622/062233.html]

correspondent, and had been out there in the Afghan capital for a few months. I thought it would be a good idea to take some vacation time to visit him and see what that life was like.

The walls of ancient Balkh as they looked in the 1990s.
Photo: Alex Shaw

I made the mistake of suggesting to my buddy, Chris (sorry it gets confusing, having two principal characters called Chris) that it would be nice to see a bit of the country outside of Kabul, thinking we would fly from one safely-held government-run city to another. Instead, we hitched a ride with an aid convoy, and bumbled straight into the war.

What followed may seem very ordinary to anybody who has lived or worked in a war zone, or who grew up in one. I have many journalist friends who have endured much more danger, hardship and terror than I encountered. I salute you all for your courage and endurance in the service of the public. Most of my friends who served in the military in Iraq and Afghanistan have of course seen far, far worse. I salute you, too, and thank you for your service. Moreover, during my career as a journalist, I have come to know hundreds of people living in war zones, and befriended not a few, as I have shared their stories.

But this was *my* experience of war, and its traumas and horrors. The blood. The helplessness. I had been a soldier and yet I was still totally unprepared for war, psychologically. I was untrained and unprepared. An innocent abroad.

Author's Note

So, after many years of nightmares and reflections, I've finally written down my experiences for posterity, principally at the urging of my daughter, Ellen. To that end, I have written this book with her in mind. I am guessing, dear reader, that you have no knowledge of the news industry or Afghanistan, or war. I want it to be accessible to all.

Afghanistan specialists might still enjoy reading this little memoir, even though it's written for a lay audience. After the shambolic US withdrawal from Afghanistan, I share my observations of the situation that unfolded the last time a superpower pulled out.

Perhaps the broader public may enjoy it, too, if you're curious to know what it's like to be helpless and adrift in a combat zone, or if you'd like to learn a little about Afghanistan. It may also give readers a little insight into the difficulties of coping with traumatic stress. I only had a taste of war, but it has echoed through my life. For many veterans and survivors of trauma, it's so much harder to come back.

I hope this little work may also serve as a timely reminder of why war and civil conflict should be dreaded. I felt real fear and insecurity over there, and so it annoys the heck out of me when people make light of starting a civil war here in my adoptive homeland, the United States. You have no idea what you're talking about. Your fear—or curiosity to see what it's like—could wreck the lives of millions, in ways you cannot imagine.

Acknowledgements
and Apologia

I must acknowledge the incomparable production team who made this book a reality: in particular my editor, Ellen Keiter, Poppy Moorhouse-Woolf, Ethan Gordon, Michael Brown, Dawn Ringel, plus the countless friends who generously gave me their advice and time. I must also recognize Ellen Keiter for her drafting skills, in preparing the maps that I hope will guide you on the journey.

Afghanistan experts may find fault with some of my observations and analyses, and I take all responsibility for that. I have researched and fact-checked as much as possible, but I do not claim to be an expert on the country's history and culture. I acknowledge I carry a massive weight of unconscious bias, having grown up in post-imperial Britain. I have tried to overcome it. I have also asked Afghan friends for help in identifying my mistakes and biases.

My particular thanks go to Qais Akbar Omar, author of *A Fort of Nine Towers,* for being so generous with his time and advice.

I'm also incredibly grateful to my old friends Jennifer Goren and Jane Selley Persad for taking the time to read the manuscript and provide so many useful suggestions. Any faults that remain are entirely mine. Finally, I must reserve the biggest thank you to my wife, Lynnie. Without her generosity, support and patience this Bumbling Book would never have seen the light of day.

Quick Reference Guide
to the Principal Characters

Chris Woolf—Me, myself and I. BBC World Service broadcast journalist, and former Territorial Army infantryman. Bumbler-in-chief.

Chris Bowers—BBC World Service correspondent in Kabul. My buddy.

Muhammad Masum—The BBC's journalist and translator (fixer) in Kabul. Our friend. Not to be confused with Massoud.

Ahmed Shah Massoud—Legendary guerrilla warrior. The Lion of the Panjshir. Leader of the *Jamiat-i-Islami* faction of the Mujahidin (Warriors of the Holy Struggle), the rebels resisting the the Soviet invasion and communist government.

Dr Abdullah, or Abdullah Abdullah—Head of the Shura-e-Nazar, or "reconstruction council" of rebel-held northern Afghanistan. Aide to Ahmed Shah Massoud. Later himself Chief Executive of Afghanistan.

Fred Estall—A senior United Nations official in Kabul; a bulldog of a man; a former soldier in the New Zealand army; always wears his Australian/New Zealand Army Corps (ANZAC) slouch hat.

Alex Shaw—Member of the HALO Trust, the volunteer de-mining group. Former British army officer in the 6th Gurkha Rifles.

Dr Haidar—Head of the Red Cross/Red Crescent in Taloqan.

Osman—A truck driver with the United Nations.

Quick Reference Guide to the Principle Characters

Islam-ud-Din / Nikolai Bystrov—A Soviet Prisoner of War / Missing in Action (POW / MIA), who became Massoud's bodyguard.

Nek Muhammad / Gennadi Tseuma or Tsevma—Another Soviet POW / MIA.

Valentin Gatsinski—The Bulgarian ambassador to Afghanistan.

Political Figures
Mentioned in the Text

Mikhail Gorbachev—The last leader of the Soviet Union, 1985-91. The man who ended the Cold War.

Muhammad Najibullah—Comrade Najib. The Soviet-backed President of the Democratic Republic of Afghanistan, 1987-92. Hanged from a lamppost in 1996, aged 49.

Gulbuddin Hekmatyar—Leader of the Mujahidin group, *Hezbe-e-Islami*, lifelong rival (and occasional ally) to Ahmed Shah Massoud. Looks like the actor, Christopher Lee. A monster.

Sayed Jafar Naderi—The rock 'n' roll governor of Baghlan province, "Jeff," son of the head of the Ismaili Shia sect in Afghanistan, who controlled the Highway to Hell. Looks like John Belushi.

Sayed Mansur Naderi—The stern head of the Ismaili Shia sect in Afghanistan; father of the fun-loving governor of Baghlan, a province in northeastern Afghanistan.

Abdul Rashid Dostum—The ultimate survivor. Warlord leader of the Uzbek militia in Afghanistan, the Jowzjanis.

Ronald Reagan—President of the United States, 1981-89.

Margaret Thatcher—British Prime Minister, 1979-90.

Prologue

It's after lunch by the time the white four-ton truck of the United Nations rolls into town. The letters "UN" are painted loudly in blue on the side and front. It's a comforting sight. Maybe we will be able to get back to Kabul before the snows close the mountain passes.

The driver pulls up to my buddy and me. The dust settles. It's Osman. And he's clearly unhappy. I'm not sure if he's been on private business or what, but I get the impression he's been sent to pick us up against his will. We're unable to communicate. He speaks no English, and we don't speak enough Dari. There's no interpreter to help us clear the air.

I can feel the tension, but I'm not sure of its source. I know it will make for an uncomfortable ride. Two days or more. I could be wrong, but it feels like the trust between us is breaking down.

There's no time to worry about it. It's already late and we're a long way from our destination. We can't be on the road at night. Far too dangerous.

We grab our packs and hop up into the cab of the truck, next to Osman. My buddy gets in first and sits in the middle. I follow and take my place by the door. Life in wartime is a lottery of simple decisions about who sits where.

I don't know exactly where we are, or the route we'll be taking. We have no paper maps and of course Google maps are a thing of the future. We just have to trust Osman.

As we drive out of town, I can't help thinking how different I feel now, compared to the beginning of our road trip just a week ago. I have lost my innocence and sense of wonder. I've seen so much blood, and felt a degree of fear and helplessness that I have never felt before.

Prologue

I am anxious to get home. At the back of mind, I am a little concerned for my safety, thinking how Mum would take any bad news. Or whether anyone would ever even know if something happened to us out here, in the violent heart of central Asia. At the front of my mind, I'm feeling more pressure to get back to work in London on time, and to simply reassure my wife and family that I'm still alive. Add to all that this new unexplained tension with Osman.

Despite all these unspoken anxieties, there is a tremendous sense of relief that we've finally begun the journey home. I push the dark thoughts away, and concentrate on the scenery.

The snow-capped mountains of the Hindu Kush lie on the horizon. In front of us, and all around us is a giant dusty plain.

This part of Afghanistan looks like the Star Wars desert planet, Tatooine—at least at this season of the year. I have traveled a fair deal in Europe, Africa and India, but this looks and feels thoroughly alien to everything I have ever experienced. You can see fields and meadows that might bloom green after the spring floods. But now, on the eve of winter, green is just a memory. Everything is dusty, dry, brown or khaki. The homes, made from adobe are the same. Their flat roofs and small windows evoke images from childhood Bible stories, or of Tusken raiders. There are few people to be seen. Not much life at all, besides the occasional herd of goats. The only signs of modernity are long, flat concrete bridges over empty river beds. It's other-worldly. It's captivating.

The rebel checkpoints come and go. If the armed men wave us down, we slow to a crawl, and lean out of the window, shouting *"Moolee-mata-heed! Moolee-mata-heed!"*—"United Nations! United Nations!" in Dari. Usually it works, but sometimes we have to show our papers. We are traveling alone, not in a convoy, so we seem to be getting flagged down more often than not. I'm grateful that we're in a UN truck, with *bona fide* papers. I can't imagine how we'd get through without them.

For our driver, Osman, the checkpoints are clearly getting tiresome. He starts to tsk and mutter at the delays.

Up ahead we see a kid.

A goat herder.

Prologue

My guess is he's 13 or 14. His clothes are a little ragged. His sandaled feet are caked white with dust. His unkempt mop of black hair is also speckled with dust. He has life and death in his hands, in the form of an ancient looking AK-47.

He is flagging us down, but he seems to be alone. There is no roadblock; his goats are off to the side of the road. Osman tsks. My buddy urges him to slow down. But Osman has had enough of delays. I get the sense he thinks this is one "checkpoint" we can afford to ignore. He curses and pushes down on the accelerator. I gasp.

As we fly by, I can see the kid pulling the weapon up to his shoulder.

He opens fire.

Bumbling Through the Hindu Kush

A Memoir of Fear and Kindness in Afghanistan

Chris Woolf

Chapter 1

Why Did I Go?

"Why on earth did you go to Afghanistan?" I have heard that question many times.

Few people in the Western world routinely live with fear and trauma. Most of us remain blissfully isolated from terror. We go about our lives in an illusory bubble of security. We don't know what it's like. Our ideas are often misinformed by Hollywood theatrics.

Then there are those of us who do face trauma, whether from an abusive partner, or a deployment to a combat zone. I don't mean occasional moments of terror, like a car crash or a mugging, but rather the state of living in a world where pain, death or dismemberment can come at any moment from anywhere. Imagine living in a minefield, where any step could prove fatal. You just never know if this breath is your last.

Unlike in Hollywood, I believe most of us deal with such mortal danger without screams and panic. Most of us meet it with courage and quiet calm. We persist. We overcome. We do our jobs. People might praise us for our strength or thank us for our service. But we still feel the terror. It will always be there. Lurking.

This is something I have felt myself. I had a taste of fear and trauma during my time in Afghanistan. I really can't complain. It was nothing compared to that faced by combat veterans or survivors of abuse. But even though it pales in comparison to these, I definitely had that experience. We drove through a minefield. We saw death. I was shot at. I had to summon all my courage to deal with certain situations. At other times I felt trapped and powerless and paranoid.

My hope with this book is that some of you might learn a little, which in turn may help you understand veterans and other survivors of trauma in some small way.

It's also a coming-of-age story. I had served in the military and yet I was quite unprepared mentally for Afghanistan and war. The experience transformed me.

Afghanistan has been the scene of America's longest war, by far. US special forces first dropped into the Hindu Kush within weeks of the al-Qaeda terror attacks on September 11th 2001. President Biden pulled the last troops out on 31st August 2021. Almost twenty years of war. Americans still need to understand the country, since it will remain an important foreign policy issue. America left a friendly regime in Kabul that fell quickly to a violent challenge from the Taliban and the Islamic State. The situation is an interesting contrast with that left behind by the Soviet Union after Moscow's withdrawal in 1989, with a friendly regime facing the Mujahidin rebels. That was when I made my trip.

The roots of the violence in Afghanistan are deep. I hope this book can also make some small contribution to understanding those roots.

ꙮ ꙮ ꙮ

In the summer of 1991, I turned 27. I was a skinny little geek, obsessed with war, history, and international affairs.

In that sense, I had the perfect job, in the newsroom of the BBC World Service. My role as a chief sub-editor was to decide what was newsworthy and write about it for a global audience. As its name implies, the World Service brings the best of BBC news to the world, in English and dozens of other languages. The job required intense depth and breadth of knowledge of world history, geography, politics and economics—as well as the ability to discern the critical elements of a story, and write them up under pressure. This was back when news was a little more newsy; when we just explained what was going on and why it mattered, instead of the occasional preference today for sharing feelings and opinions.

So I was in my element. But you don't move forward by standing still, and there seemed to be a couple of avenues open to advance my

4

career. One was to move into live programming: producing live radio news shows. The other was to try the more daring and dashing life of a foreign correspondent. It was time for me to examine that option.

I had joined the main World Service Newsroom in 1989, but I had already been working for the BBC (the "Beeb") for a couple of years prior to that. For the most part I had been at Bush House, the elegant headquarters of the BBC World Service in central London, where I began my BBC life as a humble researcher. Breaking out from that role had required entering an arena of ruthless competition.

My first break was winning a six-month stint as a sub-editor at the BBC Monitoring Service, which had its own stately headquarters at Caversham, in the countryside west of London. My job there was writing up news copy from intercepted foreign broadcasts, which seemed very glamorous, especially as we were partnered with international intelligence agencies.

I'd then spent another six months as a trainee "talks" writer back at Bush House—"Bush" as we affectionately called it—writing analysis pieces for the "Current Affairs-Talks" department.

I applied for a job in the main newsroom and failed. Repeatedly. Nevertheless, I persisted, and in 1989 I succeeded in getting freelance work. This meant working on the off days at my other jobs. So it required some stamina, determination and resilience. But I was already married and mortgaged, and had no family financial safety net. My father passed away in 1988 at the frightfully young age of 56. If I was going to succeed and be able to provide for a family, I could only do so through my own effort. That meant being willing to absorb the rejections and defeats and to keep trying, again and again.

Eventually I must have proved my worth, as I finally landed a full-time job in the World Service Newsroom at Bush House. I was honoured. It was one of the most prestigious journalism jobs in the world. The building itself, Bush House, was a thing of glory, all marble floors and Greek columns. Our motto was "Nation shall speak peace unto nation." We were trusted around the world, and feared by the enemies of truth. There was a lot to live up to.

Those were astonishing times to be in the news business, what with the fall of the Berlin wall and the release of Nelson Mandela from prison in South Africa. The old order, established in the aftermath of World War II, was breaking down. Then came Saddam Hussein's test of the new international order, with his invasion of Kuwait, and the united international response led by George H.W. Bush, still perhaps the best US president of my lifetime.

The newsroom was always filled with a thick fog of tobacco smoke. It seemed to be populated with two kinds of people. Eager young cubs, such as myself, or grizzled journalistic veterans. Most of the young cubs had solid experience in local journalism, like my buddy Chris Bowers, or backgrounds that sounded quite exotic to me at the time, such as the cluster of journalists who came to Bush House from Swiss Radio International at around the same time that I first passed through those creaky old doors.

The old grizzled set were mostly men who had served overseas for decades, usually with international wire services like Reuters or Agence France Presse (AFP), and casually exchanged stories of hair-breadth escapes from the Viet Cong or the forces of the Ayatollah, or in Biafra or the Belgian Congo. Their stories made it clear that working as a foreign correspondent could be dangerous and exciting.

It was deeply satisfying work. It felt like I could have an impact. I distinctly remember the moment I realized this, when a student dissident in Madagascar was released from jail the day after I had written a story on him.

I loved it. I found local news and British politics tiresome, and only wanted to work in international news. So I felt doubly blessed.

I did not have a journalism background, *per se*. So in that sense, I felt a little isolated, a bit of an outsider, as I have for most of my life.

৪◈৪ ৪◈৪ ৪◈৪

Let me tell you a few things about me and where I came from, so you can form some idea of this person who was about to go blundering off to war.

I've always felt like a misfit. I was a middle child, and like many such children, I felt a little neglected. I was fine with that. I learned early to rely on myself for entertainment and income.

My parents were neither poor nor rich, but at an early age I learned never to ask for anything, as the answer was invariably no. If

6

I wanted anything, I had to earn my own money. So I've worked pretty darned hard since I was about 13. At 15, I desperately wanted to go on a proposed school trip to Italy, and through hard work and saving, I was able to pay my own way. I worked on the forecourt of a gas (petrol) station; went door-to-door selling double glazing and cavity wall insulation, as well as working retail. In the UK back then, kids could work at pretty much anything from the age of 14, outside of school hours.

Another difference that I felt in my childhood was that, unlike our friends, we seemed to have no real extended family. My parents both entered adulthood as only children. As far as I knew, growing up, we had no living grandparents, no uncles or aunts, no first cousins. We were on our own. (As an adult, I found my extended family, but that's another story!)

I felt rather out of place in my school years, too. I was the smart kid at a "secondary modern" school, where the prevailing ambition was for a life of manual labour. Americans would call it a public school, although that means something quite different in the UK—a private school for the privileged. I was the first kid from that school to go to university. As far as I know, I was the first kid from my family to achieve that distinction as well.

I was not sporty, and not terribly interested in soccer. That was quite isolating in England, let me tell you, which is generally pretty soccer-obsessed. It also made me something of a disappointment to my father.

I felt I was the only kid at school who didn't smoke, as I had already made the association between cigarettes and my father's morning coughing sessions. I survived the bullying that was typical of schools back then by making people laugh; somehow that got me a pass.

I was not especially sociable. I was often happiest alone in my room with my books and notepads, reading encyclopedias and history books, and planning world domination. I preferred watching TV to going to Cub Scouts.

Like many boys back then, I had an obsession with war, from as early as I can remember. We were still in the shadow of World War II. My childhood interest in military matters remained strong, and for a long time I thought the army might make a good career for me. At 15 and 16, I crossed the country by myself by train to attend interviews, with a view to becoming an army officer.

I don't think I made a great impression at Horse Guards, the army's historic headquarters in central London. I barely knew how to tie a tie; I did not come from a family of any consequence, and I didn't even go to a "real" school. I was disappointed in them, too, and resented the idea that class or family background should have any impact when assessing merit. I immediately dismissed their suggestion that someone of my background should apply for the transport or signal corps. To my mind, if you weren't in a combat branch, then it wasn't worth being in the army at all.

The officers at the Queen's Regimental headquarters in Canterbury were more encouraging, and urged me to follow my studies, take up a sport, and maybe join the Territorial Army (TA) to get some experience. (The TA is the UK's equivalent of the National Guard.)

So I did. I applied under-age, at 17, not only with a view to trying out a possible career, but also in the hopes of getting to Buenos Aires. You see, the Argentines had just invaded the Falkland Islands, a tiny British possession off the tip of South America. The country was at war!

As a digression, I must mention how we first heard about the coming of that war. My mum was working for an engineering company at the time, and I distinctly remember her coming home and saying some Argentine soldiers had landed on the British island of South Georgia, "and stolen all our scrap metal!" South Georgia was once a centre of the whaling industry, and my Mum's employer had somehow acquired the rights to all the leftover junk. Mum's announcement didn't make any sense till the next day when we heard that the "Argies" had also invaded the Falklands. I was working on the deli counter at a supermarket, and distinctly remember pulling Argentine corned beef off the shelves. I still have one of the signs we put out to display the company's reasoning.

Naïve as it sounds, I believed that military service was in some ways the ultimate fulfillment of life. I had been brought up with the idea that public service was a higher goal. To serve and defend one's community and country from its enemies was the highest form of public service.

Recruit selection for the Territorial Army was intense. The surge of patriotism in the country had created the largest number of volunteers my unit had ever seen. We spent the selection weekend being pushed to the limit. Finally, to get the numbers down, they decided to put us through the assault course, over and over, until enough of us had dropped out. On the third attempt, I fell off the monkey bars and twisted my ankle. I tightened up my boots and started over; completed the assault course, and then did it a fourth time. I was pleased the next day to be accepted as a private soldier into Her Majesty's Fifth (Volunteer) Battalion of the Queen's Regiment of foot, the most senior English regiment in the infantry of the line. My company commander—the man who decided to accept me into Her Majesty's service—was the late, great Major Richard Holmes, future general, author, historian and TV presenter. Training began at once, even though I could not be attested (sworn-in) till after my 18th birthday.

At the time, I was disappointed there was no invasion of Argentina. The war ended with liberation of the Falkland Islands. But it's unlikely our unit would ever have been deployed. The Territorial Army, or TA, is like the National Guard and exists only to help in real emergencies. Our primary role was to prepare to fight off an invasion by the Soviet Union and its allies in the Warsaw Pact. We were good enough for that. In fact, our unit was judged so competent that we were honoured to be the only frontline, NATO-committed, TA infantry battalion. On exercises such as the mammoth Operation Lionheart in 1984, we were duly deployed by plane, train and automobile to the inner German border, to dig trenches and lay wire, to be ready to hold back the Red Horde. Or at least provide them with a speed-bump, or so we joked.

I was the only grunt in my military unit who got accepted to university. So yes, I was again something of an outsider. But for the first and only time in my life did I feel that I truly belonged. I still count my old comrades as friends and would do anything for them.

There was also the sense of trust. We were handed weapons on our first drill night, before we even got uniforms. I'd never seen or touched a real firearm before. Now I had the incredible destructive power of an L1A1 7.62mm semi-automatic self-loading rifle (SLR) in my hands. I came to love the one assigned to me, with its beautiful wooden stock.

Uniforms came soon after that, and it was about that time that the Provisional Irish Republican Army (IRA) began attacking Territorial Army drill halls. This was before I attended basic training, or "boot camp" as they say in America. I'd had just about enough training to know how to shoot my rifle, although I still had not mastered cleaning it properly. Even so, I was selected to take the first "stag," or guard duty. I was by myself, at the door, with my SLR, with five rounds in the mag and one "up the spout" (in the chamber).

Our drill hall opened right onto the Hanworth Road in Hounslow, in west London. The neighbourhood was an old Irish one. Old-school Irish, so that men and women sat in different barrooms at the pub. It was a safe bet that some of our neighbours had pro-IRA sympathies.

I had no real instruction or guidance, and remember making up my own rules of engagement. I decided I would shoo away anyone who tried to park too close, and that I could fire for effect if anyone drove toward me in a hostile fashion, thinking I would shoot the driver if necessary. I was so ill-trained at that point, before boot camp, that I did not know it's much better to shoot the engine block rather than the driver. If you shoot the driver, the vehicle will probably just keep coming at you.

It was instructive to realize that just because someone has a uniform and a weapon, that doesn't mean they have any idea what they're doing. It would be a useful lesson.

As my hour on stag passed, I remember reflecting on the destructive power of our 7.62mm rounds, and kept recalling the detail of how they could penetrate 18 inches of brick. So I'm thinking, oh, if I fire, it could pass through that house and into that one, and maybe the next. I hope I don't hit any innocent civilians.

Of course, happily, the IRA never came for Hounslow Drill Hall. And thankfully, the Red Army never crossed the inner German border.

I have digressed horribly, but I have dwelt for a while on my humble military career to show a little bit about me and the times. It shows that I knew a little about soldiering, which would be helpful to my career in journalism. I didn't know much, but I knew some of the threats one could face on different types of ground and at different times of day; I could just about distinguish the sounds of small arms, artillery, rockets and mortars; I knew the outline shapes of many Soviet tanks and other armoured vehicles. I knew how devilish the Soviets could be with landmines. It also highlights the sense of imminent disaster that hung over all of us during the Cold War, with its threat of sudden nuclear annihilation. But most of all, looking back, it makes me realize just how naïve I was about war.

I started on this military digression talking about my life as a misfit. That continued and perhaps intensified at university, where I was one of only a handful of lower-middle class kids at an overwhelmingly upper-class institution, Cambridge University. I never felt like I fitted in or belonged there.

I had been fortunate enough to get into Cambridge by the active help and assistance of a mentor at my Sixth Form college, Mrs Butler. Sixth Form is the collective term for your junior and senior years at high school. Quite often in England, Sixth Form is a different school from your secondary school, since most British kids back then were expected to end their education at age 16.

Before I met Mrs Butler, the idea of going to university had never occurred to me. I had no idea what I wanted to do, besides a possible military career. I was vaguely aware that accumulating as much education as possible was "a good thing." Mrs Butler was my history teacher, and had studied for a year in Germany soon after World War II, so she had some great life experiences to share. She ran the school's "Oxbridge" project. She helped the most gifted students apply to the greatest colleges in the land, Oxford (spit) and Cambridge. For some reason, she took a shine to me. I passed Cambridge University's entrance exams with distinction, and survived the interview.

I was also lucky that Cambridge and Oxford were under political pressure to accept more kids from state schools. About 95% of kids in England back then attended state schools and 5% went to those posh public (private) schools, and yet at Oxford and Cambridge, more than 50% of the undergraduates came from those private schools of privilege, and most others from fancy grammar schools. Privilege and discrimination have always been there.

The misfit years continued at the BBC where, as I mentioned, I began my career as a researcher, and had climbed into the newsroom without any solid journalistic credentials only through sheer persistence, hard work and my knowledge of world affairs, history and geography. My commitment to the mission of bringing accurate news to the world was deep and sincere. I yearned above all to be a truth-teller, to provide the public with reliable information. I had earned my place in the newsroom, but I still needed to prove it. Not so much to my bosses and my peers, but mostly to myself.

I was never a particularly tough guy, in terms of getting into fights and such. But I pushed myself hard in terms of endurance and stamina. In the army, I competed for, and won, a spot on the unit's endurance marching team. We got a medal for completing the Nijmegen Vierdaagse march in the Netherlands in 1983. I did a parachute course. I finished climbing Mount Kilimanjaro in 1989 despite the onset of a severe case of the runs at 17,000 feet (5200 meters). I saw myself as mentally tough. I could keep going.

So just to re-cap, I considered myself a fairly resilient, self-reliant, well-read, experienced chap, with some military knowledge, before I went to Afghanistan.

I was still utterly unprepared for war.

Chapter Two

Why Afghanistan?

But why Afghanistan, I hear you ask? Did you have to go somewhere quite so dangerous?

Well, I guess it's all about who you know. My colleague, Chris Bowers, joined the newsroom of the BBC World Service at about the same time I did. We worked together on the Arab/Africa desk and elsewhere and soon became friends. In April 1991, he competed for the post of BBC "stringer" in Kabul, Afghanistan, and was duly appointed. Chris was the connection that drew me to the Hindu Kush.

The BBC World Service at the time had the largest and most extensive network of overseas reporters of any broadcast news organization on the planet. Not many of these journalists had full-time salaried jobs as foreign correspondents. Most were "stringers" of different kinds. A reporter was considered a stringer if he or she was a freelancer who was free to file for different outlets, or "strings." Usually they would be outlets that did not compete with us on the radio, so, say, a news agency, a newspaper, or a magazine.

When the World Service wanted first-call on a reporter's time they would make him or her a "sponsored stringer," meaning they would get a monthly retainer and an allowance toward their living expenses. Then they would have to file their stories to us before filing for any of their other strings. You would still be referred to as the "BBC correspondent in XYZ" and your job back home would usually be held open for you, but technically you were freelance.

Most of the BBC's sponsored stringer posts were in unpleasant places and usually went to eager young cubs in our newsroom willing to make a name for themselves. They would be given a year's leave of absence. These positions, like everything in the BBC, were highly competitive.

If appointed, you would get the job, some recording equipment, a ticket, and then be sent on your way. There was no safety training back then to help you survive as a reporter in a hostile environment, like a war zone. There was zero instruction on how to handle potentially lethal interactions like checkpoints, or how to spot hazards, or how to react to hostile fire.

Nobody was issued personal protective equipment, like a helmet or body armour. I remember one old hack telling me that he had survived the Bangladeshi War of Independence in 1971 by wearing a pink shirt. No one, he said, would think you were a combatant if you were wearing a pink shirt.

Communications were a joke. You would have to depend on telephone landlines, or—if you were lucky—a telex machine. There were no radios to be had, no satellite phones, let alone cell phones. If you wanted to send audio, you had to send it by mail or courier.

I remember reading a management handout in which the World Service bragged that no correspondent or stringer had ever died in its service, up to that point. Looking back, given the lack of training, one can only conclude they were incredibly lucky.

Those were different times, though. In the main, journalists back then were not usually targets themselves. No one was gunning for you. Usually. The journalistic code of objective neutrality was a defence all of its own. Actors in conflict zones perceived foreign journalists as tools that could be used for conveying messages and for managing their image. Even nations and actors hostile to your own government tended to treat foreign journalists somewhat respectfully, in the hopes of making an impact on international public opinion. Look at the journalists entertained by Saddam Hussein in Baghdad during the First Gulf War in 1990-91.

There was always, of course, the risk of accidents and of getting caught in crossfire; and there was always real danger for reporters who personally witnessed an atrocity which the perpetrators wished to cover up. Some journalists might also be mistaken for spies. But we were not usually targets *per se*.

That shifted during my career, starting with the wars in the former Yugoslavia in the 1990s and during the genocide in Rwanda, as violent actors struggled to control the narrative. But the real game changers for reporter security were the attacks on 9/11, and in particular, the invasion of Iraq in 2003, when ideological extremism and desperation were added to the mix. Since then, journalists themselves have become targets for bad actors, as they were now seen as representatives of hostile powers or hostile narratives. I've lost far too many colleagues and acquaintances in the last 15 or 20 years. Good people. Sadly missed.

That was all in the future. In 1991 the main risks were accidents, crime, crossfire and suspicion of espionage. Oh, and landmines. Let me tell you, that's plenty!

Anyway, my buddy Chris was now in Kabul. Communications were impossible. There was no dependable telephone line. For weeks at a time there was no line at all. The only way we could communicate was through telex.

Now gather round and listen, children. A telex machine was a wondrous piece of technology and a mainstay of international journalism in 1991. At a time when faxes and photocopiers were still new-fangled and clunky pieces of technology, the telex machine could send messages across the world to any other telex machine. You could type into your telex machine and your words could print out on the machine on the other side of the world. They were hard-wired, needing a physical wire like telegraphs, hence "wire copy." They had this wonderful quirk where if you pushed the wrong button when sending or printing, the keyboard would flip and all your words became gobbledygook. Luckily, experienced operators could read, or at least figure out, what had been intended.

I had a fair bit of experience with telexed wire copy while "copy-tasting" in the newsroom at Bush House, and as a trainee in the Talks unit. As a copy-taster, you get first "taste" of the "copy." All the main newswires were printed in triplicate on carbon paper, and the ink on the back of each sheet instantly turned the hands and fingers of the copy-taster black. That was why one of the most important jobs in the room was usually done by junior level folks.

But I did not have free access to a telex machine to send messages. I would have to curry favour with the newsroom's telex operators, who were not the most sociable people.

After Chris had been deployed for about a month, he sent a telex message to say hello. I persuaded a telex operator to send one back saying hello, too, and asking what it was like. He sent a brief reply, to the effect that it was great, can't explain, you should come see for yourself.

From this seed, the idea took root about doing just that—making a trip to Afghanistan.

I'd been fascinated by Afghanistan since I was a kid, as it was one of the few powers on the planet that had resisted the might of the British empire at its height. Now, history appeared to have repeated itself with the Soviet invasion. Being the nerd that I am, 1 knew a rough outline of the country's history, geography and culture, the languages spoken and the main political currents. As I do for most places in the world.

A trip would do several things. It would pique my curiosity to see Afghanistan; I would catch up with my buddy; and I would see if I liked the life of a foreign correspondent.

So I started planning.

I had no idea how it would change my life.

8◊3　8◊3　8◊3

It takes a while to set up a trip like this.

First, I had to broach the idea with my wife. She definitely did not want to come. We had had a rough trip to India the year before and had got caught up in violent unrest. High-caste Indians rioted and even set themselves on fire to protest the findings of a thing called "The Mandal Commission." That was an official Commission of Inquiry that had suggested guaranteeing quotas of government jobs for low caste people and Dalits, then still known as "Untouchables"— the original outcastes. Our planned itinerary had been disrupted by protesters blocking roads, burning barricades of tires, staging mass demonstrations, and ripping up railroad tracks. At one point, government soldiers had presented their rifles, ready to fire, while we were trapped in front of them in a vehicle stranded among demonstrators on a narrow mountain road. Thankfully, the crowd dispersed without anyone opening fire.

However, my wife was supportive of a trip to somewhere like Afghanistan by myself. She understood it could be useful for my career, and my career was critical to our prosperity and plans for a family.

Next, I had to research how to physically make the journey. There were no direct flights to Afghanistan from Britain, or from any other hostile power at the time. Don't forget, the Cold War cast a shadow over things as simple as travel and transportation; and the UK under Prime Minister Margaret Thatcher had been a firm ally of Ronald Reagan's America in opposing Soviet aggression in Afghanistan.

The best jumping-off spot seemed to be India. India was a socialist country, but it was neutral in the Cold War, and maintained relatively good relations with the West, as well as the Soviet Union and its allies, such as Afghanistan. The Indian capital, Delhi, was the closest place to which I could fly directly from London, and be reasonably assured of getting an onward flight to Kabul.

There were a couple of hops from Delhi to Kabul every week. No Indian airline made the trip. The route required flying over Pakistan, and relations between India and Pakistan were pretty tense at the time. No, the only airline on that route was Afghanistan's own airline: Ariana. There was a great travel agency among the shops on the ground floor of Bush House which would be able to secure a ticket for that leg of the journey when the time was ripe.

Then I had to save up my pennies. I was pretty broke back then, and all our money went to the mortgage. My wife worked for British Airways at the time, so I had the privilege of being eligible to fly for ten per cent of the cost of the standard single fare, if I was willing to travel on stand-by. But that still added up to a fair chunk of change, about 20% of the cost of an economy fare. That could get me to India, at least.

I would need to pay full fare for the onward connection to Kabul. More money! My buddy there, Chris Bowers, had said I could stay with him, but obviously I'd have to pay for a hotel while in Delhi. On top of that, there was the cost of ground transportation and food, and all the contingencies that might come up when traveling standby. I was on a very tight budget.

Then there was the issue of paperwork. How do I legally get to visit a country like Afghanistan? There was no tourism, of course. The place was a war zone. Besides which, you can't ethically work as a journalist on a tourist visa. You would risk getting arrested, potentially embarrassing your employer and your country. It had been drilled into us that wherever we went, we were ambassadors for the BBC and in a sense, the UK.

So I applied for a journalist visa for Afghanistan. That was done via a letter written on an old-fashioned typewriter and sent by mail to whom it may concern at the Afghan Embassy in London. There were no travel websites back then, no downloadable forms. I had to look up the mailing address in a thing called a phone book—a giant tome in which were collected the names, phone numbers and addresses of residents and businesses in a particular town. I explained the purpose of my visit and gave the rough timeframe in which I hoped to be traveling. I enclosed a letter from my boss at Bush, the late lamented Val Anderson, verifying my identity and my position, and which she had very formally rubber-stamped. (Literally, an official stamp, dipped in ink and stamped on a document). Then the waiting began.

The visa was mainly a device to get permission to travel, as I expected that any news we witnessed would be covered by my friend, Chris Bowers, as the correspondent. I was there to observe, or so I thought.

Eventually a letter came back from the Afghan embassy, inviting me for an interview on November 1st—in just one week!

I had to start running around like a headless chicken.

First, I needed to get a visa for India. I couldn't be certain how quickly I could make the connection to Kabul, so I might need to stay in Delhi for a few days. Permission was needed for any kind of travel to India back then. Sounds simple enough, you might think, but getting a visa was always an adventure in itself. The Indian High Commission in London was right next door to Bush House, thankfully, but the process was comically cumbersome and bureaucratic. It involved queuing up in long lines on multiple occasions to drop off applications, fees, documents and then again, once approved, to collect the stamps in my passport. To make things worse, I needed a multiple-entry visa, as I would be passing through Delhi on the way out and on the way back. That required queuing for another window. On more than one occasion I had to apologize to my supervisor for being late back to my desk at work. Travel is so much easier today. Many of these bureaucratic obstacles have been negotiated away.

Looking at my passport, the timeline was insane. The Indian visa was issued on Thursday October 31st, and was valid for six months. That was a relief! At least I could get to India, if the Afghan visa came through.

՞◈Յ   ՞◈Յ   ՞◈Յ

The next day, Friday November 1st, is cold, grey and damp like most days in London. I put on my only jacket and tie—the same one I use for weddings and funerals and job interviews—and head across town to the Embassy of the Democratic Republic of Afghanistan. The entire embassy is just a Georgian row house in a fashionable neighbourhood. It's what Americans would call a townhouse. I'm taken aback. It looks like a private home. Do I have the right place? I check the address on my notepad. It's the right number. I straighten myself up, and knock.

The heavy black door creaks open and a young man in a suit appears.

"Yes?"

"Hi. I'm Chris Woolf from the BBC, and I'm applying for a visa."

He shows me in. It's just a dimly lit hallway, with some old black and white photographs of Afghanistan on the walls.

There are no queues, and no chaos, in stark contrast to the Indian High Commission. It's eerily quiet.

"Please to take a seat."

There are a couple of hard wooden chairs. I sit down, briefcase on my lap, as my host slips through a tall, heavy door. I'm on a deadline to get back to the office, but I know the importance of enforced waiting in certain cultures. I take a moment to breathe and study the photos on the wall. Landscapes and palaces mostly.

At length, my host returns. I'm ushered into a dark office where I meet a serious looking, clean shaven, older gentleman in a dark three-piece suit and heavy, black-rimmed glasses. I take a seat on the other side of his cluttered desk. There may even have been tea. He asks to see my passport and he politely inquires as to my intentions and my background. I charm him as best I can, but of course in that quiet, humble-brag, understated English way.

"You were at Cambridge? Which college?"

"Queens'," I answer.

He seems suspicious at first, and I feel like this could easily go either way. I can feel my stomach tightening. I suddenly realize how much I really want this.

He leans toward me, his hands clasped.

"You understand, of course, that affairs in my country are . . . complicated?"

"Yes, sir, I do. That's why I think it's important for people like me to visit and try to understand what's really going on, so we can explain it properly."

He nods. I can't tell if he thinks I'm sincere or not.

"And you are aware that life there can be . . . dangerous?"

"Yes," I reply. "I'm aware."

He unclasps his hands and reaches into a drawer. I flinch a little, unsure what he's doing. He pulls out a giant stamp, dabs it in ink and thumps it into my passport. It takes up a full page. It's in English on the left, and Dari (the official language of Afghanistan) on the right.

It's my visa!

He writes in the dates, in English and Dari. It's valid for the next six months, but it's good for only a one week stay. In other words, I can travel at any time in the next six months, but I can only stay legally in Afghanistan for a single week. Oh, the headaches that will cause!

The man across the desk smiles for the first time, as he hands me back my passport.

"Enjoy your trip!"

"I will. Thank you. I hear it's beautiful."

"It is. It is."
I am pumped! I am going to Afghanistan!

၆◇၃ ၆◇၃ ၆◇၃

I rush back to the office and call my wife. I have a week of vacation coming up, by coincidence. We have nothing planned. Should I try to go now, if I can get the additional time I need? She agrees.

I rush over to Colin, the schedule administrator, and beg and plead for extra time off. I am pretty junior on the totem pole, so I don't have much leverage. Remember, the newsroom works 24/7, and any absence makes everybody else's life much harder. He agrees to a handful of extra days, but I have to be back for a shift on Thursday, 14th November.

"No later!" Colin adds. "Don't forget any unauthorized absence can lead to disciplinary action."

I run downstairs to the travel agent in the basement and get my ticket from Delhi to Kabul and back. There's a flight on Tuesday! My wife gets me a standby ticket from London to Delhi from her friend in the British Airways reservations office.

Then I haggle with the newsroom telex operators and manage to persuade them to send a message to Chris Bowers in Kabul, that I am coming sometime in the next week.

Foolishly, I include the thought that it would be nice to see something of the country outside of the capital, Kabul. I assume it would be obvious I mean that we should fly safely from one government-held city to another. How I laugh, looking back.

I get no reply, no acknowledgement. Telexes are temperamental, so I can't even be sure that Chris has seen the message. I'm embarking on this journey without being really sure that my host will even know that I'm coming!

I get back to work. I happen to be copy-tasting that day. As I mentioned, that's where you, as a junior member of the newsroom staff, do the dirty but important work of taking a first glance at the wire copy coming in off the teleprinters. The carbon paper instantly turns your hands black.

A wire story catches my eye, datelined Kabul. It's not very long, maybe three paragraphs. A Tupelov-154 airliner belonging to Afghanistan's national airline, Ariana, has been hit by mortar fire after landing at Kabul International Airport. The story says this shows just how close the rebel Mujahidin have now penetrated toward the capital. The mortar bombs damaged the tail fin of the plane, making it unusable. The wire copy continued with the nugget that, as a result of this attack, Ariana has been left with only one airworthy plane.

Well then, I say to myself, I guess that's my ride for next week!

I decide not to share the story with my wife. I do check my company pension plan to see how much she would get if my career is cut short. Just in case. It's not bad. She would get a decent pension for life.

Chapter 3

Afghanistan in 1991

Before we get back to the narrative, let me tell you a few things about Afghanistan in 1991.

When I was born, in 1964, Afghanistan was a happy place in a hostile world.

It was still a kingdom. To the north lay the great communist power, the Union of Soviet Socialist Republics (USSR) and to the east, the People's Republic of China. To the south and west lay the then staunch US allies, Pakistan and Iran.

The Cold War was at its height. The capitalist powers of the western world, led by the United States, confronted the communist powers led by the Soviet Union, vying for world domination. The West sought to contain the spread of revolutionary communist movements backed by the Soviets. Only the fear of nuclear annihilation prevented all out war between the two superpowers. But millions died in smaller conflicts across Asia, Africa and Latin America as these competing ideologies fought for power and influence.

Afghanistan, by contrast, was at peace through most of the Cold War. It's hard to imagine that nowadays, after more than 40 years of conflict there.

From the 1940s into the 1970s, Afghanistan managed to play the role of neutral power quite well, getting aid and development from both the US and the USSR. Highway One, the great "ring road" that links most of the country's major cities, was refurbished and modernized in the 1950s and '60s by both superpowers, each working on different sections.

Afghanistan was in the Soviet Union's "backyard." More so, perhaps, than Cuba is to the US, since they shared a long common border. So Moscow had more of a vested interest in Afghan affairs than Washington.

There was even a small but thriving tourist business, once upon a time. Hippies and other westerners made the overland trip to India in search of enlightenment and spectacular scenery. Pictures of Afghanistan's cities at that time looked like anywhere else in Asia: filled with men and women—some in traditional clothes, but many following Western fashions.

Beneath the surface, however, Afghanistan was divided. The country's educated elites—those in Western clothes—were split between those who looked to Moscow, and those who looked to the West, as the best development model. Both groups were largely out of touch with most of the rest of the country, which was still very rural and much more conservative, traditional and religious. But the cities were growing fast. Change was on the horizon.

Beyond these political and urban/rural divisions, Afghanistan was, and is, a hodgepodge of different languages and ethnicities. There are two official languages: Dari and Pashto. Dari is basically archaic Farsi (Persian). I know it delights my Iranian friends to listen to Dari for its elegance and poetical sound. Something akin to listening to Shakespeare, for English speakers. Pashto is completely different. It's the language of the largest ethnic group in Afghanistan, the Pashtuns—the Pathans of Rudyard Kipling's Imperial India. Pashtuns can be found all over Afghanistan, but predominate in the south and east of the country, and also across the border in north-west Pakistan. We'll meet other groups on our journey. Tajiks speak a variant of Persian. Uzbeks and Turkmen speak variants of Turkish. Hazaras look different from everyone else. Linguists estimate there are 40 more minor languages and 200 dialects.

Pashtuns have dominated the country's politics for centuries, and provided most of its rulers. But those rulers have never been unchallenged. Afghanistan is famous for having a weak central government. Its extremely rugged geography has saved it from conquest countless times. But those same mountains and deserts have also made it difficult for its own rulers to impose their will in all parts of the country. Afghanistan is the size of Texas, but imagine the Rocky Mountains breaking up the state into isolated sections.

The dominant geographic feature of Afghanistan is the mountains, and the biggest mountain range is the Hindu Kush, or "Killer of Hindus." The name is an alleged reference to how the cold of the mountains killed off any Indians who came that far.

Tribes remain critically important in rural Pashtunistan, but not among the other cultures in Afghanistan. However, kinship groups are very important across the country. You always look out for your cousin, even if he's on the other side of a conflict.

The Pashtuns are perhaps most distinguished by their code of honour, the Pashtunwali, or Pakhtunwali. Some Afghan observers say that until the advent of the Taliban, this code often took precedence over Islamic law. The code mandates kindness and hospitality to strangers, but also encourages violent revenge for perceived injuries and insults to members of your family, clan or tribe—a revenge which can be taken against anyone in the family, clan or tribe of the person who insulted you or your kinsmen. An eye for an eye. In the British mind—framed by the imperial experience on the North-West Frontier of Britain's Indian Empire—the code is mistakenly thought to apply to all Afghans. It does not. Just traditionally minded Pashtuns.

All politics are local, or so the saying goes. And that has never been more true than in Afghanistan. Landowners, tribal and clan leaders, merchants and religious figures all have clout locally, and compete for power and influence. Given the weakness of the central government, many have long had muscle to back up their claims.

All these tensions and divisions came to a head in the 1970s. The King was overthrown in a peaceful military coup led by a Royal cousin, Muhammed Daoud Khan, in 1973. A republic was established with Daoud Khan as president. He allowed Soviet influence to increase in Afghanistan, but still strove to keep his nation neutral in the Cold War. He is famously quoted as saying he was happiest when he could light his American cigarettes with his Soviet matches.

Daoud Khan had received help from the country's communist party, the epically misnamed People's Democratic Party of

Afghanistan, or PDPA. But as time went by, the communists became dissatisfied with their share of power and felt under threat.

In April 1978, these hardline communists attempted to seize power, and Afghanistan saw its first serious political bloodshed in decades. Part of the army joined the communists and after a couple of days of hard fighting, in and around Kabul, the president was killed, along with his family and many of his supporters. In good Soviet style, a new secret police force was established, and suspected enemies rounded up. Many were tortured and killed.

The killing has not stopped. Afghanistan has seen more than four decades of war and conflict since then, with no end in sight.

The PDPA—like any radical movement—contained the usual mix of self-seekers and idealists. It's easy to demonize them with distance and time. They brought unparalleled disaster to their country, and exercised power with a cruelty and ruthlessness that sometimes shocked even their Soviet masters. But this was nevertheless a sincere, genuine, indigenous movement—at least initially. Many of its members thought they were acting in the best interests of their country and its people, to modernize its government and economy, to try to reduce inequality, to emancipate women, to bring mass education.

But the road to all kinds of evil is paved with good intentions. If individual Afghans did not approve of the Party's agenda, they must be forced to accept, for the good of the nation. The Party knows best.

Many Afghans did not accept this agenda. Within a few weeks of the communist coup in April 1978, men across the country began to take up arms to resist or obstruct the changes. Many vested interests and traditional practices were under threat. Imagine you're a land-owner and you're being told your tenants will be taking control of your property. What would you do? The atheism of the communists was seen by many as a potential threat to personal salvation. What would you do? Religious leaders began to galvanize the peasantry.

I've always found it odd that, throughout history, peasants rebel and fight against progressive revolutionary governments trying to improve life for those very same peasants. But it's well-documented. Look at the Vendée rebellions during the French Revolution, or the

Cristero uprising in Mexico in the 1920s. This is part of what happened in Afghanistan in 1978 and 1979.

The Communists may have stood a chance if they had remained united. But a house divided cannot stand. In September 1979, one Marxist faction violently seized power from another. The ousted leader soon died in mysterious circumstances. He had been Moscow's main ally, a KGB man. Moscow decided to get even.

On 27th December 1979, Soviet *spetznaz* (special forces) dropped into Kabul and killed the new ruler and his entourage, as other Soviet forces moved in to seize the airport and other key installations.

And so began Russia's Vietnam.

For more than nine years, Soviet forces and their Afghan allies attempted to suppress the anti-communist rebels. The rebels were disparate groups, but all used their faith as a unifying banner with which to confront the godless communists. They became known as Holy Warriors, or Mujahidin in Arabic. Or simply, the Muj.

The Soviets acted with astonishing brutality, as we shall see. One third of the country's population fled into exile. Resistance only hardened.

Much of the world boycotted the 1980 summer Olympics in protest against the invasion. But the US and Pakistan—anxious to prevent the spread of Soviet power—went much further. They supplied the Mujahidin with aid and eventually weapons.

The Soviets were almost immediately stuck in a quagmire. They could not terrorize the Afghans into submission. They did not really try to win hearts and minds.

It also caused trouble at home. Conscripts made unwilling soldiers. The enormous expense of the war helped bankrupt the once-mighty USSR.

By the late 1980s, the Soviet Union was being dragged, kicking and screaming, into a new era of reform by a new leader, Mikhail Gorbachev. He faced reality and started drawing down Soviet troop levels in Afghanistan.

The last column of Soviet combat troops left on February 15th 1989, across the "Friendship Bridge" over the Amu Darya river, dividing Afghanistan and the Soviet Union. They left behind a fragile communist government led by one Muhammad Najibullah. He was a former head of the feared secret police, the KHAD—the Afghan KGB.

Final Soviet withdrawal across the "Friendship Bridge,"
February 15th 1989.
WikiCommons image

The Muj and the international community had given various promises to stabilize the country. But these evaporated once the last Soviet troops had left. Instead, the Muj made an all-out effort to seize power by force. Surprisingly, they failed. The different rebel groups found it difficult to cooperate, and even clashed with each other.

Stalemate ensued. Neither side was able to conquer the other.

It was during this stalemate that I went to Afghanistan, and started bumbling through the Hindu Kush.

Chapter 4

Outward Bound!

So back to the narrative. As I was saying, I get my Afghan visa on Friday 1st November. I have to work the next day, Saturday. So the first flight I can get is a red-eye on Sunday night.

How do you pack and prepare for an adventure holiday with only 36 hours notice? Thankfully, it is not my first rodeo. As a frequent traveller to what we then called "Third World" countries, and as a minor league obsessive-compulsive, I have a handy list of what's needed. Much of the stuff is already piled together in a travel box. Proper prior planning prevents piss-poor performance, they used to tell us in the army.

My papers are in order. I have a valid visa and passport. My wife and I buy travel insurance annually, as we fly quite a lot. So that's all sorted. Remember, technically this is a vacation. Yes, I am using it to further my career, but the Beeb is not supporting the trip beyond providing a letter verifying who I am. I am paying for it all myself.

I need cash. Credit cards are as yet unknown in many parts of the world, and certainly not in Afghan-istan. I still have some Indian rupees

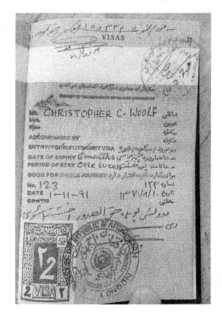

from my trip last year, and I pick up some more from the bank. Banks in central London back then always carried small stocks of every major currency. I try a few locations, but I cannot get hold of any Afghan currency. US dollars will do for now.

By the way, on a linguistic note, the currency is the only thing related to Afghanistan that is actually called Afghani. The people are Afghans. The adjective for anything pertaining to Afghanistan is Afghan. Only ignorant foreigners call the people Afghanis. Unfortunately, Afghans have heard so many ignorant foreigners say the word "Afghani" that now some Afghans say it as well.

My vaccinations are up to date. I have my certificates with my passport. You cannot travel to some countries without these certificates, proving you have been vaccinated against diseases like yellow fever. These go with my passport and wallet in a little cotton canvas bag. This has a string so I can wear it around my neck and stuff it down my shirt for security. That neck bag is something I still have and use!

I have a small first aid kit ready to go. A water bottle. Purification tablets. Salt tablets, in case of dehydration. I make sure I have extra Imodium, after my suffering in India the previous year.

I also have a sewing kit, leftover from my army days, which we called a *hussuff* (housewife). My wash-bag is quickly put in order, with a toothbrush, toothpaste, comb, deodorant, nail scissors and my little green army towel. I just need to throw together some underwear, a pair of jeans, a couple of shirts and a heavy Aran sweater for the cold I knew I could expect in the land of the Hindu Kush. I do not bring a heavy winter coat. I don't own one, and it would be too bulky anyway. So I will have to make do with just my black bomber jacket. I don't own any hiking boots either. My only shoes are a single pair of Polish-made brown leather brogues which have to make do for all occasions. I replace them every 18 months or so, through my 20s. They are cheap but sturdy. A light sleeping bag completes the kit.

I cram everything in an organized fashion into a large blue Karrimor backpack, which I still have! My kit is packed so that the stuff I will need first is at the top.

Close to the top of the backpack are my contact lenses and lens cleaning solution. I am blind as a bat without corrective help. But I don't like to sleep in contacts, so I plan to wear my glasses for the red-eye flight to Delhi.

Next to the lens case is the "Lonely Planet" travel book for Delhi. Anyone who went overseas in the 1980s and '90s will tell you how these books made impossible journeys happen. Before the Internet, information had to be memorized or printed. These guys packed key travel information into user-friendly nuggets for most places on earth. Where to go. What to see. How to get there. What to expect. What risks you might face. It was awesome. There wasn't one for Afghanistan, though.

On the top of the backpack, in the little zippered pocket on the inside, I put my little Gideon Bible. This trip to the land of Holy War was during the years that I was an upstanding leader in my local Church of England (Episcopalian) parish. I had started reading my little pocket New Testament while waiting for the bus home on the day they got handed out to everyone at my secondary school, when I was 12 or 13. Most of the other kids threw theirs away immediately. I found it intriguing that there were readings for each day, so you could read the whole thing in a year. I fell out of faith as a teenager but came back in my final year at University, and started reading that little Bible again every morning and evening. It was a practice I kept up into my late 30s, when I fell out of faith again.

Incidentally, that falling from faith took place after my first divorce, which coincided with the Church abuse crisis in the US, and also a personal realization and acceptance that no single teaching can have a monopoly of truth and virtue. I have met good and bad people of all faiths, including in Afghanistan. Since then I have been an ethical atheist. I still have that little Gideon Bible. As I write, it's sitting right by my computer. I don't open it much any more, but I still use Christ's life and teaching as a moral compass, if not as a pathway to salvation. I can no longer accept the illogicality of religion and I reject its claims to exclusive morality. I consider myself kind, honest and polite in a world full of . . . well, you know where I'm going.

But that's now. Back in 1991, I was still a believer. Carrying a Bible into a Muslim land can cause problems, but I am willing to risk it, for my faith. Besides, I am not expecting to run into any Mujahidin, or Holy Warriors! So I don't think the risk is severe. I am not seeking converts, only to practice my personal faith, which I always do discreetly.

Anyway, packing and preparation does not take long.

I think I stopped by my mum's house, which was just round the corner from ours. But I'm not sure. I was not a very good son until I became a father.

On Sunday night, my wife drives me the short distance to Heathrow Airport and drops me off where I can pick up the shuttle bus to the international terminal. I have to be well dressed, as I'm travelling standby on an airline staff ticket. You have to be smart in the (unlikely) event you're upgraded. So I have cleaned my shoes, put on my nicely pressed pair of khakis, plus a shirt and sweater. I look like an eager schoolboy in the photo of that moment.

The author, ready to take on the world, 1991

I also wear a poppy. It's a week until Remembrance Day, November 11th, when the UK honours those who made the supreme sacrifice in war. Red paper poppies are sold and worn to support disabled ex-servicemen. I wear mine proudly every year, and not just because I'm a veteran myself. It's how I was brought up.

In the distance we can hear fireworks. Guy Fawkes night is also coming up, when Brits celebrate a successful counter-terrorism operation, way back in 1605. Religiously motivated terror-ists, led by this guy, Fawkes, attempted to blow up the King and Parliament. This fire festival is also known as Bonfire Night.

It's also Diwali. The neighbor-hoods around Heathrow had a high concentration of immigrant families, and Diwali is the Hindu festival of light. It's also celebrated with fireworks. Many towns where

I grew up combined Bonfire Night and Diwali into one big explosive party.

The bang and crackle of fireworks would never sound as pleasant to me, after the trip.

୫◈୬   ୫◈୬   ୫◈୬

The stress of getting the visas, getting ready and getting to the airport is over. Now there's a new challenge. I have to wait and see if I can get a seat. Flights are never guaranteed when traveling standby: if the flight is full, I will have to wait, or come back for the next one. And keep my fingers crossed.

On this night, I am lucky.

I don't remember much about the flight out to India. I wasn't upgraded, that's for sure. That only happened to me once while I was flying standby, coming home from Zimbabwe a few months before this trip.

I probably re-read my Lonely Planet book on Delhi, to prepare for getting into town and finding a place to stay, and I typically make a short-list of sights to see, to make the most of my time. I'm hoping to get a flight to Kabul on Tuesday, so I'll have one full day to explore the Indian capital again.

I can't claim to know India very well. I can only record the impressions of a traveller. But India is a staggering place, if you've never been. Staggering beauty, staggering spirituality, and staggering deprivation.

The first thing I notice on all my visits to Delhi are the bright white cows wandering safely and happily onto the main highway between the airport and the city. Cows of course are sacred to Hindus —they're the original sacred cows. Then there's the bright skies, made hazy by pollution, the dazzling architecture—ancient and modern— the chaotic streets, the jostling markets, with their persistent hawking of wares. You can see incredible opulence cheek-by-jowl with the most awful poverty. Outside luxurious bejeweled tombs and temples, limbless waifs lay beside half-starved women, with hands out-stretched, begging. Flush toilets are more common now, but back then they were pretty much unknown outside of tourist hotels and the homes of the wealthy. Little children would squat and defecate in the street. I've seen poverty elsewhere, in Africa and of course Afghanistan, but I'm sorry to say that—to my mind—poverty in India feels inexplicably harder to bear

India in 1991 was still a socialist republic. Despite the chaos, everything was, at one level, regimented and bureaucratic. Old-school bureaucracy: with forms, long lines, clerks at windows, stamps in hand, allocating seats on a train, or whatever. Thuggish men in uniforms, with long canes called *lathis*, would enforce public discipline. Only two types of cars were allowed on the streets, and one kind of bicycle. You couldn't rent a car unless you also rented a driver. He would often bring a friend. The Indian economy was opened up to free enterprise later in the 1990s, and has since taken off. But back in 1991, resources were much more limited.

To a westerner, India can be disorienting, initially. The crowds, the noise, the hustle. But at the same time, some things are recognizable and relatable. A great many Indians speak or understand English. It's an official language, alongside Hindi. Most signs are in English—or at least in the Latin alphabet—as well as in Hindi or other local languages, with their very different scripts. India in general, and New Delhi in particular, has a lot of places named after British imperial officials and members of the UK's Royal Family. To a Brit, this can make India seem both familiar and alien at the same time. My hotel for example was close to "Connaught Place"—a name you could expect to find anywhere in the British Isles. The place names, and the language, are legacies of centuries of British imperial expansion into the Indian sub-continent—an expansion only checked by the warriors of Afghanistan.

I take the bus into town from the airport. I check my map in the Lonely Planet book, and walk several blocks to the same hotel in New Delhi that my wife and I visited a year ago, the Metro. They have a room.

The Metro Hotel's most noticeable feature is the fuse box on the hall of the second floor, hanging off the wall, with wires spread this way and that. Clearly, no one has tended to it in the twelve months since I was last here. *Plus ça change.*

I drop my backpack and go explore. I walk mostly, but also take an auto-rickshaw when necessary. These are motor scooters with little seats attached, like the pedicabs of some US cities, except motorized. The ride is always exciting. The traffic flow is Darwinian.

The streets of Delhi are full of people dressed and ready for the Hindu festival of Diwali, the festival of Light. Many wear fine clothes and ride in brightly decorated donkey carts, or ride gilded white horses, bedecked with flowers.

White horses and donkey carts decorated for Diwali

I visit some popular tourist attractions: the *Purana Qila* fort and mosque, and then the tomb of the 16th century Mughal emperor, Humayun. It seems appropriate, given my ultimate destination. The Mughals were the last imperial dynasty in India before the British. They were Afghans, who conquered northern India in 1526. They claimed to be descended from the great medieval Mongol conquerors, Genghis Khan and Tamerlane. The British executed the sons of the last Mughal emperor during the rebellion of 1857. Hollywood gets the term "mogul" from these Mughals.

Other critters are hanging around in Humayun's tomb: bats. Thousands of them. I take a picture with a flash and they swarm after me.

The tomb of Mughal emperor Humayun

Snake charmers in Delhi

I also pause to enjoy the snake charmers. My wife did not let us linger with these reptiles on our last visit.

I'm pretty careful when it comes to food. I love Indian food but I had a pretty severe case of the runs on my trip the year before. I don't want to go into a war zone with that kind of disability, so I stick mainly to plain rice.

There may have been fireworks that night, I can't recall for certain. I fall asleep early, exhausted.

Tomorrow, Afghanistan!

Chapter 5

Go! Go! Go!

Finally the day has come. Tuesday, November 5th. I'm flying into a country at war, for the first time in my life. And not any country. Afghanistan. The legendary land of the Hindu Kush and Kipling's Pathan warriors. The violent epicenter of the Cold War for the last 12 years. I've been curious about war and Afghanistan since I was a little boy. Now I'm about to get a firsthand view of both.

I get the bus to Delhi International Airport and seek out the single desk checking in passengers for the Ariana flight to Kabul. Security is no different than elsewhere, and I'm soon at the gate. There aren't many of us heading to Afghanistan. Almost all men. Many of them are Sikhs. I am not surprised. Being the nerd that I am, I already know that the small community of Indians living in Kabul are mostly traders and mostly Sikhs. Sikh men are known for their beards and turbans, and as such are often mistaken for Muslims by Americans. Nothing could be more wrong. The Sikh faith is quite different, although it is seen by some as a bridge between Islam and Hinduism.

Sikhism developed in northern India about 500 years ago, and soon won a few converts in Kabul. Merchants followed. A significant new influx occurred during and after the partition of Britain's Indian empire in 1947, with many Sikhs becoming refugees from the new proudly Muslim nation of Pakistan.

The Sikhs had a mixed relationship with the Afghans. The great Sikh king of the Punjab, Ranjit Singh, fought repeated wars with his Afghan neighbors in the early 1800s. His successful campaigns to a large extent define the borders of Pakistan and Afghanistan today, leaving many people who identify as Afghan living in Pakistani territory.

Some of my fellow passengers are in Western clothes, but most are in traditional plain Punjabi clothing, with long collarless shirts called *kurtahs*, with flared sleeves. These *kurtahs* hang down to the knees in some cases, half-concealing baggy cotton trousers.

I don't remember the flight being called, but all at once there's a movement toward a door. I follow. Down the stairs, and out into the bright morning light of autumn in the north Indian plain.

We walk across the tarmac toward the Ariana plane: the pride and joy of the Afghan airline. You could call it the Ariana "Grande." (Sorry. Couldn't resist.)

My ride is indeed the flagship of Ariana. It has to be. There is no other. It's their only remaining airliner after last week's mortar attack on Kabul airport. It's a Soviet-built Tupolev TU-154.

There's something invariably grim and utilitarian about all things Soviet. Beauty and form surrender all hope in the face of brutal practicality. I can't bring a perfect picture to mind, but the imagery in my memory is of unpainted steel, and uncovered rivets and bolts. It feels somehow unfinished, or maybe a little ratty, like an old beater of a car. It goes. It gets you from A to B. It gets the job done. But aesthetically, it's just grim.

It doesn't inspire confidence.

We climb the steps of an old-fashioned movable airport staircase. The stairs lead to the middle door of the old airliner, just in front of the engine. That's odd, I think. As I enter the dim cabin, I can see the reason why.

The entire front half of the plane is filled with wooden crates and boxes. Many are marked in Russian Cyrillic lettering. That's unusual, I think to myself. My first guess is that these perhaps are luxury goods, destined for Kabul's communist elite. Then among the lettering I make out some numbers—Russians use Arabic numbers, just like we do in English. I squint. Oh—7.62 mm and 5.45 mm. These numbers can only mean one thing.

Ammunition. My flight is stacked floor to ceiling with bullets! Who knows what else?

That's a little unsettling. I mean, it won't make a difference if the plane crashes. But it could make life trickier if we come under fire on landing, as had happened last week with Ariana's other plane. Or if there was a fire inside the plane. There is no prohibition on smoking on the flight. But thankfully not many people take advantage.

The plane's lethal cargo reminds me of my army training, when we were told how everything Soviet is dual-purpose; how everything can be quickly switched to military use in the event of war. I recall airliners being a particular example, in that all the seats can be quickly ripped out to make way for military purposes. I can now see that in action. I am naïve enough to think you can't do that with Boeings and Airbuses as well!

The cabin is dim. There's enough light to see. But the interior seems to be an orangey brown. Must be another Soviet utilitarian thing. Or it could be tobacco grime. It feels grungy.

There are no allocated seats. In fact, I don't recall any kind of flight attendants at all. So I grab a window seat for the two-hour flight. I'm keen to see the landscape, if I can.

A very tall Sikh man in a dirty *kurtah* plops down next to me. He's carrying a huge metal bowl, maybe two or three feet wide, covered in cloth. He hoikes up his baggy trousers and kurtah to make himself comfortable, and sits cross-legged the entire journey, the metal bowl in his lap. His legs are bare and hairy, and rather close to mine.

I am not uncomfortable. I'm an experienced traveller. But some readers might need to be told that many other cultures have a very different sense of personal space, and happily encroach into yours without any concern. My neighbor's leg is a prime example. I'm not bothered. It only makes me uncomfortable when these strangers are touting Kalashnikovs and rocket-propelled grenades, as will happen later on my trip.

Readers might also need to be reminded that deodorant was quite uncommon outside the US and Europe at this moment in history. As a matter of fact, it's not even that universal in continental Europe to this day.

I smile and say hello, but we have no language in common.

The takeoff is uneventful, and before we've reached cruising altitude, my Sikh neighbor takes the cloth off his giant metal bowl. It's brim-filled with sweet-smelling food. At first glance it looks like a gigantic pile of fried or barbecued chicken pieces, but that doesn't jive with what I know about Sikhs being largely vegetarian. I later learn it was more likely *pakora*, spicy vegetable fritters. My neighbour promptly starts handing out pieces to his friends, amid a great deal of loud banter. He is the plane's impromptu, self-appointed galley. The oily fritters are passed from hand to hand across the plane to those entitled to the bounty. I politely decline when he offers me one. About half the bowl is emptied before the cloth cover is re-attached.

Ariana does not provide pretzels.

It's the first image of the trip seared into my memory. It's surreal. The orange-brown light. This tall, intense-looking Sikh man, sitting cross-legged, holding up these greasy snacks with his outstretched arm, as if to say "Whose piece is this?" while a couple of rows ahead are stacks of wooden ammunition crates from floor to ceiling.

In keeping with the Soviet utilitarian tradition, the aircraft designers at Tupolev have also not bothered much with sound proofing. It's one of the loudest flights I've ever been on.

From my perch at the window I can see Punjab below me, as we fly northwest. Flat dry plains as far as the eye can see, irrigated by the five rivers that give Punjab its name, flowing south toward the mighty Indus. That's the river that gave birth to civilization in India, five thousand years ago, and the river that finally put a stop to the expansion of Alexander the Great in the fourth century before Christ.

Soon I can see mountains on the horizon. At first I think it's just a line of clouds on the horizon. But on closer inspection, I can make out snow-capped peaks. I smile. It's a joy I always feel when flying. Having grown up in England, which is mostly monotonously flat, it's always a treat for me to see mountains. Seeing them from the air is a bonus.

But I also feel a little knot of excitement in my stomach. There before me lies the mighty Hindu Kush.

As we begin to pass over the foothills, I scour the landscape below to try to make out contours. I checked the route on the map before-hand so I know that somewhere below me is the Khyber Pass. In English memory—at least for people of my generation and older—the Khyber Pass is legend. Poetically, it is the edge of civilization, the limit of British power, the terminus of law and order. Beyond the pass are ruthless, cunning enemies, and death. A place where Rudyard Kipling warned young British soldiers to always save the last round for themselves, so they don't fall prey to the knives of the locals. The poetry and literature of empire, its imagery and psychology, have long fallen out of fashion in the UK, and for good reason. But it seems a little sad that my generation will likely be the last that can quickly decode the meanings we read in historical documents and literature.

As a historian and geographer, I know the significance of the Khyber Pass is largely symbolic. There are plenty of other passes. Afghanistan is not uncivilized. British law and order might mean safety for British passport holders, but did not necessarily mean justice for their enemies or even for their subject peoples of colour. But anyway, for me, passing over the Khyber symbolizes a psychological step over the line from safety to danger. I am beyond the Pale. North of the Wall.

The action begins at once.

కఁ౩   కఁ౩   కఁ౩

Kabul is surprisingly close to the border with Pakistan, only 140 miles (225 km) from the Khyber Pass. So we reach it quickly. The plane descends fast and is soon making tight corkscrew circles, getting lower and lower.

I try not to dwell on the fact that the Mujahidin are close to Kabul. Given that an Ariana plane had been hit just the week before, I know that our flight could be targeted as we come in to land. That's unpleasant enough. Worse, the ammunition on board our flight makes us a legitimate military target, and adds an extra hazard. The results of an attack could be catastrophic for us, but I rely on hope. I hope that the odds of anything happening are low. War is full of such calculations and hopes. I push the thoughts to the back of my mind, and try to focus on the scenery.

The sense of risk increases as we begin to land. You can feel the tension rising in the cabin. I think everyone knows what had happened to the other Ariana plane last week.

As soon as the wheels hit the ground, the brakes are screeching. We're all thrown forward by the violent deceleration. I've never felt anything like it in my life. I hear a whirring noise from the back of the plane. I look around and see the rear door opening—one of those old cargo gangplanks, like on a transport plane. We haven't even stopped moving.

There's no time wasted on taxiing. We just shudder to a halt.

Go! Go! Go! Everybody bolts for the gangplank. There's no panic. No shouting. But everyone is moving with urgency and determination. It feels like everyone is off the plane and running across the tarmac just seconds after landing.

It is the most satisfying deplaning I've ever witnessed or been part of.

୧◈୨ ୧◈୨ ୧◈୨

The crowd scampers and trots toward the terminal building. Presumably they're as conscious of the recent mortar attack as I am. I follow on, at a pretty good clip. Thankfully, there's no incoming fire today.

The terminal building is a cross between a warehouse and a Quonset hut, or what Brits call a Nissen hut. I pass through the door. It feels like one big open space, with crowds and queues and officials. I don't remember interacting with anyone resembling an immigration officer, which is strange, as it must have been my first official interaction in Afghanistan. I guess I am distracted by the adrenalin rush of the sudden deplaning. But I do have an extraordinarily vivid recollection of what came next.

My papers must be in order, as I pass through immigration and I am admitted to the Democratic Republic of Afghanistan. I'm still in the warehouse-like terminal building. Since my BBC chum, Chris Bowers, didn't know when I'd be arriving, or even what day, there's no one to greet me. Not a problem. I assume I can simply just grab a taxi.

I look up for a sign saying exit. Or taxi. Or anything.

Problem.

All the signs are in Dari, the official language of Afghanistan, and written in the Persian script. Everything is unreadable to me. Some signs are in Russian, but the Cyrillic script is also foreign to me. Nothing is in English or even in the Latin alphabet. Worse, there are none of the pictographs or symbols typically seen at airports today. It's a moment of complete and total culture shock, and personal disorientation.

I realize I am alone in a completely foreign and dangerous land. No one even knows I'm here.

I don't panic in moments of acute stress. I get this overwhelming feeling of serenity, and time slows down. I might even feel a little giddy, almost euphoric. That calm helps me keep a clear head and make decisions fast. The stress and trauma is there in my body, but suppressed, and comes out later in nightmares.

This is one of those moments.

I look around and ask for help. I try various counters and official looking people. No one speaks English. Nobody. I try French. *Pas de joie.* I have no phrase book for Dari.

A few minutes seems like an eternity.

I've never felt so alone.

I'm scratching my head, when I hear a soft-spoken voice in good English, with an Indian accent, ask, "Do you need help?"

It's a short, slender man, in smart Western clothes.

My relief must have been evident.

"Yes, please."

He introduces himself. I cannot now recall his name, but I will always remember the importance of kindness to strangers. I'll call him Anil.

"I'm with AFP, the French news agency," Anil explains.

"Oh, yes? Are you based here?"

"Yes, but I also work in our Delhi bureau. I split my time between India and here." He seems very intense and serious. I notice he has a thin mustache, and his skin is smooth and delicate. He wants to be taken seriously, despite his youthful looks. I instantly empathize. I know that feeling.

"So you must know Chris Bowers from the BBC?" I ask with a smile, trying to lighten the mood.

"Of course, of course." The corner of his mouth creases with the first hint of a smile. "I wouldn't be very good at my job if I didn't. There are only two or three of us foreign correspondents in the whole country!"

I did not know that, I thought to myself.

"Well, now there's one more," I joke. "At least for the next week. I'm with the BBC as well, and I'm here to visit Chris."

I introduce myself, and ask for directions to the taxi rank, but Anil insists I travel with him. It's a good thing, as I don't even have Chris's street address!

I'm so lucky and grateful. I really don't know what I would have done otherwise. And I've only been "in country" for less than an hour.

He leads me toward the exit.

"Whereabouts are you from in India?"

"I am not Indian," Anil says acidly. "I'm from Sri Lanka."

Sri Lanka is an island state off the south coast of India. It's sometimes called "the pearl of the Indian Ocean," but it's another war-torn country. That might also account for his seriousness.

"My bosses think it's safer to send me here to Afghanistan than to send a European or an Indian," he explains. "The Europeans are seen as too close to the Americans. And the Indians are seen as too close to the Russians. I'm kind of a neutral."

I like the way he says Afghanistan. The "gh" is softer than we say it in the west, more glottal, so it sounds more like "Af'kh'anistan." That would become quite familiar.

At the exit, my new pal from AFP is greeted by a friend who's come to pick him up. We squeeze into his little white car, and head out onto the airport road and into the legendary city of Kabul, capital of Afghanistan.

I suspect that my first impressions of Afghanistan are the same as others. My eyes are drawn first to the mountains. They lie in all directions; all are a dusty brown, except for the tops. It's November, and snow already crowns the summits. They all seem to be treeless. The sky is an incredibly clear blue, with none of the pollution so visible in India. And the light has this crystal sharp quality that can only be found at high altitudes. I don't know how to describe it better, but as a life-long flatlander, I always find it breathtaking.

The skyline of suburban Kabul between the airport and the old city is dominated by grim, Soviet-style tower blocks of apartments. They're a very visible reminder of the Soviet intrusion into this spectacular land, and their failed attempt to rebuild it in their image. They were built specially for the thousands of Soviet civilians brought in to help transform the country after the invasion. Many Afghans viewed them as colonists. The height, industrial quality, and off-white colour of these apartment blocks makes them stand out from an otherwise fairly low-rise city, of mostly old, tan-coloured buildings.

There are not many people to be seen. The roads from the airport are not teeming with life, like Delhi. The faces are different, too. Afghans, as a rule, do not look like Indians. Some Afghans look quite European. Most are something in-between, which makes sense, given the geography. The clothing is a mixture, too. Those in uniform look quite Soviet, as you'd expect after 12 years of domination from Moscow. Civilians wear a mix of Western and local styles. Jeans and t-shirts side by side with turbans, skirt-like *kurtahs,* and waistcoat vests without buttons. The mood of the faces generally seems serious and reserved. There isn't much inane smiling at strangers, as you sometimes get in the West.

On the ride, after the usual small talk, I ask my friend from AFP about the progress of the war. I'm keen to get a sense of how safe the city is.

"The airport road is considered safe during daylight," Anil tells me. "The city can get 'noisy' occasionally, but nothing to worry about, really."

Folks who were there at the time, and who know Kabul now, say it was a very different war back then. Much noisier. If you visit Kabul today as a foreigner, your life is in serious danger from extremists looking to kill or kidnap you. As a result, your movements are extremely restricted. But you will almost never hear gunfire or explosions. It was the reverse in 1991. Gunfire and explosions could be heard on an almost daily basis, but the danger you faced as a foreigner was no greater or less than anyone else. You could move about pretty freely.

In terms of noise, one aid worker who was there in 1991 recently described to me how his office in Kabul was close to a battery of

Scuds, which would roar into life almost every day, sending long-range missiles across the country.

As I enter Kabul, I am more concerned about incoming fire than outgoing. The guerrillas—the holy warriors, the Mujahidin—have most of their heavy weapons in the hills to the west of Kabul and occasionally lob shells and rockets into the city. The Intercontinental Hotel is on that side of town and, being a rather tall building, it often interrupts the flight of these shells and rockets. The hotel would not rent rooms on the side of the hotel which faced the hills, just in case.[4]

The InterCon is about four miles (6 km) from where I will be staying; four miles further away from the heavy weapons of the Muj. Relatively safe. Life in wartime is all about relative risk.

Chris's home is in the diplomatic and government quarter, known as Wazir Akbar Khan. This district is not hermetically sealed like the Green Zone in Baghdad during the US occupation of Iraq. But it is by far the safest and most heavily guarded section of town. Just how I like it!

The shelling of the city had begun in 1989, and had killed a couple thousand people by the time I arrived. It's almost forgotten now, as it was just a tragic foretaste of the devastation that would be unleashed on Kabul after the regime collapsed a few months after my visit.

I must have known about this occasional shelling before I came to Afghanistan, from my job in the news business. But it never registered as a significant potential risk for me personally. Life for millions of Kabulis was going on as normal. Nobody in the government/diplomatic quarter was taking any precautions, although that would change by the end of my visit. But I'm getting ahead of myself.

To be honest, I myself never heard any "bang-bang" in Kabul itself. I was to hear plenty outside of the capital, but I heard no explosions on the days I was in the city.

Apparently, I was lucky.

੪◈੩　੪◈੩　੪◈੩

---

[4]See "Afghan Rebel Rockets Kill 3 at Kabul Hotel," by UPI, printed in the Los Angeles Times, May 24th 1990. [www.latimes.com/archives/la-xpm-1990-05-24-mn-307-story.html]

The AFP car brings me to Chris's home in Kabul's diplomatic quarter, just across the street from the Mongolian embassy. The little house is the BBC bureau in Afghanistan.

Like so many others in the city, Chris's house is square, flat-roofed, and once whitewashed, with a dry front yard, where I'm greeted by a cat. The cat gives me a pleasant reminder of domestic life. But the illusion is punctured when my AFP buddy says he must wait for me to be admitted before he will depart. We knock.

"How do you say thank you in Dari?" I ask, while we wait at the door.

"*Tashakor*," smiles Anil.

"*Tashakor!*" I reply. "Thank you! I don't know what I would have done without you. *Tashakor!*"

The door is opened by a weather-beaten man with a Mongolian-looking face. His clothes are worn and patched. He speaks no English, and appears stern and humourless. My AFP colleague explains the situation, and the gentleman admits me. My BBC buddy, Chris Bowers, is out at the moment.

I learn later this gentleman is Chris's cook and housekeeper. I'm shocked. Wait, what? You're a poor stringer, and you have servants? Yes, even the poorest Western reporters can afford to employ multiple people here, it seems. And have a nice house. I get my own room!

The cook's name is Tajmuddin. I learn that he is a Hazara. I had read about the Hazara as part of my research, but I didn't expect them to look so different from other Afghans.

Tajmuddin, smiling!

The Hazara can be found all over Afghanistan but predominate in a mountainous region in the heart of the country, known as the Hazarajat. At its centre is the province of Bamian, home to the giant statues of Buddha famously blown up by the Taliban in 2001. The Taliban saw these magnificent ancient works of art as idols, forbidden under Islam.

The Hazara are said by some to be the descendants of the armies of Genghis Khan, the Mongol conqueror of half the world, 800 years ago. Their origins are probably not quite so exotic—given the geography it's likely many have been here since time immemorial. But any past glories have meant little since Hazarajat was subjugated by Kabul in the late 1800s. Today, Hazaras face discrimination and prejudice from many fellow Afghans. Their East-Asian faces make them a visible minority in Afghanistan. Besides their looks, many are also followers of Shia Islam, rather than the predominant Sunni form of Islam found through most of Afghanistan.

Hazaras are often obliged to take the most menial jobs. In newsreels from the Soviet war, you would see a squad of Muj troops moving through the mountains in single file, and there was always a guy at the tail end stooped down, carrying a load much larger than anyone else. Always a Hazara. Even in a liberation struggle, it seems, there is an underclass.

I will always remember Tajmuddin. He was kind, if stern-looking. A no nonsense man. And a tease.

As we wait for Chris to come home, Tajmuddin prepares lunch: my first Afghan meal. Afghan food is pretty simple. One friend says there really are only about twenty dishes, despite the variety of climates and cultures found in the county. I am a complete novice and know nothing. This is something I have not researched.

Tajmuddin soon produces a small bowl of yellow stew, and puts in front of me as I sit at the kitchen table. He also plops down an oval-shaped piece of flatbread that I recognize from India, called *naan*.

"*Tashakor!*" I say. "Thank you." Tajmuddin ignores me.

I look around for a spoon or fork. There is none. I make hand signals for eating. Tajmuddin grunts, and pushes the piece of *naan* bread closer to me.

Ahah, I think. Maybe this is a test? I'm certain Chris has cutlery in his kitchen drawers, but I guess they're not commonly used here in Afghanistan, just like in India. Tajmuddin wants to see how I manage.

OK, I think to myself, I'll play. I've attempted this in India and Tanzania. I can do this.

Tajmuddin watches with his arms folded as I tear off a piece of bread and dip it into the stew. I want to get a taste of the spice level before digging in. The hot spices of Indian cuisine sometimes upset my stomach, so I proceed with caution.

The yellow stew is delightful. Not spicy at all, but full of flavour from herbs. Maybe parsley and coriander (cilantro). It has diced pieces of lamb, carrots and some other vegetables, and best of all some nuts, raisins and even apricot.

I feel like a champ as I chase a cube of lamb into a piece of *naan* that I've folded into a scoop. Tajmuddin is not impressed with my efforts. He unfolds his arms with a sigh and pulls a fork from a drawer. I ignore it and finish the stew with the bread. It takes a while. I make a mess. But I succeed. I wipe the bowl with a tiny last sliver of *naan* bread, triumphant. My host remains expressionless, but I feel pleased with myself.

This kind of stew is known as a *korma*, and remains one of my favourite dishes to this day. All Afghan food is made to be picked up by hand. The base of any meal is the carb: either rice or a flatbread made from wheat, maize or barley. *Naan* bread is common and is definitely the easiest thing for the novice to use to scoop up a *korma*. Sticky *pulao* rice can also be used, but it takes some getting used to!

The main meat in Afghan cuisine, I would learn, is lamb or mutton. Sheep and goats are much easier to raise than cattle in the dry mountainous terrain. Beef is rare, and even chicken is not that common. Lamb can be ground, but more commonly diced for stews and kebabs. But, overall, there's a lot less meat than in a Western diet.

୧◈୨   ୧◈୨   ୧◈୨

I don't have to wait long after lunch for my old friend to arrive. Chris comes in, beaming as always.

"You made it, then?" he asks, with classic northern English warmth. I am the first person to visit him since he arrived in-country seven months ago.

Chris is a wiry northerner, a little taller than me, with a mop of curly dark hair, and an irrepressible spirit. His Lancashire accent is thick, at least to my ears. He's gregarious, warm and friendly. But sharp as a tack, and cunning. The jollity is sincere but it masks a mind that can penetrate the cold reality of a situation, where I would be clouded with innocence and idealism.

He's originally from the Wirral, near Liverpool. He had been living near Manchester when I met him, but he refuses to be called a Mancunian. Tribalism remains an issue in England's northwest, and it's all to do with the religion of soccer.

As I mentioned, Chris had joined the World Service Newsroom at around the same time as me, and we had quickly bonded. He'd come from the BBC's local news services in the UK and he had an endless collection of hilarious stories. I remember vividly one incident he recounted while he was a local reporter during some coastal flooding. He needed to figure out just how deep the water was. It was dark, but he bravely waded in. Ankle deep. Knee deep. Sploosh, right into a duck pond. Neck deep!

Another time he was working for a local music show up north in Lancashire somewhere. During the news bulletin at the top of the show, they heard that Fred Astaire had passed away. The DJ rushed downstairs to the music library to pick up anything by that musical legend. He got back just in the nick of time, before the end of the bulletin, and threw the album to the studio manager. The DJ got the thumbs up just as the newscast ended, but without any time to be told the name of the track that had been lined up. He tells his listeners, "now, here's our own special tribute to the late, great Fred Astaire," and up comes the opening words of "Cheek to Cheek."

"Heaven, I'm in heaven . . ."

I'm betting that story is apocryphal. But knowing Chris, you could never be sure.

Afghans and English share a passion for tea, and a kettle is soon boiling.

With Chris is an equally cheerful Afghan gent.

"This is my fixer, translator and friend, Masum," says Chris. Muhammad Masum, whom everyone knew simply as Masum. A fixer is a local journalist who helps a foreign correspondent find and report stories.

"How do you do?" says Masum in perfect if slightly accented English, as he gives me a solid handshake. He snorts and laughs a little. The first thing I notice about Masum is his wry, infectious smile, and the twinkle in his eyes. He laughs often. He is the perfect fixer, by

all accounts. He seems to know everyone, or have a connection with everyone, and he has a charm that could smooth out the most serious of situations. He is lean, but with his receding hairline, silver sideburns, and his wisdom, he seems old. I later learn he's only 33.

"How was your trip?" asks Chris.

"Uneventful," I lie. It's an English custom to underplay everything. "The descent into the airport was steeper than I expected. And the deplaning was fun. Very efficient. I wish we could do that everywhere."

He nods toward the empty bowl by the sink. "Made yourself at home, then?"

"Yes, thanks to our friend here." I smile toward Tajmuddin, who keeps himself busy moving plates. "How the devil are you? How are you enjoying life here?"

"I love it. The people are so nice. The food's amazing. The scenery is mind-blowing. I can work on whatever I want, whenever I want. There's no bosses breathing down my neck, telling me what to do. And yet the story is one of the biggest in the world. I love it."

"And you can afford all this?" I wave my hand around at his house.

"Aye," he grins. "More or less. The Beeb covers most of it. I'm stringing for Reuters as well, now. That helps."

Chris Bowers in his home/office in Kabul

They show me around the house/office. It's a fairly spacious, modern, two-story home. It feels square and boxy. A lot of white paint. Kind of clinical. Perfect for a young, single reporter.

There are a couple of bedrooms and an office. The office is rather spartan. Chris has a primitive word processing computer and a phone, to which he can attach a device called a Mutterbox to try to improve audio quality, if the phones are working.

The centerpiece of Chris's work station is a huge old East German telex machine. As I mentioned earlier, the telex was pretty much the only semi-reliable way to communicate with the outside world. But the machines were notoriously clunky and temperamental. Besides the issue of occasionally randomly converting one's messages into gobbledygook, they also relied on a physical wire lines, just like an old telegraph or telephone line. So these could often be overloaded, or damaged or broken in a war zone. But unlike phone lines, the message would eventually get through when traffic eased or the line was restored.

Chris says he likes it this way, as he can plausibly tell head office in London that there is trouble with the line. That way, he can keep the office in London off his back, and file his stories in his own time.

The telex is also somewhat more secure than the phone lines, which are all bugged by the secret police. There are only landlines, of course. If you are placing a call or picking one up, you can hear a click, indicating the spooks have started listening. These wiretaps are all simple ones, where the monitors are just another party to the call; if they push the wrong button, they unmute themselves and you can actually hear them. Chris says it happened to him once, when he heard the agent saying, "He's just calling the ministry again." I heard the same story from other internationals who laugh about hearing the secret policemen coughing and sputtering sometimes. I am shocked by how amateurish it sounds.

It should be obvious, but it bears repeating that in 1991 the Internet is just a twinkle in the eye of Tim Berners-Lee and his team at CERN, and mobile phones are still the realm of science fiction.

That physical separation and the lack of communications meant a reporter in a tough location back then was extremely isolated. It was obviously difficult to get advice, guidance, or instructions. The journalist needed to be thoroughly self-reliant, to find, write and edit his or her stories. That's where a good fixer became priceless. A fixer is vital for a successful assignment anywhere in the world in any age. But before the advent of the web, it was a *sine qua non*—without which there is nothing. Thankfully, Chris has Masum.

He's dying to show me his city.

Chapter 6

The Woman on the Bridge

Chris has to work, so I spend my first day in Afghanistan out and about with Masum. He is so kind and funny, and generous with his time.

He takes me out to his little yellow car: a Soviet-built Lada, I think.

"It says 'Taxi' here?" I say, surprised.

"Yes!' Masum snorts a laugh. "You're correct. Working for a foreign journalist is a great job for an Afghan. I love it. It's what I want to do with my life. But the pay . . ." He tilts his head and makes a gesture with has hand as if to say "so-so."

"So like many Afghans, I have another job." He waves expansively at his little Lada. We climb in.

"You know, it's funny, though. The two jobs go together quite well. Who do you suppose uses a taxi in Kabul?"

"I don't know. People with money?"

"Exactly. And here in Kabul these are usually government officials, and businessmen. So I hear things. News. Stuff that is useful to BBC."

Ahh, I think to myself, as light dawns over Marblehead. Driving a taxi generates quite a lot of leads for a journalist.

Today though, Masum is off the clock, and he turns off the meter. I'm grateful to him for sharing his time.

The first order of business is to get my papers in order, a process called accreditation. Getting a visa prior to travel is just a first step. Then usually a journalist needs to get approval from the authorities in-country upon arrival. In Kabul in 1991, this means a trip to the Interior Ministry.

I need to get my passport stamped, authenticating my journalist visa and allowing me to work. It also registers my presence in the country with the authorities.

The Interior Ministry is housed in a large imposing building. I wait in the car, while Masum goes in to collect the stamps. I am a little anxious. If I am not approved, I could be on the next plane out.

Thankfully, all goes well.

A foreign journalist without papers can be locked up for working illegally, and potentially sentenced to a term in prison, or deported. That's true in any country. I had to get a journalist visa when I first came to work in the United States, for example. It can be a tiresome process, and sometimes countries will say no. But it's rarely worth the risk of skipping the step. This is especially true for me in Afghanistan, as this is not an official BBC deployment. I am way too junior to be embarrassing "Aunty Beeb."

More seriously, a foreigner in a war zone can easily be mistaken for a spy, and justice can be executed summarily. I am not expecting to be in a combat zone but I don't want to risk any unnecessary trouble. Foreign reporters had seriously embarrassed the Soviets and their Afghan allies by exposing how badly the war was going, so they are not popular. Reprisals have been threatened against any foreign journalists found with the Mujahidin without papers.

There's no way I could have known, but within a week I'd be thanking God that I took the trouble to get that stamp.

Information control had been a vital part of the Soviet war effort in Afghanistan. Chris told me how the government from time to time would announce successes about this or that village being liberated. They would take all the journalists they could find to prove it. Cheerful villagers would show their gratitude. After a few times, Chris noticed they were usually driving in the wrong direction to the places that had allegedly been liberated. There was no GPS back then of course, but good map readers would know they were being deceived. He also said they went to the same village a couple of times. I was not surprised by the story, but I was surprised by the apparent clumsiness and amateurishness. Just like the phone-tapping. I had expected more of the Soviet security colossus.

There's even better news than simply getting my stay approved. I am not assigned a "minder." A minder is an employee of the Information Ministry who accompanies a journalist while they're working. Depending on their degree of dedication to the job, the minder might tell you where you can and can't go, and who you can and can't talk to. In Afghanistan, it's always a man. Obviously, he can also listen in to your conversations, and the expectation is that he will report anyone who speaks out against the government. The public knows this, and the presence of a minder will stop most people from talking freely. So not having a minder is a good thing.

The day is now ours and we are free to explore and do a little sightseeing. Masum is excited to show off the capital city of the country he loves so much.

It is the only day of my trip where I don't feel like there's an immediate existential threat to my life. Everything is new and exciting. The sun is bright. The sky is blue. The mountains are spectacular. The temperature is delightful. The city of Kabul and its people are charming.

ε◊з ε◊з ε◊з

I am keen to see the old city and the old fortress, the Bala Hisar. I'm of course a huge history buff, and I already knew the importance of the fortress, particularly in the epic British disaster of 1841.

The Brits invaded Afghanistan for the first time in 1839, to head off the danger of Russian influence. A dispute over the succession to the throne gave them an excuse.

But what on earth—I hear you ask—were the Brits doing there, so far from home, so long ago?

Well, funnily enough, I've always been fascinated by how such a poor country with such a weak state had been able to resist the most powerful empire of its day. So let me share the story with you!

By the 1830s, the Brits were the dominant power in the Indian sub-continent. The British had come to India to make money, and their takeover had begun as a security measure to protect trade. But in the 1750s, the business of conquest also became hugely profitable for the individuals in charge, from bribes, tribute and plunder. So expansion proceeded rapidly over the next few decades from a mix of greed and duty.

The Indian Empire became a central driver for the British economy, and India's security became a paramount concern for imperial policy makers in London. One of the threats to that security came from other European powers. The French had been driven out, but by the 1830s a new threat was seen from Russia, which was expanding rapidly into central Asia. The invasion of Afghanistan was ordered in 1838 after Russian agents were reported to be active there.

The invasion itself was an undertaking of staggering magnitude and endurance. The army assembled around Delhi in 1838, along with thousands of contractors and camp followers. These men and women then marched 1,500 miles (2400 km) over the next six months, most of them on foot, taking a roundabout route through the independent kingdom of Punjab, through Quetta in Baluchistan, across the Bolan Pass to the important Afghan city of Kandahar and then finally on to Kabul. That's the equivalent of walking from Tulsa, Oklahoma, to Los Angeles, through similar terrain of mountain and desert. Or from Madrid, Spain, to Vienna in Austria. My flight earlier today had made the same journey from Delhi to Kabul in just a couple of hours.

The British invasion was initially successful. Regime change was achieved. Much of the army was withdrawn over the next year or two, but Kabul remained occupied by 4,500 troops and 12,000 contractors and dependents.

That's where the Bala Hisar comes in—the main citadel of Kabul.

For diplomatic reasons, the British had not occupied the Bala Hisar. The fortress doubled as a royal palace, and the Brits wanted to give their puppet ruler a fig leaf of independence. The mistake proved fatal. The fort was the only place that could have withstood a siege. When the inevitable revolt erupted in Kabul late in 1841, the garrison was trapped in their huts on an indefensible plain on the outskirts of the city. A deal was cut for a withdrawal back to India. But the column was attacked and massacred before it reached the safety of a secure base at Jalalabad, 90 miles (145 km) to the east. Only a single Brit made it, a Dr Brydon.

Masum is delighted that I've even heard of the Bala Hisar and we drive across town to go see it. As a history buff, it is a remarkable feeling to be standing on the ground where the tragedy of that First Anglo-Afghan War had begun to unfold, and at the exact same season, early November.

The author at Bala Hisar

Bala Hisar means "High Fort," and the reason for the name is obvious. It sits on a steep hill that dominates Kabul, on the south side of the river.

The fort itself does not appear remarkable. Stone ramparts line the slopes of a dusty khaki-colored hill overlooking the city. Despite the name High Fort, the walls are not especially high, with no particularly tall towers. But to be fair, it's difficult to explore properly.

The Soviets, presumably learning from history, had occupied the Bala Hisar. After they left, the fort became a headquarters for the army of the Democratic Republic of Afghanistan. So obviously we cannot look inside, or even get very close. Masum says there are minefields closer to the walls, a reminder this is an active war zone. But we walk around, looking down on the ancient city.

The lower parts of the hill contain cemeteries, decorated with small colourful flags. Masum explains it is the custom to mark a family member's resting place with these prayer flags. They will become all too familiar on this trip.

The hill and the cemeteries are quiet, with almost nobody around.

The Bala Hisar is still there today. It survived the colonial wars pretty well, and the Soviet occupation. But it was badly damaged by fighting in the civil war in 1994.

We head back towards downtown. I start to notice more prayer flags for the dead. By the side of the road is a burned out bus, decorated with 20 or 30 prayer flags. Each one represents someone who had died.

"Is that what I think it is?" I ask Masum.

"Yes," he sighs. "The war came here."

༄༅ ༄༅ ༄༅

We drive into the old city and park near the river. The city is abuzz: open air market stalls, selling everything from carpets and calicoes to pomegranates and peaches. Shoppers mill about, some in traditional clothes, some in Western clothes. There is some traffic noise, but the hubbub comes mostly from voices. Chatting. Laughing. Hawking, Haggling.

We walk onto an old stone bridge.[5] When I am told its age, I calculate that it would have been here when the Brits first invaded. Sorry, but that's how I roll. It's small, maybe just a footbridge or maybe wide enough for a single vehicle. It's crowded.

I am surprised how broad and full the Kabul River actually is. I imagined Afghanistan as an arid country, and from my travels elsewhere, I expected the riverbed to be dry, given how late it is in the season. But the river is in flood, and looks to be about the same width and depth as the River Thames, back home in sunny Shepparton.

The river is the heart of Kabul. Looking at a map, especially a topographical map, you can see why Kabul became an important city in ancient times. River valleys and mountain passes funnel traffic here, the Kabul river flows from the southwest, giving you access to

---

[5]*On a side note, one of the wonders of the internet in 2020 is being able to geolocate images, especially if there are prominent buildings in the background. I did not know where we were at the time, other than downtown in the Old City. The open air market is on the left, as you look downstream. The dome of a mosque is on the right side of the river, close to a larger road bridge. I'm pretty sure we're looking southeast and that's the Pul-e-Kheshti mosque, and that other bridge downstream is on the Nadir Pashton Road. Google Maps lists the bridge where I met Masum's friend simply as "Brige."*

Ghazni and Kandahar; then after passing through the city the river flows east towards Jalalabad and Peshawar; another river flows down the Salang Valley to join the Kabul river from the north; another route takes you south to Gardez and Khost.

The rivers of Afghanistan are fed mainly by the snows that fall in the Hindu Kush in winter. They flood in spring and many dry up as the summer advances. The Kabul river is an exception and, as I can see, remains flowing all year round. Water is precious everywhere.

While I'm getting over my geographical sense of wonder at the breadth of the river, something even more astonishing occurs: Masum shouts hallo to a friend on the bridge.

A woman.

She is in a sharp-looking business suit, her hair is uncovered and styled, and she's wearing makeup and a modest amount of jewellery. Moreover, she is unaccompanied. A professional woman, just going about her business.

I never knew her name. Masum of course says it, when he introduces us. But I am unfamiliar with it, and I'm too polite to ask again after two attempts. She smiles politely and we shake hands. I try out some of the pleasantries Masum has been trying to teach me in Dari. Unsuccessfully. But she's happy for me to take her photo.

They chat and catch up. They are clearly good friends. I'm unable to join in the conversation, but even so, this lady changes my view of the world.

She would have been at home in any western city. But this was Kabul. To be honest, I did not think it possible. I understood Afghanistan to be a very conservative society, which had shown itself willing to oppose outside influence with extreme violence. I knew the cities were different, but I had no idea an Afghan woman could be this liberated.

Traditional Afghan culture, reinforced by Islam, gives a special status to women. A positive interpretation would say women are protected from abuse, by being shielded from men outside of their family. A negative interpretation would say they are inherently abused by being denied their own identity and agency by a violent patriarchy.

Both interpretations are gross over-simplifications, of course.

Afghan culture, contrary to stereotype, has shifted significantly, especially in recent decades. Significant parts of the country were not converted to Islam until the late 1800s. Until 1896, Nuristan, the Land of Light, was known as Kafiristan, the Land of Unbelievers, with a distinct religion, similar to Hinduism. In many other areas, some scholars say Islam was secondary to local cultural practice, giving women, for example, different degrees of autonomy, and the ability to dress and socialize more freely.

The twentieth century saw Afghan society torn in polar opposite directions. Urban populations embraced literacy and European values and ideas, while a religious awakening, funded by oil money from Saudi Arabia and other Gulf states, empowered a more conservative interpretation of Islam, especially in the countryside. This divide was accentuated by the Soviet invasion, and later climaxed in the Taliban government from 1996 to 2001, with its violent imposition of a very Saudi/Wahabi interpretation of Islam, with women utterly sequestered from the workplace, or any form of public life, or from being seen at all.

Much of this divide was now embodied right here in front of me on this bridge over the Kabul River. However awful the Soviet occupation had been—and there is no denying its horrors—this woman had been protected by it to some extent. Afghan women of a certain class, I am told, had been educated and dressing in Western fashions for decades before the Soviet invasion. But the Islamic revival was now putting that in question.

Afghanistan had been on the nightly news in the West since the Soviet invasion in 1979. Our view of the nation had been largely shaped by that coverage. A plucky, pious people taking on our common communist enemy. The godless Soviets were portrayed as trying to Sovietize Afghan society by force. Our sympathies were supposed to be with the resistance. But those comfortable truths fell apart for me on that bridge. If "our" side won, then what would happen to this woman? Would she ever be able to be outdoors again, uncovered and unaccompanied by a man telling her where she could go and what she should do? Those simple freedoms would be lost. Was that the liberation we in the West were supporting? Would she be able to work? Would her daughter be allowed to go to school?

We had no idea at the time, but just six months after that meeting on the bridge, the communist regime would fall to the Mujahidin. This woman would have had to flee, or start a life wearing a *burqa*.

One of the joys of travel is to have your assumptions challenged, and your misconceptions exposed. If you have an open mind, it can become a vital part of a good education. I wouldn't have missed this experience on the bridge for the world. I resolve to never take anything at face value ever again.

ЄѺӠ   ЄѺӠ   ЄѺӠ

I realize I need money. I need to get some of the local currency. As I mentioned, I was not able to get any "Afghanis" in London or Delhi. I ask if we can go to a bank.

Masum laughs, snorting uncontrollably.

"No, no, no." He struggles to speak between chuckles. "We must go somewhere special."

"Oh? Where?" I'm usually uncomfortable changing money on the black market when traveling. I'm even more skeptical of doing it in a police state.

"Chicken Street," says Masum. "It's where you can do any kind of business in Kabul."

He sees my face and puts a hand on my shoulder: "Don't worry, my friend. It's very safe."

Chicken Street can only be described as a wild place. It's the heart of Afghanistan's black market. Everything feels dodgy, underground, sketchy, mobbed-up. There are jewellery stores, pawn shops, spice stores, rugs, trinkets, money lenders. No chickens, though, I notice. I heard it got spruced up after the US invasion and became trendy with foreigners. But back in 1991, it is all Afghans.

We enter a store selling trinkets. A guard opens a door and we climb up a dark stairway. Another guard opens another door to a small office which seems gloomy despite the large window. The window is wide open, and the bustle and hustle of Chicken Street reverberates through the room.

Sitting behind a desk is a paunchy middle-aged man in a Western business jacket, over a black sweater and a nice white shirt. He's very polite. We all shake hands, but he looks a little nervous and sweaty. He has big tinted glasses, and his long jet-black hair seems slicked down.

Money-changer, Kabul, 1991

Masum explains my situation. The money man seems skeptical but, as always, Masum wins him over. We get tea. I hand over my pathetically small handful of US dollars, and receive an impossibly large armful of Afghanis. The exchange rate is ridiculously better than the official one I had researched before leaving London.

The money changer is much more relaxed now, and chats with Masum over tea. He lets me take his photo, and another from his window. There's a rug stall below, and I notice I'm the centre of attention for several men sitting on the carpets below. It feels like the wrong side of curious—almost intimate. I am very fair, and I look quite young, with what some might call girlish good looks. Not for the last time in Afghanistan I feel a little uncomfortable.

※ ※ ※

When we get back to the house late in the afternoon, Chris announces we are going out for supper. It's a dinner party, at the home of the Bulgarian ambassador. Chris tells me he is the best-informed person in Kabul. An excellent source. I put on my one clean shirt.

Bulgaria, in 1991, is still an ally of the Soviet Union. It's a small country in the Balkan region of southeast Europe. It had only won its independence from the Ottoman Turkish empire a century before. Since 1945 it had been held tightly in Moscow's empire, through the Warsaw Pact treaty. Each of the Warsaw Pact nations had contributed in one way or another to the Soviet occupation of Afghanistan. Since the departure of the Soviets, Chris explains, the Bulgarian embassy has become a key conduit for diplomacy and intelligence in Kabul. A democratic revolution is taking place back home in Bulgaria, but out here, the old diplomats from the old communist regime remain firmly in place, for now.

At the appointed time, Masum drops us off and then heads home to his family. He's been such a kind and affable companion for my first day in Afghanistan.

The ambassador's house sits on the corner of a street and is not especially grand for the residence of a senior diplomat. It seems not much bigger than Chris's.

We knock. The door is opened by perhaps the most beautiful woman I've ever seen in my life up to that point. A stunning blonde. In an older time, she would be described as a perfect ten. Her looks were an asset and she knew it, but I'll get to that in a little while.

She hugs Chris and shakes my hand. Chris introduces her. I'll call her Ana. She is the Bulgarian ambassador's assistant. I've always been clumsy and awkward around women, especially beautiful women, but I manage to retain my composure. Wine helps.

Inside, the ambassador's residence is furnished elegantly, with good furniture and the finest Afghan rugs and artwork on display.

"Nice place," I blurt out.

"Thank you."

I turn and see a bright smile.

"Valentin Gatsinski, at your service." The ambassador's English is impeccable, with a hint of an eastern European accent. He's a portly man, with thin grey hair, maybe in his late 50s. His heavy jowls shake when he laughs.

Drinks appear from somewhere as introductions are completed.

I am the first topic of conversation.

"What are you doing here?" asks Valentin, in a tone that suggests only a fool comes to Kabul willingly.

I explain that I'm here to see my friend and to see if I would like the life of a foreign correspondent. The ambassador looks at me with pity, but he says he understands.

We dine at a table. That would become unusual as my travel progressed through Afghanistan. But it seems normal enough in the moment. Unlike lunch with Tajmuddin, there is cutlery.

Chris and I are the only guests besides the ambassador and his assistant. We are served by an Afghan man. The ambassador helps, which impresses me. The food is a mix of Bulgarian and Afghan. Curiously, there are similarities.

"My country, Bulgaria, is right next to Turkey, as of course I'm sure you know," explains Valentin. "The Ottoman Turks even owned my homeland for a couple of hundred years. So of course they influenced our culture, in food and music and so on. And the Turks, as you know, were originally from here in central Asia. The Silk Road connected us all."

We're served a variety of small plates, a saffron-coloured stew like I'd enjoyed at lunchtime. Lamb, of course. Then different plates of vegetables, like eggplant, okra, lentils, carrot and cauliflower, mixed in rice and some blended to my delight with nuts and fruits like raisins, grapes or slices of apricot, and maybe some yoghurt or goat cheese curds. Everyone helps themselves to a spoonful of each.

The conversation turns from personal chit-chat to politics. Mostly about the situation here in Afghanistan, and the current state of the United Nations peace plan.

"If only we could hear from Ahmed Shah Massoud," laments Valentin. "He's the only player who has yet to respond. He keeps saying the UN should go to him, but who can get to him in those mountains?"

"Have you ever met him?" I ask. I'm fascinated by Massoud. The man is a living legend.

Valentin laughs. "I'm on the wrong side."

"What do you make of him?"

There's a brief pause.

"He has caused our friends a lot of trouble. He's good at that.'

"Do you think the UN plan could really bring peace?" I ask.

Another pause. Valentin purses his lips while he's thinking. "It might. It could bring change. But I don't know if it can bring peace. There are so many strongmen in the country now, on the other side. I don't know if any of them want to be told what to do by any of the others."

The conversation soon turns from local news to affairs in Moscow and eastern Europe more broadly. Change is in the air. It's only been two years since the Berlin Wall fell. The old world order is collapsing. It's unclear if aid will keep coming south to prop up the communist regime here. It's unclear if the Soviet Union itself will even survive. We also discuss Iraq. The First Gulf War had been fought earlier that year, and the wisdom of not advancing on Baghdad is still being debated. Saddam Hussein is another friend of the Soviets.

As a diplomat from a Warsaw Pact country, Valentin's future could be jeopardized by the collapse of the old order. He could lose his job or his pension, or worse. Many regime figures in Bulgaria's neighbour, Romania, had been killed or jailed after a revolution there at the end of 1989. However, if Valentin is concerned by any of this, he does not show it. He's the perfect diplomat.

Ambassador Gatsinski is very charming. He puts everyone at ease, and recounts marvelous stories, none of which I can remember. Chris does the same job on our behalf. Ana and I are fairly quiet.

There is also a little gossip, about this aid worker sleeping with that diplomat and so on. I learn that for most organizations, Kabul is considered a hardship posting. Because of the danger, spouses and families are discouraged or prohibited. That leaves a lot of young and fit "internationals"—aid workers, diplomats and journalists—with a lot of temptation. The danger of the war hangs over everyone like the sword of Damocles, adding an impulse to enjoy every day you are given, while you can. I am surprised to be on the inside of this particular information loop. I listen, gobsmacked. Again, not what I expected from a war zone. It seems logical, if a little shocking.

I ask if any internationals develop relationships with locals, and I'm met with howls of derision. Local women are strictly out of bounds. No one even thinks about it. Everyone recounts the story of an aid worker who developed a crush on an Afghan woman. I don't think the relationship was ever consummated, but it was enough to attract the wrath of her family. The aid worker had to flee home to England. I am assured that one of the woman's brothers tracked him down and killed him. In Birmingham. Everyone had that particular detail. The story sounded like folklore, but hearing it from multiple sources, with the same details, made it feel plausible. Even if it was just a fable, the lesson was clear. If you're a foreign male, never try to reach out to Afghan women, even platonically.

Our meal ends with fruit of the unforbidden kind. The Kabul valley is famous for its fruit. Pomegranates, apricots, melons and grapes are pure delight.

Dinner wraps up quickly. We're heading out.

"Out?" I ask. "Where to?"

"A bar."

Wait, what? A bar? In a war zone? In a Muslim nation?

Yes. Afghanistan under the communists does not count itself as Islamic. In fact, one way for Afghans to prove their loyalty to the regime is to drink. The problem is—as one source told me—most of them are not very good at it.

We jump into the ambassador's car and he drives us all to a bar attached to a hotel. Only "internationals" are allowed. Aid workers, diplomats, journalists. It's not large, but it's hopping.

Lights are flashing. Western music is pulsing. People are dancing. There's even a little sexual tension. The drinks are unbelievably cheap.

I'm introduced to countless people. There seems to be an even number of women, which is not what I had expected. Everyone seems to have a story about a recent close call with danger. Or gossip about who's hooking up with whom.

The other subject of gossip is who is spying for whom. No one admits to being a spy themselves, but it seems that everyone thinks everybody else is a spy. Now, the word spy in the Western imagination conveys James Bond or Jason Bourne. In reality, it's much more mundane, meaning you might just share information that you gather in the ordinary course of your day with your own government, or occasionally somebody else's government.

However, in this bar in Kabul I am introduced to some individuals whom I'm told are more in the mould of Bond and Bourne. One such unlikely candidate is a petite, mature European woman. I won't give her name, but let's call her Françoise. Officially, she works for the United Nations, but behind her back, everyone tells stories about her courage under fire, and her connections with the Mujahidin. In particular, I hear the same story from a couple of people about how Françoise kept her cool during a battle involving tanks while she herself was stuck in quicksand or a swamp, depending on the *raconteur*. It's only bar-room gossip, and is at best exaggerated. But it gives you a sense of the milieu of the international community in Kabul back then. Sex, spies and danger.

Another, more mundane, surprise comes in a conversation with another UN employee. This one is a chap from Zimbabwe. We have a longish chat about his terms of employment, as I am keen to compare notes with the BBC's package. Now, you should know that the average wage in Zimbabwe at this time was about one hundred times less than the average wage in the UK or the US, and yet this chap is making a full Western salary. I was happy for him, and it seems perfectly fair and reasonable. But what a lucky break, compared to his countrymen? Besides the salary, all his living expenses are paid for; there is hardship pay on top, and then there is a month or more "convalescent time" after every two months in-country—basically extra vacation—even though his particular job does not sound especially hazardous. It sounds like a wonderful gravy train, even for a Westerner.

In the next few days, I will meet and travel with individuals who more than earn such pay and benefits, risking their lives to help people in desperate need. But in that moment, I was kind of aghast at the waste and abuse of some of these international organizations. The perks of being a foreign correspondent pale in comparison.

Of course, being the virtuous public servant I am, it never occurs to me to try to jump aboard this gravy train.

Eventually we leave the bar, and everyone is feeling peckish. So somebody suggests we go looking for street kebabs. By now, we're all pretty buzzed, to put it mildly. We're young, loud and drunk. We're laughing and stumbling around. Somehow we find a kebab stall, and get a bucket full. We wind up back at the ambassador's residence, stuff our faces with the kebabs, and wash them down with vodka shots.

Life here in Kabul is a blast. I could get used to this!

Chapter 7

Road Trip!

I wake up next morning, not surprisingly, with a slight headache. (And yes, I wake up alone, in case any of you are wondering. I'm a married man, and I try to live as a man of honour). Thankfully the window in Chris's guest room has been left ajar, and a night of fresh air has taken the sting out of the hangover. I'm pleasantly surprised it's not worse, when I review the long evening we had.

I get up a little after dawn, just to open the window wider. I take in a deep draught of the chill morning air. It feels clean and fresh and invigorating. I look up. I can see the mountains from the window. I notice the snow has crept a little further down the mountainside.

Over breakfast Chris nonchalantly drops into the conversation that we had been lucky with the curfew.

"The what?" I ask.

"The curfew. From dusk to dawn."

To me, the word curfew was only known through reading military history, where it is usually accompanied by a shoot-on-sight policy for curfew-breakers. I ask Chris if that's the case here.

"Well, yes," he replies. "But it's usually fine in the diplomatic quarter, where we were."

Usually fine. That's only mildly reassuring. I'm a little shocked. I had no idea there was any risk at all.

"By the way," says Chris, changing the subject. "You remember Ana, that nice young lady who works for the Bulgarian ambassador?"

Of course I do. We exchange compliments about her beauty.

"She is a real diplomat. And smart." His mouth curls with mischief. "But did you know that part of her job is to sleep with guys here who might be useful, to get leverage: compromising information or pictures? Diplomats, aid workers, journalists. They even have a word for it: *kompromat*."

I'd heard similar stories from other BBC veterans who'd worked in the Soviet bloc, so I should not have been so totally surprised. She seemed like such a nice girl.

I scoff. "How do you even know that?"

He raises an eyebrow. "Let's just say I was tempted."

My eyes open wide in shock.

"But I did the right thing. I have a girlfriend back home. I knew what Ana was about. The point is to be able to blackmail someone into doing what you want."

I don't push the subject. I'm sure he did the right thing.

ೋ ೋ ೋ

I don't remember exact details about the rest of that second day in Kabul. I think I spent most of it with Masum, again, sightseeing. I know we headed back to Chicken Street on an errand, and I felt myself being gawked at again.

At some point during the day, Masum hears rumours of fighting. We pick up Chris and head over to the Bulgarian ambassador's place again. The ambassador knows everything. The rumour is confirmed. There's some fighting a little to the north of Kabul, around towns called Golbahar and Jabal-os-Saraj. Too far for us to be able to hear anything. The names mean nothing to me, but there's a large map on the wall and Chris points out where we're talking about. I ask him about which factions might be involved. They're impressed with my knowledge of the country and its ethnic and political groupings.

At another moment during the day, Masum and I are out walking in the city. My eyes are drawn upward by the rare sound of a plane.

While I was in Kabul, the skies seemed to be always blue, free from pollution. Only once or twice a day would you see an airplane. I remember looking up and seeing my old friend, the last airworthy

Ariana Tupolev-154 airliner, and I am stunned to see it start to drop flares, in pairs. As a veteran, I know this can only have one purpose: to decoy heat-seeking missiles. Like, for example, the Stingers given to the Mujahidin by the CIA.

I'd been on that plane yesterday! Presumably we were dropping flares, too, on our approach. I realize for the first time that, out there somewhere in those mountains, are people who not only might be willing to take pot shots at a plane, but have the full capability to shoot it down.

To kill me.

It's odd that it should be this moment that I first think about possible mortal peril on this trip. I had been quite aware of the mortar threat at the airport. I was aware of the occasional shelling of the city by the rebels. I was shocked when I learned we had risked our lives by being out after curfew. But those were theoretical threats. Now before my eyes, I see an actual moment of danger that I had lived through, without knowing it. The pilot of the airplane that I'd flown on is concerned enough to drop flares to decoy heat-seeking missiles.

It makes perfect sense, as a newsman and military analyst, but it is an unusual feeling to realize that I could have become collateral damage.

My mind starts whirring.

"I noticed while we were coming in to land yesterday, that we descended in these tight circles. Is that to minimize the amount of time we spend low over the mountains, so that we would be less vulnerable to hostile fire and missiles?"

"No," Masum answers, laughing slightly. "That's just because they don't want to hit the mountains themselves. The Stinger can get you anywhere."

Not very comforting.

Stingers are US-made, man-portable, surface-to-air missiles which were supplied to the Mujahidin by the CIA at the prompting of Charlie Wilson, the Texas congressman made famous by the Tom Hanks movie, *Charlie Wilson's War*. In the movie, and in Western propaganda more widely, the Stingers made a decisive difference to the course of the war in Afghanistan, ending Soviet air supremacy. The truth is a little more complicated. Historians have found that the

Soviets had already begun their withdrawal before the Stingers started hitting their planes and helicopters. But, still, they had a significant psychological impact. Previously, the skies had been relatively safe for Soviet airpower.

Stingers were never used against a civilian airplane by the Mujahidin. But of course, we couldn't know that at the time.

8◈3   8◈3   8◈3

In the evening, it's back to the bar. It's not so lively today. The music is quieter. I take it pretty easy after last night's excess.

Mingling is easy. People are curious about who I am. My buddy Chris is off gadding about by himself.

Halfway through the evening, Chris runs over, excited.

"Hey, guess what?"

"What?"

"Well, you know you said you wanted to see more of the country?"

"Yes," I say cautiously.

"Well, it looks like we can make that happen."

"Oh yeah?"

"Yeah. Françoise says there's an aid convoy heading out of town tomorrow, and they've agreed to let us tag along."

"Convoy? By road?" I ask.

"Yeah, yeah," he says, brimming with characteristic enthusiasm. "Fantastic, eh?"

"How safe is that?"

"They know what they're doing, the blokes running the convoy," Chris assures me. "They wouldn't go if they couldn't handle it. We'll be in good hands. I've weighed it all up. Seems good."

I trust him. My gut is a little nervous. I put it down to excitement. Maybe it was telling me I should be a little more careful. When I wrote that telex message to Chris saying I'd like to see more of the country than just Kabul, I had assumed we would fly from one safely held government city to another. To Kandahar or Herat, for example. I had never thought we'd be taking a road trip. Oh well, if Chris has weighed it all up and is happy, then I'm okay. Not happy, but okay.

"How long will it take? Don't forget I only have a week. I have to get that flight out on Tuesday. Can't be late for my shift at Bush on Thursday."

"Oh goodness, yes," Chris assures me. "A day or two, up and back."

"So we're going soon?"

"Hopefully first thing tomorrow."

"Crikey. Alrighty, then." As Brits will always say in such a situation, I add: "Better get another round in!"

I don't think to ask how we will get back.

"Come on," says Chris after we've refilled our beers. "Let's go meet the blokes we're going with."

Chris introduces me to a couple of guys that I will get to share a lot with, over the next few days.

First I meet Fred Estall. He's in his late 30s, a little bulldog of a man. He's a Kiwi, a former officer in the New Zealand army. I don't think I ever see him not proudly wearing his olive green slouch hat, the trademark image of the ANZAC soldier since World War I. (Aussies usually fold one side up, while New Zealanders wear it with all sides down). He has a thick Saddam Hussein-style mustache. He has a face like a rugby forward or a guard on the offensive line in American football: somehow flattened. He's short but solid. A brusque, no nonsense kind of guy, with a dry sense of humour. Bulldog seems very *apropos*: when necessary he barks orders, and takes no guff. I take an instant liking to him.

He works for the United Nations now, and he will be in charge of our little convoy.

The other man is a fellow Brit called Alex Shaw. He has the accent and carriage of a gentleman who went to a good school. He too has a confident air. He's more slender than Fred. Unshaven, but without a full beard. Dark hair. He is not as direct.

Like Fred, Alex is a former infantry officer, although he was in the British army. He works for an independent NGO, a non-profit non-governmental organization.

"An aid worker?" I ask.

"Not quite," he says. "I'm a de-miner."

I think I've misheard.

"A miner?" I'm baffled. There are mines in Afghanistan with foreign workers?

"No. De-miner," says Alex. "I find and remove landmines."

My jaw drops.

"You know. The exploding kind," he adds. I must appear slow.

I'd never heard of such a thing. Western volunteers, working for peanuts, risking their lives, finding and removing landmines in an active war zone?

"Plus other unexploded ordnance, like artillery shells," adds Alex.

I am impressed with his altruism and courage, and that of all his comrades. The organization that Alex worked for is the HALO Trust.[6] They are still going strong, actively helping people and communities across the globe deal with the horrors of landmines.

Alex tells me he's a former officer in the Gurkhas. I'm fascinated by this. I had grown up on tales of the legendary courage of the Gurkhas. They have served the British Crown since 1815, and most recently in the Falklands War of 1982. Their close combat weapon is the curve-bladed *kukri*, which allegedly must taste blood whenever it is drawn.

"Well that's not strictly accurate," explains Alex. "They have to clean them every day, so it would get a bit messy if they're pricking their fingers all the time."

Gurkhas are soldiers recruited under contract from the Himalayan country of Nepal, to serve in the armies of India, the UK, Singapore and Brunei. In the British army, about a third of the Gurkha regimental officers are white British men, but they are first required to learn the language and culture of their soldiers. The other officers are Gurkhas who have risen through the ranks.

My dad had embarrassed me as a teenager, by posing for pictures with a paraded detachment of Gurkha soldiers, during a visit to the Sandhurst military academy. That was back when I was considering a military career. But besides that, I had never met one. They were not entitled to settle in the UK, back then, after their service. Moreover, they were only paid a fraction of what British squaddies made until 2007, when they were granted equal pay, after something of a public outcry in the UK.

---

[6]Find out more about the HALO Trust and its vital work at HALOTrust.org

The Gurkhas are in a sense, the final remnant of Britain's once mighty imperial and colonial armed forces. It seems appropriate that a former Gurkha officer should find work in Asia.

"By the way," Alex adds, "there's a detachment of Gurkhas here in Kabul, guarding the British embassy. Retired, of course, but you're never really an ex-Gurkha."

"There's a British embassy here in Kabul? I thought it was closed way back when, to protest against the Soviet invasion?"

"It was," Alex explains. "But it's still there. Still British. Just unoccupied. The Gurkhas maintain it, and keep out any unwanted visitors."

"Really?"

"Absolutely," he says. "Let's go, and you can see for yourself. It's a beautiful building anyway. It's pretty close, too."

We find our way into somebody's car and drive a few blocks.

The Afghan caretaker is brusque and unwelcoming but he is overruled by the Gurkhas, who have come to know Alex pretty well since he arrived in-country a few months ago.

True to form, the Gurkhas at the embassy are immaculate and sharp. I'm slightly disappointed they are not uniformed and armed. Alex chats with them in Gorkhali. It occurs to me later that I should have asked Alex to wish them a happy Diwali from me. Most Nepalis are Hindu, and this week is the festival of light, Diwali. But as usual, I don't think about it in time.

The embassy itself is grand. It's dark, so I didn't get a clear image of the outside, but the inside was pretty spectacular, as one would expect from a relic expected to demonstrate the Izzat, or prestige, of the British Raj. The Empire. A long wide hallway stretches seemingly endlessly into the interior of the building. Much of the artwork has been removed from the walls, but thick Persian rugs, predominantly red in colour, cover the floors. I am told some factoid about the rug in the hallway being the biggest rug of its kind in the world, or some such thing. I'm told how they have trouble with the roofs from the weight of snow in winter, and how the Gurkhas need to shovel it off. This was many years before I moved to New England and lived through a real winter—which is very different from the cool damp season we have in old England and laughingly call winter.

It is bizarre to run into Gurkhas in Afghanistan. One of the supporting characters in Rudyard Kipling's novel, *The Man Who Would Be King,* is a Gurkha soldier trapped alone in wildest Kafiristan. It is yet another level of surreal.

Back at the bar, it's noisy. We crack a few more beers. Yes, we have to get up early. But we have no idea how long it will be before we can grab another beer. We're young, we'll bounce back. It's another late night, although not as insane. No vodka shots.

It helps me, too. I get to sleep without reflecting on what tomorrow might bring.

Chapter 8

The Running Man

The next morning, Thursday November 7th 1991, seems a little cooler and crisper, but still bright. The snow has crept even further down the mountainsides.

I had no idea, but today was to be one of those days that change your life. Perhaps define it.

I'm dressed for the road: jeans, black shirt, brogues. I have my thick, white aran sweater handy for when it gets cold. Chris has a similar take: brogues, khakis, yellow shirt and funnily enough, a similar aran sweater. Our sleeping bags, wash gear and clean underwear are in backpacks. I'm excited. A little nervous. But mostly excited.

Chris the author with Chris Bowers, ready for the road trip

Masum drives us over to the United Nations compound. Chris and I grab our packs and jump out. Masum stays in the car, then gives a friendly wave and drives off.

"Where's he going?"

"Oh, he can't come with us," says Chris, matter-of-factly. "He was in the army once upon a time, you see. If we run into the wrong people, it could be awkward," he said. Talk about classic English understatement. It was only later that I realized how chilling those words were. I didn't really understand at the time.

Masum's departure leaves me feeling slightly uncomfortable. It hints that there could be some danger on this trip. Perhaps we will run into "wrong people." It also leaves us at a little disadvantage. How do we function without a translator or fixer who knows the country and has all the contacts? Chris says it will all be fine. I trust him.

Masum had never mentioned his military service to me. Chris explains that being an Afghan male of a certain age, he had had no choice. All Afghan men at that time were conscripted into the army, or drafted, as they say in the US, and had to serve two years. I later learned he was proud of the fact that he'd never actually killed anyone in the service. But he had been part of the army fighting the Mujahidin.

Masum's military service also reminded me of the arbitrary nature of war, and how it can sweep up ordinary, mild-mannered people like him. He was a conscript. No volunteer. Service was just something you had to go through. As a soldier in Germany during the Cold War, waiting for the Warsaw Pact to come over the horizon, it had been easy for me to visualize potential enemy soldiers as mere targets. Now, here was a thoroughly pleasant chap who had himself served in one of those armies allied with the Soviet Red Army. It seemed impossible to imagine a world in which I should have to try to kill him.

I also later learn that Masum's background in the military and his connections to the regime do not sit well with certain people at the UN. Chris later explained that Masum probably has to tell the government where he's going and who he's meeting. It's a fact of life for people in a civil war that they have to make compromises to stay safe. There's a lot going on that I don't know about.

The convoy is assembling.[7] It's not very large. There's a big army-style four-ton truck, loaded with supplies. It's painted white and marked in blue with United Nations insignia. The tarpaulin cover is also white. There's another truck, a little smaller, marked with the insignia of the HALO Trust—Alex's de-mining outfit. It's also painted white, and covered with an olive green tarp. Then there's a white Toyota pick-up truck, with a double cab. It's carrying supplies on the bed at the back, covered with a white tarp. And that's it. Three vehicles.

I'd been told we are bringing vital supplies to some isolated places to help them last through the winter. There doesn't seem to be a lot here. I'm told it's mostly low-bulk goods like medical supplies, plus a little fuel for generators and some food.

I'm told that children will die over the winter if we don't make it through. The winter is severe enough to close the mountain passes

---

[7] *It was only while researching this book that I learned just how rare and unusual it was for the United Nations to try to move any kind of vehicle through the Salang Pass at this moment in history. It was simply too dangerous. The Salang was the Soviet supply bottleneck and the Muj kept it under near constant attack. Fred himself was in charge of UN security and routinely blocked such trips. For example, normal protocol for travel to Pul-i-Khumri, at the far end of the Pass, was to fly over the Hindu Kush mountains to Mazar-i-Sharif, then drive back south. It seems only the dire nature of the humanitarian situation in Taloqan and Kunduz forced them to act.*

where we're going, so this is the last opportunity to push through without getting stuck on the wrong side of the Hindu Kush, or risking too much danger from the ice and snow.

Fred is there in his trademark Kiwi slouch hat, army boots and lightweight army trousers. His military look is only broken up by a coarse brown shirt, untucked. His face is pure, barely restrained bulldog. Confidence and aggression. You can tell he's itching to get moving.

Alex is dressed more casually, in jeans, a sweater and sunglasses. He has a couple of days growth of auburn stubble on his face. He's one of those men who seem to look cool however casually they dress. His lips purse often, when trying not to laugh or while composing his thoughts before speaking. He's scruffy yet very put together; he reminds me a little of the actor, Hugh Grant, in the way he speaks and carries himself.

Fred Estall of the UN and Alex Shaw of the
HALO Trust, the de-mining organization

Some of the other UN workers we had met with over the last couple of days are also milling about. Most are there just to see us off. The mood is alternately playful and solemn. Françoise, the alleged agent from the tank fight in the swamp, is also there. The convoy is her brain child.

I think to myself: if the convoy is so safe, why all the hugs?

ℰ◈℈ ℰ◈℈ ℰ◈℈

Time to go! Afghans will be driving the trucks, while Fred will be behind the wheel of the pickup, with Alex riding shotgun, and Chris and me in the back seat. Shotgun is just a metaphor. None of us are armed. I put aside a feeling of foreboding and I am filled with wonder, curiosity and excitement.

We jump on a main road heading out of town. It's called a highway but is only big enough really for two lanes. I don't actually know where we are going. I'd been told the names of a couple of towns, but they are unfamiliar. I do not know where they are. North, but I don't know how far, or how long it will take.

Kabul then was a lot smaller than it is now.[8] Traffic was light compared to today and we soon reach the edge of town.

We stop at a casual-looking checkpoint on the edge of town. It's unfortified. Just soldiers waving us down.

The soldiers have the uniforms of the Afghan army, which look uncomfortable, as if made from coarse, heavy wool, like the old British battle dress from World War II. I was familiar with that personally, having been issued a set when I attended my Territorial Army recruit selection weekend, back in 1982. Talk about itchy.

The Afghan army's uniforms are coloured a plain dark brown or maybe it's a brownish olive green. Brown remains the main colour in my memory. There's no disruptive patterning on the uniforms; no attempt at camouflage. I also notice there's no body armour of any kind—not even any helmets in sight. To be fair, I was never issued body armour while in the British Army in the early 1980s. It seems unthinkable nowadays.

Only a couple of the soldiers are carrying their weapons. Nobody is wearing the webbing-belting which we almost always had to wear when we were on duty. That meant these Afghan soldiers have no quick access to spare ammunition, grenades or first aid kits if they are surprised. So, either this is a very safe and cushy post, or their discipline is very poor.

---

[8]*Kabul had about 1.6m people in 1991, compared to 4.2m in 2020. Source: UN World Population Prospects 21 Sep 2020* [www.macrotrends.net/cities/20002/kabul/population]

These soldiers look relaxed. Fred opens his window and I hear a phrase that will become our catch-call for the next week.

"Moolee matta-heed! Moolee matta-heed!"

The soldiers wave us on.

"What's '*Moolee matta-heed*'?" I ask.

"United Nations," replied Fred and Alex in unison.

"Oh," I say. "So the UN is pretty well known, then?"

"Sort of. Not perfect," explains Fred. "But good enough."

We enter the flat, fertile plain of the Kabul river valley. It's known as the Shomali Plain. The fields and meadows are a mix of green and khaki. The mountains are still some miles off, bare and brown as always, except for their white caps of snow. The sky remains a perfect blue, with the occasional fluffy white cloud, and that wonderful hazy light provided by the altitude. Kabul is several hundred feet further above sea level than, say, Boulder or Denver or Davos, Switzerland.

It's only a couple of minutes since we passed that first checkpoint —buildings have just given way to fields—when I suddenly notice a man jogging across the field from a square, flat-roofed adobe farmhouse. He looks like a farmer. He's not the most dramatic thing I'm about to see, but his image is the first that is seared into my mind. To this day.

The old farmer has a dark turban, with a tail of cloth swinging beside it; a white and black chequered scarf—known as a *shemagh*— coiled loose around his neck. He has a dark gray *kurtah*, the long shirt, girded up over his knees. He's clutching it with one hand in front of him, so he can run faster. I can see his bare knees and lower legs, brushing through the long grass, as he jogs forward. He has a long salt and pepper beard, and a weathered face. His eyes are looking straight ahead and they look troubled. Why is he jogging? Why does he look alarmed?

It looks like the old man is moving in slow motion. But it's just my mind. Everything seems to be slowing down.

Just at that moment, Fred the Kiwi tilts his head forwards. "Looks like trouble."

I take my eyes off the old farmer and see other people moving in the fields. Men and boys mostly, but a couple of women, too. They are all converging on what looks like an accident ahead. If you've ever come across a vehicle accident you will know the kind of motion I mean, where residents and passersby start to converge on the scene. But this is no accident.

I lean forwards and see some sort of military vehicle on its side. As we got closer, I recognize it as a BTR-60, an armoured personnel carrier, or APC. An APC is designed to carry infantry into battle, as its name implies. A BTR-60 has a crew of two and can carry 12 fully armed infantry soldiers. Some APCs have tracks like a tank, some have wheels. A BTR-60 has wheels, four big ones on each side, and a tiny armoured turret on top for a machine gunner. I had been trained to recognize them when I was a young rifleman in the British Army, using pocket sized cards filled with black silhouettes of different Soviet vehicles. But this is the first one I've seen in real life.

And it's in a bad way.

It's dark green, like the ones we might have seen in the North German Plain, had the Red Army decided to roll across the Inner German Border. It looks to me like this BTR-60 had rolled off the road into the dirt. It's badly knocked about. Tires are missing. Wisps of black smoke hang in the air. Smouldering.

Then I see the blood.

Not a little spatter like you might see in a Hollywood movie. I mean an ocean of blood. The entire side of the dust-caked highway is covered in blood. It is fresh and bright-red, a stark contrast to the khaki street, the green fields and the clear blue sky. I've never seen so much blood and hope I never will. We cross to the other side of the road to avoid it.

In the center of the ocean of blood is an island. A man. He is wearing the plain, dark brown uniform of the Afghan army. Not a kid, an older man, maybe in his early 30s. He appears to be asleep on his side. He looks quite comfortable. Except for the fact that half his face is missing. His head is split neatly down the middle, from the crown to the jaw. So half of his nose and mouth have survived, and half of his handsome moustache, and half of his neat black hair.

I could not imagine an injury that could create such a neat wound. It's an image I have never been able to get out of my head.

What's left of his face is white. I mean white. Paper white. Snow white. I've never seen anything so unnatural. I see the blood, and think: so this is what the phrase "bled white" actually means.

Beyond the sleeping man is another figure, also in the dark brown uniform of the Afghan army. This one does not look comfortable. Arms and legs are twisted in unnatural directions, like a rag doll thrown to the ground. I can't see his face. Does he even have a head?

The old farmer in the *kurtah*, whose image I still recall so vividly, was just a witness; a portent of trouble. His face had told me something was wrong.

That we had left safety behind us.

Everyone in the pickup is silent. The air is tense. The mood serious.

We are riding on a humanitarian convoy, packed with medical supplies, and carrying several men with excellent first-aid training.

"Shouldn't we stop and help?" I ask.

There's a moment of silence

"They're past helping," says Fred, nodding towards the fallen. It dawns on me the men in the brown uniforms are dead.

Up to this point in my life, I think I'd only ever seen one dead person in real life. I'd been to several funerals, but open caskets are not a thing in England. My father, however, had passed three years previously. It was tragic loss, that upsets me to this day. He was a kind soul, taken much too young. But he'd had a hard life, and lived hard. I saw him about an hour after he'd passed. He seemed smaller than life, yellow, cold, limp. But at least he was clean; lying on white sheets; his glasses neatly folded by his bed; the machines finally quiet. It was heartbreaking. But it was all very neat and clinical, and respectful, in a way. Not at all like what I see now.

I go silent. I know a BTR-60 can carry 12 more men besides those we can see. I am wondering about asking whether we should stop to check and help them if we can, when Fred adds: "Besides, it's unsafe."

I'm not sure if he's worried about the risk from fire, or from ammunition or ordnance exploding, or from the villagers, or from the authorities when they arrive.

Thinking it's the latter, I say, "It was just an accident." I'm still thinking the APC has just rolled over.

"No," says Fred, his jaw tightening. "Landmine."

I go quiet again. My mind whirring. Wait, what? Landmine? This close to Kabul? We have literally just passed the city limits. The Muj can penetrate this close?

And then there's the matter of coming face-to-face with death. (Or should I say, face-to-half-face? Sorry, the only way to cope with death and trauma sometimes is to joke about it. Ask any emergency room surgeon.)

I suddenly realize that this trip will not be as safe as I had expected.

I had had plenty of life-threatening misadventures and accidents in my life up to this point already. Eleven stitches on my face and some broken teeth in a bike accident. Twice I'd nearly been struck by lightning. I had lived down-and-out in Paris for a week. I'd climbed Mount Kilimanjaro, back when the guides carried rifles to fight off bandits. I'd sailed in a leaky, overcrowded, badly-captained dhow across that part of the Indian Ocean that's the breeding ground for Great White sharks. I had run into violent demonstrations in India against the caste law (the Mandal Commission). I'd been robbed by fake cops in Nairobi. I'd been a soldier on guard against possible IRA attack in London. Plus all the stupid shit you did as a drunken teenager in Britain back in the day. These were all things that could have gone badly. But this? This was suddenly different. A whole different league. I had just been confronted with mortality in real time. And it had come totally out of the blue.

I had not expected this. I had assumed our journey was not going to be especially dangerous. Instead, this is the real deal. I could actually die. I am shocked.

Had I been brought up as an American I might have said, "You're not in Kansas anymore, Dorothy." Or maybe, "Shit just got real."

Instead, I am quiet. As I have mentioned, I usually get kind of serene in these moments, which helps me think quickly and take action as needed. Keep busy and focus on doing your job. Outwardly I might look like I have retained my composure and appear unflappable. But all the terror and trauma is being internalized and stored away for later, I promise you!

For a moment I feel like I'm out of my body, looking down at myself, sitting in the back of that pickup. A skinny guy in black shirt and jeans, looking a little lost.

It was an interesting moment. A sense of personal security and safety is so profound in most of us, most of the time, that we rarely give it any thought. In fact, it is a privilege. A privilege we just take for granted. To lose it suddenly and unexpectedly is profoundly disorienting and disturbing. Our assumed anchor is ripped away. In an instant, you are alone at sea, and in peril. Maybe feeling helpless. Your world is upended. It feels like the floor you're walking on has been ripped away and you're now just out there, floating in the air. Exposed and vulnerable.

Anyone who has endured a trauma, or suffered violence, or even witnessed it, has suffered that sudden disorientation. But not many then go on to realize they are just at the beginning of their peril. A car or bike accident, or even an assault, is sudden and awful; the injuries may last a lifetime; the psychological scars may never heal properly. But once you're out of immediate danger, your brain can switch back to that safety mode. The immediate threat is over. It can't get worse. In a war zone, once you lose your sense of personal security and safety, you have no idea when you will get it back. If ever. The threat not only continues but may well intensify. Your mind is filled with what might happen. My head, in that moment started to feel giddy, I guess from the rush of blood or adrenaline. I feel like I'm free-falling.

Of course, I don't say any of this. I couldn't have articulated any of it, anyway, at the time. My priority is to maintain my composure in front of my traveling companions. My friends who are ex-military say that in a war zone you just focus on doing your job. They chose this life, they knew what it might cost. But I didn't really have a job to focus on at that moment. I did not choose to be here. I had thought we would stay in securely-held government territory. I didn't understand what I was getting myself into.

I had bumbled into war.

Chapter 9

How to Pee in a Minefield

There is no going back now. Must keep a stiff upper lip. Our journey has only just begun.

As I'm processing what I've seen and heard, it occurs to me that maybe the mine that wrecked the BTR-60 is not alone.

"Landmine?" I ask, as casually as I can. "On the road?"

"Yep," answers Alex. Alex, as I hope you remember, is a former British army officer and an expert in landmines. He's a volunteer with the de-mining group, the HALO Trust. His job is literally to look for these things and get rid of them. So he knows his onions, as we say in the UK.

"See all the potholes?" he asks.

I nod.

"They bury them in those. Sometimes four or five on top of each other, deep down to avoid mine detectors."

"I see," I say as matter-of-factly as I can.

After a pause, I ask "Aren't we on the same road? Couldn't there be more?"

"Perhaps," chimes in Fred. "but they are typically placed to target a specific vehicle." They've clearly seen all this before. "I'll try to steer clear of the potholes, just in case," he adds cheerfully.

"Must have been an anti-tank mine to have flipped it over," clarifies Alex, grinning as he looks at Fred. I think these veterans of life in Afghanistan are amused by my innocence. "Anti-tank mines need more weight."

"Yes, I remember that from army days."

Landmines come in two main varieties. One is designed to kill people, the other is designed to destroy heavy vehicles, like tanks and APCs (armoured personnel carriers). Most are pressure activated. You don't want to waste your big expensive anti-tank mines on a couple of foot soldiers or civilians, so they are designed to be activated only by the weight of heavy vehicles.

Russian anti-tank mine
Photo: WikiCommons

I start rationalizing to myself that our little pickup is therefore not heavy enough to set off an anti-tank mine. So being in a road with anti-tank mines isn't as scary as I first thought. But then I remember that behind us in the convoy is a four-ton truck, fully laden with supplies. An armoured personnel carrier, like the BTR-60 we are leaving behind us, can't weigh much more than that. I now know that that Soviet APC is only ten tonnes.

But I keep quiet. Our veterans don't seem too troubled.

It was only in 2020 that I finally researched the numbers and discovered that most US and Soviet anti-tank mines only need a few hundred pounds of pressure (200-300 kg). Our fully laden Toyota pickup by itself must have been north of 4,000 lbs (1,800 kg), with us, our kit, and the supplies in the back.

We would have been toast, had we hit an anti-tank mine, anywhere on our trip. I now know that Alex and Fred were bluffing to stop me panicking and keep me quiet. It worked. Realizing this today fills the pit of my stomach with horror. We were navigating through a literal minefield on a hope and a prayer.

We drive on.

֎֎֎   ֎֎֎   ֎֎֎

After a short while, Fred announces we will be making a pit stop. We pull to the side of the road in a very rural area, with a clear field of view. There are no houses to be seen. No people. A good place for a rest stop in Afghanistan.

I can still see in my mind a green field, and beyond it a rare copse of trees and bushes, maybe 50 yards away. I start heading towards the copse.

Alex grabs my arm. "Where the hell do you think you're going?"

"To pee," I reply, trying not to sound embarrassed.

"Oh no you don't," he says. Everyone is smiling, knowingly. "Mines. Anti-personnel mines. This is Afghanistan. They're every-where. Nowhere is safe except where it's paved." Alex should know. That is his specialty, after all.

So we line the side of the road and pee into the dirt.

This is fine for us, I remember thinking, but what about the poor farmers who have no choice?

It's a useful lesson for me. A few years later, in 2003, I was in charge of correspondent safety for a BBC program called *The World*, a co-production with US public radio. We had three people in and around Iraq, waiting for the invasion. One in Baghdad itself, one in Kuwait, with US and British forces, and a talented young fellow called Quil Lawrence in the Kurdish autonomous area of northern Iraq, where he was waiting for the US Army's Fourth Infantry Division to appear from Turkey. It never came.

A few days after the US-led invasion began in the south, Quil called in to say the Iraqi troops across the line-of-control appeared to have gone. He told me he was with a farmer whose home and farm had been in no man's land for more than ten years—since northern Iraq was divided after the end of the First Gulf War in 1991. It was split into an autonomous region controlled by the Kurds, and the rest of the country still under the Iraqi dictator, Saddam Hussein.

OK, I say, you can go, but here are the ground rules. I reminded him of what I'd written in his risk assessment prior to deployment. "Don't touch anything. Don't pick anything up. And most of all, don't stray off the pavement or tarmac. Don't step on any soil or dirt."

Saddam's forces had been trained and equipped on the Soviet pattern, and I said, if I was them, I would have mined and booby-trapped everything. He managed to complete his assignment safely. Elsewhere in Iraq that week, a regular BBC team dismounted from their vehicle in a field. It was mined. One died. One lost a foot.

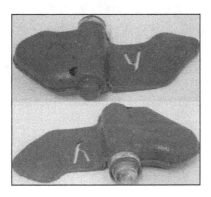

PFM-1 butterfly mine
Photo: Juergen Schomp,
CreativeCommons

Mines are a nightmare. They kill and maim indiscriminately, for decades after a conflict has ended. The Soviets deployed millions in Afghanistan. Millions. Each mine was its own little war-crime-in-waiting. I say "was"—actually, most are still there. Some were allegedly disguised as children's toys, although I now believe that's CIA propaganda. There were things known as "butterfly mines," like the PFM-1. Their hard plastic look gives them a toy-like quality.

Under international law, even back then in the 1980s, you were supposed to mark a field if you mined it, keep a record on a map, and write a document on how they were distributed. The idea is that they could then be safely removed after hostilities have ended. The Soviets and their Afghan allies, I have learned, were very good at keeping such records. Every hilltop entrenched position kept good notes on the layout and composition of its defensive minefields. These maps and papers were used by the HALO Trust in their mine clearance efforts. Sadly, it seems most of this documentation was lost after the Najibullah regime collapsed in 1992.

The mines that chilled me the most in my army training were the anti-personnel mines that bounced up to a certain height before exploding, spraying shrapnel out to all 360 degrees. These were aimed at taking a leg off. Soviet doctrine emphasized wounding rather than killing enemies, as it took two or more unwounded men to take a wounded comrade off the battlefield. A dead man does not need to be moved immediately.

The Muj had mines, too. Some they captured or bought on the black market. Others were supplied by Pakistani intelligence and the CIA. They generally preferred anti-tank mines like the one we had seen used against that BTR-60 on the outskirts of Kabul.

As kids in the West, most of us have played the game where the floor is lava, and we can't step on it. It's great fun! For children in Afghanistan and many other countries wracked by conflict during the Cold War, that game is a deadly reality even to this day. If you're a farmer, you have no choice. You can't avoid the dirt. You can't stay on the pavement.

In 2018, some 6,900 people, mostly civilians, were killed or injured by landmines across some sixty countries.[9] Almost one third of these casualties were Afghans. Most of these are victims of legacy mines from the Soviet war.

As a soldier, landmines form an essential part of position defense. For example, they would be essential in delaying any sudden attempt by North Korea to capture Seoul, the capital of South Korea. But if they are not removed, the cost to future generations is appalling.

Thankfully, anti-personnel mines were outlawed by international convention in 1997. The Mine Ban Treaty is "a legally binding international agreement that bans the use, production, stockpiling and transfer of anti-personnel mines." It also "places obligations on countries to clear affected areas, assist victims, and destroy stockpiles."[10] There are a few states that are not party to the Mine Ban Treaty: China, Egypt, India, Israel, Pakistan, Russia and the United States. Ironically, Afghanistan is a signatory.[11]

---

[9]See: Landmine Monitor 2019. [14 Sep 2020: the-monitor.org/en-gb/home.aspx]

[10]There are a few states that are not party to the Mine Ban Treaty: China, Egypt, India, Israel, Pakistan, Russia and the United States. Ironically, Afghanistan is a signatory. See the Treaty page of the International Campaign to Ban Landmines [icbl.org/en-gb/the-treaty.aspx], and also the Anti-Personnel Mine Ban Convention [apminebanconvention.org]

[11]While not a signatory, the US has made commitments limiting the production and use of landmines. But these were overturned by President Trump in 2020. See Human Rights Watch "Questions and Answers on the new US Landmine Policy," Feb 27th 2020, [hrw.org/news/2020/02/27/questions-and-answers-new-us-landmine-policy]

ဧဝဒ   ဧဝဒ   ဧဝဒ

The pit stop over, our leader, Fred, announces he wants to re-arrange the passengers. My buddy Chris and I are to be separated —"just in case." They tell me it's not smart to have people from the same organization in one vehicle, to make sure they don't both get "lost." That seems eminently practical, I think to myself.

Nothing to worry about. Just a precaution, they say. Better safe than sorry.

I fail to connect the dots with the danger from anti-tank mines. I'm still reassured by their advice that our vehicles are not heavy enough to trigger them. When I figure it out later, I feel foolishly clueless.

Chris goes on the HALO Trust vehicle, the smaller of our two trucks. I stay with Fred and Alex in the UN pickup. We drive as fast as we can, but we also have to keep the convoy together. We can only go as fast as the slowest vehicle, the four-tonner. The fertile plain stretches to our right, the mountains rise to our left.

All of a sudden, I feel the pickup slowing down.

"Bugger," mutters Fred, as he eases up on the gas. I follow his gaze.

There's a checkpoint ahead. More delay. No uniforms here. Just men in local clothes, toting AKs and RPGs.

"Militia," explains Fred.

Militia, in Afghanistan at this time, means pro-government irregular forces. A regular army comprises organized, uniformed troops. An irregular force is one outside of that organization. An auxiliary force that helps the regulars. They may be part-timers, they might be volunteers. They are often local and their first loyalty is usually to their neighbourhood, clan or religious sect, or to some area strongman. They rarely have uniforms. They don't have any real discipline, but their firepower is all too real.

A quick digression on Soviet-era weapons. I use the phrase AKs for all Soviet-era assault rifles: the famous Kalashnikovs. The first design produced by World War II veteran Mikhail Kalashnikov was the AK-47 which, as its name implies, emerged in 1947. Many people mistakenly use the term AK-47 for all types of Kalashnikov, but that's incorrect. There are multiple designs. More common than the AK-47 is the AKM, and more recent is the AK-74, which—you guessed it— emerged in 1974. I'm not a big firearms buff, so I'm not very good at telling them apart, so I use AKs wherever needed.[12]

The only thing you need to know about all Kalashnikovs is that they are simple to use, simple to maintain, and almost indestructible. They were designed to be easily mastered and maintained by illiterate peasants. Comrade Kalashnikov succeeded wildly. Thanks to massive Soviet exports and cheap copies made locally by allies, they are easily the most common firearm ever seen on the planet. You can get one in a marketplace here in Afghanistan in 1991 for about $10 US.

They're extremely resilient. There's a joke that four years after he was buried, they dug up Mikhail Kalashnikov, scraped off the mud, and he worked as well as he ever had.

The downside to the AKs is their accuracy. The AK-74 is much better in that regard, as it fires a smaller round at a higher velocity. But overall, the tactic employed by guerrillas the world over, but especially in Afghanistan, is "to spray and pray."

The Mujahidin had started the war with whatever weapons came to hand. Plenty were using various rifles captured from the British over the previous century. Mostly Lee-Enfields, but also a few ancient muzzle loaders. As the war progressed, the rebels quickly came to prefer AKs. Many were captured, but most were supplied by the Pakistani intelligence service, assisted by the Central Intelligence Agency of the United States. Some AKs were made by the blacksmiths of Peshawar, across the border in Pakistan, but these were much less reliable.

(left) AK-47 rifle, (right) RPG-7
Photos: WikiCommons

---

[12]If you really need to know the differences between the different types of Kalashnikov, you can find some entertaining explainers on YouTube. [For example, here: youtube.com/watch? v=v8CFBH0JQQU&app=desktop]

The other weapon of choice among the Muj was the RPG-7, or simply, the RPG. It's known in the West as a rocket-propelled grenade, but RPG is really an abbreviation of the Russian words for "hand-held anti-tank grenade-launcher." It's man-portable, reusable, recoilless. You fire it from the shoulder. Like the AK, it's rugged, simple and cheap. I have no personal experience with them, but my friends who served in Iraq say many of the RPGs fired at them were (thankfully) duds—they failed to explode.

In Afghanistan, when I was there, you would see squads of six to eight men on both sides, Mujahidin and pro-government militia. They would all be armed with AKs; a couple would be carrying RPGs; and typically you'd see a Hazara man at the end of the column carrying all the heavy stuff, including spare rounds for the RPGs.

We slow down for the armed men at the checkpoint.

"Moo-lee matta-heed! Moo-lee matta-heed!" we shout. They give us the once over then wave us on.

Every few miles there's another checkpoint. Usually, they wave us on. Sometimes they look at our papers.

Occasionally we see burned-out civilian vehicles, a bus or van or car, with the usual colourful prayer flags for the dead. The buses have at least ten, sometimes 20 or 30 flags. But besides those, and the militiamen, it seems peaceful.

We trade stories to pass the time. Alex tells us a story about the first time he got shot at in Afghanistan. He was mapping a minefield on a hilltop with a Colonel of the KHAD, the Afghan secret police. As they're coming back down the hill, Alex is a little in front when he suddenly hears the distinctive crack-thump of a bullet passing very close. The crack is the sound of the bullet passing you by; the thump is the sound of it being fired. A bullet travels faster than the speed of sound, so you hear it being fired after it's hit you, if you're still alive. Anyway, being a trained soldier, Alex recognizes the threat. The round is extremely close. He dives for cover.

The KHAD colonel takes the situation in hand. The shooter was a member of the local village militia who had been tasked with guarding their Land Rover. He had seen Alex's white face and assumed he was a Russian. The man's two older brothers had been in the Muj and had both killed Russians, and he wanted a share of the bragging rights in the family. He assumed any European faces in Afghanistan must be Russian. The fact that the shooter was working for the pro-Russian regime himself was irrelevant. Family and personal pride comes before any other kind of loyalty for many Afghans.

The moral of the story, Alex tells us, is that you never know what the man with the gun is thinking about you, as a foreigner. Government troops might think you are American spies. The Muj might think you're Russian military advisers. Most can't tell a Russian from an American, and many don't even know there's a difference. Or care.

Alex rounds off his parable by saying that after the situation was explained to the shooter, they all drove home together, as if nothing had happened.

I find nothing about the story to be very comforting. So any of these gunmen we see on our journey might choose to take a pot shot at us? This is not something I had considered.

The checkpoints quickly become tediously familiar. The usual squad of militia with AKs and RPGs. *"Moolee-matta-heed! Moolee-matta-heed!"*

As we drive, one of my hosts points out that five or six miles to our right lies the famous Bagram military airbase. This helps me figure out a couple of things. One is that we are clearly headed north. I also remembered reading about Muj attacks on Bagram, which had been one of the main bases of the Soviet army during their ten-year occupation. That knowledge and our proximity piques my curiosity.

"So when might we get close to rebel-held territory?" I ask.

Everyone laughs.

Apparently, every other checkpoint that we have passed through in the past couple of hours has been manned by the Mujahidin! We'd crossed through hostile territory multiple times and I didn't even know. The Mujahidin rebels and the pro-government militiamen look indistinguishable to me.

The rebels do not really control the territory that we just passed through, except at night. They do control the mountains, to the west, just a mile or two to our left. They come down from the mountains and set up these checkpoints on the road as temporary irritants, to make life difficult for government supporters. It's unlikely they would try to engage government combat troops. Not intentionally. Not in daylight. At night, the rebels own the roads, as the government forces invariably retire into the nearest fortified town around 4 p.m.

It seems funny now, but at the time I was shocked to learn we had just met the Muj. Remember, I had no real idea where I was going or what lay in front of us. The names of the towns they had mentioned meant nothing to me. I really was just bumbling through the Hindu Kush, a right innocent abroad. Now these places are all seared in my memory.

My whole life I have been kind of obsessed with war and conflict. As you know, dear reader, I had even contemplated a military career. I did not see myself as naïve. I knew the costs of war and its consequences. I was fascinated by the science and art of war, of tactics, of learning what made men tick in combat. Yes, I'd served a little in the reserve force of the British army. But all that reading and thinking and even my "hands-on" part-time military experience did not prepare me very well.

In reality, I knew nothing of war.

Suddenly, here I am. An observer to an all too real war. One I was not really expecting to witness quite so closely. The shock is profound. But of course, I keep quiet. My role model growing up had been the fictional naval officer, Horatio Hornblower, whose only reaction in combat was to stand firm on the bridge of his ship, clasping his hands behind his back, and say "Hmm, ahh," as bad news was delivered.

After what seems like a few hours we reach a place called Charikar. More delays. Apparently we have to pay our respects to the governor, and get clearance to continue north up the road toward the Salang Valley and the famous pass over the Hindu Kush.

8◉3   8◉3   8◉3

I am excited to hear we will be passing through the storied Salang. It's one of the few places I've heard of in Afghanistan, outside of the major cities.

I was still a schoolboy when the Soviets invaded Afghanistan in 1979 but I was already an avid consumer of international news, especially military news. The Salang was a critical early battlefield, and remained so throughout the Soviet occupation and especially now under the successor regime of President Najibullah.

The reason the Salang was, and is, so important is geography. The Hindu Kush mountain range is the spine of Afghanistan, pretty much dividing the country in half from east to west for 500 miles (800 km). It's an extension of the Himalaya, and it's a steep, jagged, cruel, freezing set of mountains.

Most of the Hindu Kush lies above 20,000 feet (6000 meters). Commerce and travel depend on a handful of passes through the mountains. The same is true for warfare. The most important of these passes is the Salang. It carries the only real paved road northward from Kabul to central Asia. In simple terms, it's a giant bottleneck.

Modern warfare requires enormous amounts of ammunition and fuel. Afghanistan has very little energy infrastructure of its own, and not much of an ability to manufacture weapons beyond Kalashnikovs. Everything else has to come from outside.

During the US presence in Afghanistan, even the mighty US Air Force could only bring in a fraction of the needs of the coalition forces, and at huge expense. Practically everything else had to be trucked in, from the Pakistani port of Karachi. There are no railways in Afghanistan. No ports, obviously. What can't be flown in, must come in by road.

For the Soviets, and their communist allies, supplies were trucked in across the northern border from the Soviet central Asian republics. Everything needed in the southeastern half of Afghanistan - which was where much of the fighting took place—had to be funnelled through the Salang. All the fuel and the ammo. Even food.

The Salang Pass sits at 12,700 feet (3870 meters) and is often blocked by snow, so in 1964 the Soviets built a tunnel at the much more accessible altitude of 11,155 feet, (or approximately 3400 metres.) The tunnel was bored through 1.7 miles (2.7 km) of the Hindu Kush. It was an engineering triumph, and as soon as it opened, it transformed north-south commerce in Afghanistan.

Naturally, when the war started, the rebels saw its importance and immediately began attacking the Russian convoys in the Salang. The Soviets responded with astonishing ruthlessness. Understanding

Mao's maxim that a guerrilla is a fish swimming in a river of civilians, the Soviets decided to drain the river: they systematically depopulated the valleys either side of the Salang Tunnel, for 50 miles (80 km) in each direction.

Atrocities like this created a massive refugee problem. The Afghan people fled to the cities, to rebel areas and, above all, to neighbouring countries. In all, some five million Afghans, or about one third of the pre-war population fled abroad after the Soviet invasion. Most went to Pakistan, and the rest to Iran.

Naturally this featured prominently in Western news coverage, keen to highlight Soviet inhumanity. That was how I had first heard of the Salang.

Now I am on my way there, to this storied battleground.

ε◊з   ε◊з   ε◊з

Just past Charikar, we see signs of a serious, in-depth, defensive line, starting with entrenched artillery, facing north.

Up to now, we had only seen small arms, like AKs and RPGs, among the soldiers, militia and Mujahidin rebels we had encountered. Now we're looking at much heavier weapons in a more conventional military posture. The line of howitzers—big guns—seems to stretch across the plain to the west as far as the eye could see. There's no netting or camouflage.

I had not had any training in the army to recognize Soviet artillery, but comparing what I remember to images on the internet, I think I was looking at a battalion of D-30 howitzers. That's an artillery piece that can lob a 122mm explosive shell about ten miles (16 km). It was already an old weapon by 1991, but reliable.[13]

A sight like this can help a trained observer quite a lot. In late Soviet military organization, an artillery battalion of 18 guns was considered enough to support a motorized rifle regiment, roughly

---

[13]The D-30 was considered obsolete by the Soviets by 1991, but was still widely in use, especially among allies. In fact, many D-30 howitzers are still in service with the Afghan National Army in 2020. For more see "U.S. Troops Are Training to Operate Cold-War-Era Howitzers," by Kyle Mizokami, in Popular Mechanics, January 24th 2019. [popularmechanics.com/military/weapons/a26028078/us-troops-d30-soviet-howitzer/]

equivalent to a brigade in NATO organization, usually combined with a tank battalion. In other words, one could estimate that maybe 3-5,000 men were deployed in this defensive line.[14]

Artillery used to be known as the queen of the battlefield. That honour probably now goes to close air support, which fulfills many of the same roles. For centuries, artillery produced the most battlefield casualties, through its ability to hit targets a long way away, and hit them hard. Artillery was particularly venerated in the Soviet tradition. The Soviet dictator, Josef Stalin, called it the God of War. The Red Army was described by Western analysts during the Cold War as "an artillery army with a lot of tanks."[15]

A D-30 howitzer is moved by being towed by a truck, then man-handled into a firing position. The ones I see are in dugout positions, a couple of feet deep, some with sandbags for added protection. There looks to be a couple of hundred feet between each gun emplacement. They are dark green. The gun crews are lounging around, waiting for orders. The trucks are dug in as well, a little further back.

I reach for my camera.

"Whoa! Be careful," warns Fred. "You don't want to have any pictures like that on your camera, if you're stopped."

Whatever your documents might say, images of military positions count as spying in anyone's book. You could easily be jailed for a long time or even face execution. The danger is that if you give the images to an enemy, they can figure out precise locations, look for weaknesses and find ways to kill the soldiers defending the positions you have photographed. I put my camera in my lap.

A little further up the road we see a platoon of tanks, T-62s, resting in a column along the side of the road. It isn't a military position, *per se*, so I take a gamble and take a snap with my camera. The crews are lounging on top, in mismatched uniforms. The only thing they wear in common is a khaki-coloured fatigue cap that looks something like a *képi*, the kind of hat favoured by the French Foreign Legion.

---

[14]For details of late Soviet orders of battle (ORBAT) and tables of organization and equipment (TOE), see the US Defense Department's 1991 handbook on the Soviet Army. [https://fas.org/irp/doddir/army/fm100-2-3.pdf]

[15]For more on the Russian military's obsession with artillery check out the Global Security website's data page for Soviet Rockets and Artillery. [globalsecurity.org/military/world/russia/artillery.htm]

Having not long been out of the military myself, I am appalled at how ratty and beat-up these tanks look. Then it dawns on me—oh, these guys are probably just out of combat. In my picture, you can see the front left track protector has been knocked off. The faces of the crew look weary.

Still further along the road, there are several more tanks, but these are dug in, like the howitzers. Like the artillery, they are all facing north, in a line, perpendicular to the highway. They are dug in deep, so that just their turrets are above ground. I do a double take, just to confirm they are tanks, as I've never seen or heard of tanks being dug in like this.

Yes, they're tanks, not SPGs. Most armies have artillery weapons mounted on tracked vehicles. These are called self-propelled guns, or SPGs. They look like tanks to the uninitiated, but they are very different. I can tell the difference, and what I'm looking at are definitely tanks.

This puzzles me. I had always thought of tanks as manoeuvre weapons. Tanks are by definition already armoured against most threats, so why waste effort digging in? Why waste tanks on position defence, like this? It's not something I had seen in NATO, but I wasn't a tankie and so I'm not familiar with their drills.

One thing it does demonstrate is that government forces are concerned about incoming fire. That means the Mujahidin must be capable of deploying and supporting heavy weapons themselves.

I can see that the war here in Afghanistan is becoming much more conventional than was generally supposed in the West at the time. In a guerrilla war there is, by definition, no front line. And yet here I can see a very conventional linear defensive position. I soon learn, in fact, that the Muj have been taking and holding ground since the mid-1980s.

Beyond the line of dug-in tanks, I expect to see a line of infantry posts. Foot soldiers are always the first line of defence. I scan the ground intently for the next mile or two, as we drive on. But I see nothing. That might well be a compliment to their skill at digging in and using camouflage. They are probably there, but I can't see the front line or the forward edge of the battle area.

I had no idea at the time, but this defensive line was probably around a place called Jabal-os-Saraj. I can see on a map today that this town was on our route, just past Charikar. Again, I did not realize it at the time. While we were in Kabul, we had heard that there had been fighting around Jabal-os-Saraj and another place called Golbahar, a few miles to the east. I had thought these places were a lot further away from our route!

I'm not sure how keen I would have been to pass through here, had I known this was the battlefield we had been hearing about for the past few days. But ignorance is bliss sometimes, especially in wartime.

In fact, we have just entered a significantly more dangerous zone. Presumably a little to the north are strong Mujahidin forces. We are now in a kind of no man's land. Talk about lack of situational awareness!

Looking at a map today, you can see that Jabal-os-Saraj has a pretty important strategic significance to the government in Kabul. You have to pass through it to get to the Salang Valley and the main supply route from the Soviet Union. The Kabul government has no choice but to pour its limited military resources into defending the supply route. That means there were fewer troops to defend other parts of the country, making it easier for the Mujahidin commanders to make gains elsewhere.

Golbahar lies just five miles (8 km) to the east of Jabal-os-Saraj and guards the entrance to the Panjshir Valley. The Panjshir had been a rebel stronghold since the beginning of the Soviet invasion. Under the leadership of the now famous guerrilla leader, Ahmed Shah Massoud, the local Tajik population had withstood no less than nine assaults by Soviet army divisions in the early '80s. Now Massoud's forces were probing for weaknesses around Golbahar and Jabal-os-Saraj, to find a way to break out of the Panjshir, while raiding parties crossed the mountains to harass the supply route through the Salang.

Little did we know that one of those raiding parties was at work just ahead of us.

Chapter 10

Into the Valley of Death:
The Salang Pass

After Charikar, the plain narrows and the mountains start to close in. After Jabal-os-Saraj, the foothills start to encroach on the road and you are clearly in a valley.

Soon we come to another checkpoint. This one is different. The checkpoint has a few militiamen but it's mostly manned by regular army soldiers in uniform. We are not allowed forward. There is fighting ahead.

We can't hear any shooting or explosions, so it's a little mystifying. Alex says that just means the fighting is several miles up the valley.

Again I'm speechless. This is not what I expected. I'm excited and curious, but also at a loss to know what we can do now. There is only one road north, and warring factions are currently fighting for control of it.

However, those warring factions have not encountered Fred Estall.

Fred jumps out of the pickup and demands to see the local army commander. He knows enough Dari to communicate his key points personally. I don't recall there being an interpreter. Fred is not especially tall, but he's thickset and gets like a bulldog when needed. This makes it seem like he towers over the officer at the checkpoint. Fingers are pointed. He's not afraid to be loud. Radios crackle and we are allowed to move forward to another checkpoint, to meet with the local commander in person.

Here, the unfortunate Afghan army officer gets a severe talking-to, partially in English, partially in Dari. I can hear Fred not quite yelling, but very forcefully, ordering the Afghan officer to reach out to the rebel commander and arrange a ceasefire long enough for us to pass through.

I can't quite believe it. The nerve of asking commanders in combat to stop fighting? It's a perfect example of a Yiddish concept I learned in America: "chutzpah."

I also can't quite believe that the Afghan army commander has a line of communication to his Mujahidin opponent.

I can hear Fred stating that the supplies we are carrying must get through before the snows close the passes, or innocent civilians will die. And reminding the officer of the power and influence of the United Nations, and asking if he wanted to be personally responsible for the damage to the government's international reputation if he blocked the supplies from getting through.

I'm skeptical if Fred will succeed, and resign myself to a quick drive back to Kabul. Maybe we'd get there in time for a drink at the international club?

We wait. Radios crackle. Fred looms over the radio operator. I don't know Dari, but I know radio protocol from my time as a radio operator in the infantry. You can hear callsigns being exchanged and so forth.

I don't recall how long we wait but finally the radioman looks up and says something. There is nodding, checking of watches and some haggling.

Fred jumps back in the pickup.

"We're off in ten," he announces. He has done it! A ceasefire starts in ten minutes and will last two hours. That should give us time to get past the danger zone.

If I hadn't seen it, I wouldn't have believed it. I knew humanitarian ceasefires could be arranged, and happen all the time. But for some reason I had assumed they were set up way in advance, way above Fred's pay grade.

I push him on the communications issue. I've never heard of such a thing. "You mean to say, this guy has a direct line to the chap he's fighting? The man who's trying to kill him?"

"Yes," says Fred. "Matter of fact, this one was a little easier, since they're cousins."

"What?"

"Yes. He's fighting his cousin. Happens all the time here."

Again, I'm speechless. It makes sense. But I am bewildered.

I have to take my hat off to Fred and the countless other men and women like him, who for decades now, have risked their lives to help others—strangers—enduring hardships and dangers in ways we cannot imagine, while we've been sleeping comfortably in our beds.

I've read countless books on war and insurgency, but my experience of the real thing so far has resembled nothing like the writings of many military historians. I make a note to be wary of those armchair warriors in the future.

8◈3   8◈3   8◈3

We are now in the foothills of the Hindu Kush, and entering the infamous Salang Valley. Were it not for the ugly footprint of war, it would have been beautiful. Not picturesque like the Swiss Alps, but a primitive, raw kind of beauty.

The Salang river winds its way down the valley floor, bringing life to little scrubby trees and bushes, mostly in various shades of brown, but some green. Grey rocks. The ubiquitous khaki dirt.

Almost immediately we start to see the wreckage of 12 years of war. Colourful broken pieces of metal that were once civilian cars and trucks. Hulks of freight trucks, four-tonners and 18-wheelers, burned out. Some recently, some long ago. There are few prayer flags, though. No one is allowed into the valley to mourn.

More terrifyingly, we see the rubble where villages once stood. This is the awful reality of the Soviet attempt to clear the civilian population from this strategic bottleneck, the Salang Valley. Between Jabal-os-Saraj and Pul-e-Khumri, one hundred miles (160 km) to the north, we do not see another civilian. But at every turn we see the devastated remains of farms, homes, stables, sheds. Mostly just khaki rubble now. It's been ten years since the Soviets went house by house, blowing them up and driving away the people who had lived there for countless generations. We see narrow fields marked by stone terraces painstakingly built up the sides of the hills, now empty and lifeless. The Soviets did not want the people or the buildings providing shelter and sustenance for the "dushman"—the guerrilla.

Rubble of villages destroyed by the Soviets, Salang Valley

As a counter-insurgency tactic, it was a disaster. The people—at least those who survived—became embittered and cried out for vengeance. The men came back and fought. They are still fighting. The evidence is all around us.

We see a lifeless tank in the river bed. Fresh green paint indicates it's not been there too long. Then an abandoned armoured personnel carrier, like the one we'd seen on the outskirts of Kabul. A military truck, upside down. A self-propelled gun (SPG), trackless and wheelless. Another tank, pushed off the roadway. And then another. And another. And another.

The Salang is littered with these metallic skeletons of Soviet military power. Dozens upon dozens. There are even three tanks still in a perfect v-formation, abandoned in the middle of the river. I can see unexploded ordnance just carelessly lying around. Big grey bombs dropped from an aircraft who knows how many years before, that failed to detonate. Here lies the turret of a tank, but with no chassis nearby.

Sometimes it is hard to see why a particular vehicle had been abandoned, as it looks okay. Others have clearly been ripped apart.

The war is still ripping the valley apart. The road starts to zig-zag, following the course carved by the river. At each turn is an Afghan army outpost. It's interesting to note how they use the ground—the geometry of war. I had assumed you would build your outposts on the high ground, in the angles of the zig-zags, to get something like 360-degree visibility. But the Afghan army posts are on the valley floor, in the acute angles of the zig-zags. You could immediately see why. There are heavy weapons like tanks, anti-aircraft guns and howitzers tucked into these corners. These weapons and their ammo are heavy. They are easier to deploy and easier to supply on the valley floor, beside the road. More importantly they have a clear view. These

positions are at the apex of a v-shaped field of fire; as the road zig-zags, it obviously creates these v-shapes. If you stand at this apex, you can simultaneously see down the valley in one direction, and up the valley in the other.

In some places you see stone-built machine gun posts and strongpoints, half-buried into the ground. The heavy weapons are usually protected by barricades made from sandbags or rocks. Stone huts provide shelter for their crews and other troops. Each post is surrounded by a cluster of wreckage from burned and broken vehicles.

The soldiers seem good-humoured whenever we are required to stop. This must be a rough assignment. The Salang Valley starts in the south at about 5,200 feet (1600 meters) above sea level, and rises over 40-50 miles (60-80 km) to the tunnel at 11,155 feet (3400 meters). It's November. It's cold and damp. The threat of attack is ever present. The debris and signs of death among your predecessors at these posts are present everywhere. It occurs to me now that perhaps we were the source of their good humour, since Fred had negotiated this two-hour ceasefire.

Of the Mujahidin, there is no sign. Of course. This is not like the Christmas truce of 1914, in World War I, where the combatants came together to sing carols and play soccer. No, the Muj are out of sight. Even in combat it's unlikely you would be able to see them. My military training had long ago shown me just how unreal is Hollywood's idea of warfare. You almost never see your enemy in real life. Maybe a muzzle flash would give you a hint of their location. But

111

Hollywood requires a much more intimate image of war to sell its product.

We zig-zag our way up the valley, occasionally stopping at checkpoints or whenever a curious officer wants to check us out. I try to take a few photos, but I am now supremely conscious of the need not to snap actual military outposts. The wrecked tanks and APCs seem like fair game. But it's hard. You have to keep the camera out of sight, you bring it up ready when you see a wreck, but sometimes you've flown by too fast, or there's a soldier watching, or brush or rocks obscure the view. I surreptitiously snap another live T-62 tank standing guard, partially covered with a camo net.

The foothills get higher and higher, and the valley floor gets narrower and narrower. The clouds close in, making it gloomy and misty in places. For many miles there are no spectacular views to enjoy, as the hills crowd us in. But finally we round another corner, and get a view of the high snow-capped mountains before us. We can faintly make out the road zig-zagging up the mountainside a couple of miles in the distance.

Boy, is it starting to get cold. I can't tell if that shiver is cold or adrenaline. But it rattles the knot in my stomach.

There is almost no brush now. Just dirt and rocks. Above us, ice and snow.

The final approach to the tunnel is along a spectacular set of hairpin turns. They are exciting enough to negotiate in a pickup. I cannot imagine what it's like for the drivers of heavy trucks. There is plenty of evidence that for some it's too much. We can see several 18-wheelers tumbled down the mountainside; we know not whether from accident or attack.

At the top we must wait. The Salang Tunnel is a marvel of engineering, and was a state-of-the-art piece of infrastructure when it opened in 1964. But still to this day, it can only comfortably accommodate one lane of vehicles. Traffic takes turns to flow in each direction, changing every day. Today is a south-to-north day.

Hairpin turns on the Salang Pass
Photo: Google Maps

We still have to wait our turn, as they only allow so many through at a time. We soon attract a crowd. Members of the garrison of this godforsaken mountain eyrie decide to come and fraternize with us. A collection of boys mostly, with perhaps the roughest assign-ment of all, given the constant cold and damp at this altitude. There are few Muj attacks this high up. The soldiers are clearly bored out of their minds most of the time. We pause for a photo op. You can see just how uncomfortable I am.

There's a tank, dug in up to its turret, facing down the valley. Its 115mm gun would have been able to use its full range. You can see for miles.

There's an 18-wheeler, a fresh one, a few hundred yards down the cliff.

The Salang Tunnel is itself a place of death. Avalanches are not uncommon. In November 1982, there was an incident that blocked the tunnel. At the time, Western media claimed it was the result of a Mujahidin attack, but it now appears to have been a traffic accident. More recent sources say there was a fire. But regardless of the cause, drivers were stuck in the

Chris Bowers with crashed 18-wheeler

tunnel and kept their motors running for warmth. The carbon monoxide killed many. Pro-rebel sources say 2-3,000 Soviets and Afghans perished from the fire or from choking. In reality, it may have been fewer than 200. Nobody knows for sure. The Soviets never released details, so the event hangs over the Salang Tunnel like a legend. A myth. Part of local folklore. The story fades or grows depending on the storyteller.

I am passing through the Salang Tunnel exactly nine years after the disaster. I am well aware of that grim event. I had read a novel mythologizing the Mujahidin's courage in taking on the Soviets, and that work of fiction had depicted the tunnel disaster as a result of an attack by the rebels. I did not know the less glamorous truth.

So it seems perfectly reasonable to me that what has happened before can happen again. Entering the tunnel produces an interesting feeling of awe and trepidation in me. I am told the ventilation system is much better now, as if that would help.

The tunnel is built in the best Soviet style of architecture. Grim and practical. Dirty concrete. For the first few hundred yards you pass through a section that is only semi-enclosed. Dozens of large arches are open on one side as you hug the mountainside on the other. Then suddenly you enter the darkness. It's very poorly lit, so it's hard to make out details. It seems to last forever but it really is only 1.7 miles (2.7 km) underground. You can almost taste the exhaust fumes. They create a permanent fog that is alternately white, gray, blue and purple. Soviet-era trucks and cars are not known for their clean emission standards. I can't help thinking of those hundreds of poor people who choked to death on fumes here in this tunnel during the disaster just nine years before.

Suddenly we emerge from the tunnel into misty sunlight. We are now officially north of the Hindu Kush.

In central Asia.

࿊   ࿊   ࿊

Fred is starting to get rattled. His composure has been remarkable up to this point. But now he is getting anxious. I don't know why, so I ask what's up.

"It's getting late. Anything on the road after dark is considered fair game by both sides. Anyone trying to get into a town after dark is going to be shot to pieces. And we still have a long way to go."

Oh, I think. I didn't know that. Makes sense, though. I hope we're okay. LOL. This is becoming my life now, being surprised to learn about new life and death issues every hour or so.

The north side of the Salang is pretty similar to the approach on the south side. The road descends from the tunnel mouth, at over 11,000 feet, down a series of hairpin turns. The mountainsides are similarly decorated with broken trucks, cars, buses and military vehicles. I can't help thinking that a scrap metal merchant will one day do a roaring trade hereabouts.

Soon the hairpin turns become more gentle and the road starts to zig-zag, following the river. A different river, of course. This is one of several small tributaries that run roughly northward to join the Kunduz river, and eventually the Amu-Darya: the legendary Oxus of Alexander the Great's time.

There's also the same 50 miles of devastation as there is on the south side. When you read in military history books about a region being "laid waste," this is what it looks like. Overgrown fields, broken walls. No signs of life: no cattle, no sheep, no goats, no dogs, no people. Or at least, no civilians.

Our two-hour ceasefire expired some time ago. Some of the soldiers are now looking more attentive, surveying the hills. We get a good look at them at each of the usual checkpoints that we must pass through. *"Moolee-matta-heed! Moolee-matta-heed!"*

As we descend, the mist thins out and the sun breaks through in patches. The road drops 9,000 feet (2700 meters) in the 50 miles (80 km) or so from the mouth of the Salang Tunnel to the city of Pul-i-Khumri at the northern end of the pass. Ears pop constantly. Slowly, the valley begins to broaden. The turns become less pronounced. More curves than zig-zags. Ultimately, the road opens to a narrow plain, a few hundred yards wide. Long, low bridges criss-cross the mostly dry river beds.

A pale orange glow begins to cover the landscape. The sun is going down. We're entering the dangerous time of twilight.

As the shadows begin to lengthen, the truck carrying my BBC buddy, Chris, starts to fall behind. I can't help thinking about Fred's warning, about the vulnerability of vehicles on the road after dark. I dread to think what might happen if they don't keep up.

Each time we make a turn round a foothill, I look back until Chris comes into view. Each time it's taking a little longer.

Then ultimately there's a moment when we don't see him at all. "Where is he?" I'm thinking to myself. As we make the next turn, he becomes visible, thanks to a fold in the elevation. But it's not good. His truck is halted, maybe half a mile back.

"They've stopped," I announce.

Fred's lips purse. He and Alex exchange half a glance, as if to communicate something.

I see the driver opening the hood on Chris's truck. "I think they've broken down."

There is silence. If anything, Fred is driving faster. Every second takes us further away from my friend.

"I guess we should go pick them up?" I offer, naively. There's a pause before Fred answers.

"There's no time."

The pit falls out of my stomach. There's nothing else to say.

"It's almost dark," adds Alex.

I say nothing. I'm thinking: I know, I know. It's too dangerous to be out after dark. But what the fuck?

There's no radio in Chris's truck. No way to make sure they're okay.

The last few miles seem to take an eternity. My stomach still feels like it has no bottom. Imagine the way you feel on the biggest drop of the biggest rollercoaster you've ever ridden. My head is spinning. I cannot imagine how Chris and his driver can approach any checkpoint safely after darkness falls.

"So," I think to myself, "in a short while I could well be the new *de facto* BBC correspondent in Kabul."

And my first story might have to be of my predecessor's untimely end. I feel nauseous.

The sky is still light as we approach a substantial looking checkpoint. It's on the defensive perimeter of our destination. Once we're through, we should be safe for the night.

Unlike my buddy Chris.

୫◈୨ ୫◈୨ ୫◈୨

I'm told we've reached our destination for the day: the city of Pul-i-Khumri, capital of Baghlan Province. It's the guardian of the northern end of the Salang Valley. It's firmly under the control of the communist government. I thought I knew all the major cities of Afghanistan, but I've never heard of Pul-i-Khumri till this moment. In my notes I spell it as Pol-e-Xhumri. Everyone calls it "Pully."

There's not much to it. "Pully" appears to comprise mostly low-rise, square, flat-roofed cement buildings. It's a long, thin town, stretched out along the river. The hills don't seem very far away, and I feel like they are close enough to command the town if you could get artillery up there.

There are lots of soldiers. Their faces clean shaven, showing their support for the government. There are plenty of military installations, fuel and ammo dumps, presumably supporting the garrisons of the outposts along the Salang.

It's getting dark by the time we pull up to our home for the night, a white-washed two-story office block. It's Alex's base, the headquarters of the "International Mine Clearance & Safety Team," which is led by the British charity group he works for, the HALO Trust.

"What about the other truck?" I ask, as I grab my backpack, trying not to let my anxiety show.

"I spoke to the guards at the checkpoint," answers Fred. "Hopefully they'll keep an eye out for them."

I feel that it's a slim hope.

Inside, I'm having a hard time keeping feelings of grief at bay. I'm also feeling a little anxiety about the prospect of taking on the awesome responsibility of running the BBC bureau, for which I am clearly unprepared. Mentally, I'm thinking through how to notify Chris's next of kin if necessary. I don't know his family personally, so I assume the BBC would do it. I do know his girlfriend.

All we can do is wait, and trust that the sentries aren't too jumpy tonight.

We make a base in a large room on the second floor, which is crowded with a mix of desks and office chairs, as well as a couch and armchairs. Everything seems very black and white. The walls are clean and whitewashed, the furniture black. The two-tone look is unnatural and feels uncomfortable.

Alex's colleagues are pleased to be reunited with him. I can't recall how many there are, maybe two or three, but I do remember they have the same background as Alex. They're all former British military officers in their late 20s.

I am a little skeptical that such young former officers should all wind up here, as poor volunteers, doing extremely dangerous work for a charitable organization. But they really are those kind of unsung public servants. Apparently, the KHAD—the Afghan secret police—is also suspicious of them and believes they may well be still working for Her Majesty's Government on the down-low, doing the de-mining work as cover. Their phones are constantly tapped.

Whatever the case, their de-mining work is nothing short of heroic. Mines are everywhere in Afghanistan, as I had learned through the course of this long day. The HALO Trust itself would lose three volunteers to an anti-tank mine just eight months after my visit.[16]

We sit around on the couch and armchairs, or perch on the desks, chatting. Drinking tea. They're interested in me and my experience as an infantryman in the Territorial Army. I'm fascinated by their work. I'm trying to keep my mind busy, trying not to worry about Chris until I have to.

---

[16]Timothy Goggs, Julian Gregson and Shah Muhammad. [See tribute here: HALOtrust.org/ latest/HALO-updates/news/a-tribute-to-humanitarian-colleagues-friends-and-comrades/ and a story about a memorial fund here: gazetteandherald.co.uk/news/7345660.tims-fund-is-helping-afghans-a-decade-on/]

The chit-chat is suddenly interrupted by a loud popping and banging, very close by.

Despite the horrors of the day, I am still the little lost naif, who's been bumbling across a war zone all day, blind to so many terrors.

"Is that Diwali?" I ask. Diwali, as I've mentioned before, is the Hindu festival of light, celebrated with fireworks, at this time of year.

"No, Chris," says Alex. "That's the war."

I half-leap out of my chair, ready to dive to the floor for cover.

Alex and the other HALO officers don't even flinch.

"How do you know about Diwali?" asks Alex, leaning forward, very curious. Most Gurkhas are Hindu, so would be celebrating the festival of light, Diwali, this week.

"But, but . . . what's that?" I gesture with my thumb out the window to "the war" that they just so glibly announced was taking place, seemingly across the street. I can make out heavy machine guns and small explosions, like mortar shells.

"Oh, don't worry!" says Alex, about the gunfire. "Most of it is outgoing. Tell us how you know about Diwali."

Most of it is outgoing? That means some of it is incoming. Why aren't we taking cover? What the heck have I gotten myself into?

For Brits of a certain age, like myself, I can only think of the dinner party scene from the campy 1960s comedy film, *Carry On Up the Khyber,* where are a party of British officers and their wives nonchalantly carry on as if nothing is happening, while their compound is under assault from Afghan tribesmen. One civilian, the Reverend Belcher, is the only one who seems to feel the gravity of the situation, ducking for cover and flinching at every artillery blast. Everyone else is oblivious, from the Governor, Sir Sydney Ruff-Diamond, to the young Captain Keene.

I am become the Reverend Belcher. I'm thinking, "You're all stark raving mad!"

I'm also thinking of Chris and the other truck, out there. Did they make it through yet? Are they still out there? Are they the target of this shooting?

"No, seriously," insists Alex, the former Gurkha officer. "How do you know about Diwali? I was with the Gurkhas, so it's obvious to me. But it's so rare to run into someone else from the UK who knows what we're talking about."

I sit back down. I breathe. I accept the situation. I realize these guys are experienced enough to have made a real risk calculation about this location and the sounds we can hear, rattling the windows. I appreciate the distraction offered by the conversation.

"I used to live in Hounslow," I explain. "Big Indian community there. The town even has a joint fireworks display for Diwali and Guy Fawkes night."

"Ahhh," they all say, knowingly.

"Plus, I was just in Delhi where they were all getting geared up," I add.

I feel like I have scored some brownie points, with my cultural knowledge, and also from being able to regain my composure.

Why the heck did I think it was Diwali, I'm thinking to myself. I know for a fact that Afghanistan is just about 100% Muslim. I realize it's just cognitive dissonance. I've heard plenty of gunfire in my time, while safely on an army range. I've never heard weapons fired in anger before, at any other point in my life. My brain just reached for the first thing it could find—fireworks. There's no Guy Fawkes here, so it must be Diwali. Oh boy. I don't realize just how familiar I am to become with the sound of flying lead.

The banging and popping intensifies. Glimmers of flashes can be seen between the buildings. A giant BM21 "Grad" multiple rocket launcher is stationed on a platform on some high ground not far from the HALO Trust building. You can see it from the window. It shrieks a salvo into the night.[17] The gunfire is constant. They tell me the shooters are mostly just letting each other know they're there. The HALO guys tell me the only time they hit the deck is during weddings. I have no idea what they are talking about.

⊱◈⊰   ⊱◈⊰   ⊱◈⊰

---

[17]You can find the awful sound of a BM21 being fired on YouTube. [Here's one from Ukraine: youtube.com/watch?v=0-SN9Cxao5M]

Just about that time, the other truck pulls up. It's undamaged. Chris and the driver are fine. Praise be!

It seems that Fred's heads-up to the sentries at the checkpoint did the trick. Chris appears oblivious to the risk he had faced. To this day, he can barely recall the incident. The driver had fixed whatever needed fixing with the truck and they had set out again, maybe only half-an-hour behind us. But they'd been slowed down by the need for caution in the dark.

Needless to say, I'm relieved. I think I punched Chris on the shoulder. I told him I thought he was a goner, had bought the farm for sure, gone west, had shuffled off this mortal coil and gone to meet his maker, and that I had been ready to take over his job. I'm pretty sure he thinks I'm joking. Just another day on the job.

&⊙3   &⊙3   &⊙3

That evening I learned something of the power of what we did at the BBC World Service. At that time, Bush House[18] provided about 30 minutes of programming each evening in the Afghan languages of Pashto and Dari. As I sat in that room with the HALO Trust folks, there was a perceptible drop in the amount of firing outside. It went from a constant rattle to an intermittent cracking.

It's noticeable enough for me to ask "What's that now?"

"That's you," says one of our hosts, with a very straight face.

"What do you mean?"

"It's 8 o'clock. The BBC news in Pashto has just started." Gesturing a hand toward the men shooting outside somewhere, our host adds: "They tune in to find out who's winning."

I'm not sure if he's joking. I am pretty sure that even the BBC Pashto service wouldn't have much granular detail about a skirmish in one small town. But they would be able to give listeners the big picture, and that was clearly enough to make Afghans on both sides of the war stop and listen. To prove the point, literally as soon as the broadcast ends, the firing immediately picks up again.

---

[18]Bush House was synonymous with the BBC World Service for decades. The first overseas broadcast from Bush House was in 1940 during World War II and the last on July 12th 2012.

That was the power of radio, in the pre-Internet age.

We talk for a long time. Mostly about the hows and wherefores of de-mining. I find it fascinating how they do the work. How they recruit and train local help. The risks they take. Not all mines can be found with a metal detector. Some anti-personnel mines are plastic. The metal detectors don't always work. How you have to probe around the suspected mine with a knife to find it and determine its type, age and condition, and the best way to deactivate or remove it. Each act of removal is a masterpiece. Then there are the dangers of piling up the cleared mines in trucks. More than once something has gone wrong and a truck full of mines has blown up. Cleared areas are mapped and marked. The tragic reality is that for all the art and science and courage needed to clear a minefield, it's really all just a drop in the bucket when compared to the millions of landmines that still remain.

The fighting outside continues. Our hosts explain that the rebels come round after dark to take a few potshots or drop in a few mortar rounds from the hills on either side of the town. The garrison fires back, pretty indiscriminately. Sometimes they're just shooting at shadows. It's not very deadly, they assure me.

Eventually it's time to hit the sack. We have another long day ahead of us. I learn that Pul-i-Khumri is not our final destination. Just a stop on the way. We're planning to hitch a ride with the UN much further north tomorrow. To another city I've never heard of. That's the place where the people need the humanitarian aid—the fuel, food and medical supplies—that the UN vehicles are carrying.

A place called Taloqan.

Chris and I unroll our sleeping bags on the floor of the HALO Trust office with the armchairs. It's been a long and traumatic day. Images fill my mind. The smouldering wisps of smoke from the overturned BTR-60 near Kabul. The old farmer running towards the scene. The split head of the soldier lying nearby. The whiteness of his flesh. Bled white. The other corpse. The ocean of blood. The checkpoints. The green field where we peed off the side of the roadway, for fear of mines. The line of howitzers. Fred blaring into the radio to demand a ceasefire. The unbelievable amount of battle wreckage along the Salang. The purple haze of fumes in the Salang Tunnel. The villages laid waste.

Then the feelings well up. There's the shock from that moment of realization that we were leaving safety behind us, after we saw those first casualties, right on the outskirts of the capital. The helplessness. The visceral fear when my buddy's truck broke down. The relief at being reunited. The minor panic when the gunfire erupted. The nonchalance of my colleagues.

These images, these feelings, have not gone away. They've stayed with me all this time, seared into my brain. Sometimes they lie dormant for a long time, until a sound or a sight brings them back.

That night of Thursday, November 7th 1991, was the first night in my life that I fell asleep to the sound of guns being fired in anger.

It would not be the last.

Chapter 11

Behind Rebel Lines

I sleep surprisingly well on the office floor, despite the lullaby of battle. I don't remember breakfast the next morning, but my buddy Chris recalls being disturbed by gunfire and explosions one night in Pul-i-Khumri. "When I came down for breakfast," he wrote in 2020, "and I asked about the 'noise' during the night, there was a degree of chuckling and it was explained that the miscreants—bearded Muj types—were precisely the folks who had been gathered round for breakfast—goat's head soup."

We can't be certain this is the same night that I was there. I think I would have remembered goat's head soup. But the anecdote gives an interesting insight into the complexities of warfare in Afghanistan: that Mujahidin warriors and government soldiers could be exchanging fire overnight, then sharing jokes and breakfast the next morning.

Baghlan province, of which Pul-i-Khumri was the capital, belonged to the Naderi family more than the government, at this time in 1991. The Naderis, father and son, held government positions and rank in the government's army. But that was not the source of their power. On the contrary, their power was rooted locally, in the Ismaili Muslim population, of which the Naderis were the hereditary leaders, or Khans. Their followers provided them with revenue and foot soldiers. That hereditary power was what had led to the family getting co-opted by the government. They weren't even communists. But while they may have been "loyal" to the government, the Naderis didn't fight unnecessary battles on Kabul's behalf. They defended themselves when attacked. But if the Mujahidin wanted to move troops and equipment through their territory, they just had to ask and, I assume, negotiate a price.

Of course, I had no idea of any of this at the time. My thinking about war was conditioned by what I'd read about the total wars of the 20th century, where the textbooks never mentioned fraternization or cooperation or negotiation or turning a blind eye. Just fighting. The reality of war, as I was slowly beginning to learn in Afghanistan, was very different.

As for myself, this Friday morning, I am feeling pretty collected. Surprisingly so, given the shocks of yesterday. There's something invigorating about living through dangers. I enjoy the good natured banter of men in the morning who are sharing hardships. I'm a little nervous to see what the day might bring. But I'm telling myself to simply accept it without complaint, like my traveling companions. It is what it is. What choice do you have? Remember Horatio Hornblower. Ha-hmm.

We pack up our kit, and climb back into our vehicles. Chris and I are separated again. Presumably that means there could be danger ahead.

I am surprised to see Alex, the de-mining guy, jumping into our trusty pickup. I had assumed he would remain in Pul-i-Khumri, at the field headquarters of his organization, the HALO Trust. He has business further north.

At the north end of Pul-i-Khumri, the road splits. The fork to the left is Highway One, the main ring road around Afghanistan—the one built by the US and the Soviet Union in the 1950s and 60s. That road leads toward Mazar-i-Sharif and the ancient Bactrian capital of Balkh —the one captured by the army of Alexander the Great. That road also leads to the so-called Friendship Bridge connecting Afghanistan to the Soviet Union, near the city of Termez in what is now Uzbekistan. Termez was the railhead and jumping off point for the logistics machine that had supported the Soviet occupation of Afghanistan, and now supported the Afghan communist regime of President Najibullah. From Termez, supply convoys drive across the Friendship Bridge, bringing their vital supplies of fuel and ammu-nition to the beleaguered armies of the communist government and their militia allies. It was over the Friendship Bridge that the last Soviet combat troops had left Afghanistan on February 15th 1989, almost three years before my visit. Their commander, Lieutenant-General Boris Gromov, symbolically walked across the bridge, the last to leave.

We are not following Gromov's footsteps. We take the fork to the right. That road leads to Kunduz and the wild northeast of Afghanistan.

There's a saying in Afghanistan: "If you want to die, move to Kunduz." It's a reference to the malaria that hits migrants from the highlands. But Kunduz has also been the scene of some of the most violent fighting over the last forty years.

We are planning to go through Kunduz and then some.

I didn't know all this geography at the time, dear reader. I am just a passenger. I have a vague idea where we were, but I have no map to study, as I would like. I have to trust my traveling companions, and try to enjoy the views, and not think about the war.

After you pass the last checkpoint at Pul-i-Khumri, on the road headed north, you enter a different Afghanistan. You are not only leaving behind the rugged, barren mountains of the Hindu Kush; you are leaving behind the 100 miles of manmade desolation along the Salang.

You start to see fields that are cultivated; irrigation systems that work; flocks of goats and sheep, tended by solitary shepherd boys; villages filled with people. The sky is bright and blue. It's good to feel the warmth of the sun again.

But the scene unfolding is like nothing you can see in the West. It's as if time has stood still. Besides our vehicles, there are long stretches where you can see nothing mechanical, nothing electrical. Transport is by horse and donkey, or on foot. Work is done by hand without the benefit of modern machinery.

It's past harvest time, and villagers are using the tarmac of the road to thresh wheat and barley. They toss it in the air and beat it with a wooden flail, to loosen the husks of grain from the straw. It's the ancient way of threshing, developed by the first farmers, thousands of years ago. It's an incredibly labour-intensive exercise. Except for the use of the roadway, it's a scene that could have been witnessed at any time in the past three or four thousand years. The same crops, the same tools, the same techniques.

The square, flat-roofed stone and abode houses complete the ancient imagery.

It's a humbling and beautiful moment. A moment in which I felt really connected with the past. At the same time, it illustrates how far Afghanistan needs to travel to catch up with modern technology and the modern economy.

The war seems further away than it did yesterday, in the Salang Valley. Here and there, tanks and armoured personnel carriers intrude on the eye, and bring you back to the present. But a moment later, even the military can look ancient.

At one pit stop, we're doing our business as usual from the edge of the tarmacked roadway, when I hear Alex say something. "Wow! Take a look at that!"

I look up. We're facing a broad plain of bright yellow crop stubble. Marching across the field, as far as the eye can see, there is a line of horse soldiers. They are riding in extended order—about 50-100 feet (15-30 meters) apart—I assume that's to minimize the risk from anti-personnel mines. They are not uniformed, but dressed in traditional baggy clothes, wearing turbans. They're bearded, so I assume they are Mujahidin, but out here they could just as well be pro-government militia. AKs are slung on their backs or in pommels on the sides of their ponies. Their mounts are white, brown or mottled. They move at a very slow walk. Their spacing is good. I turn and see a couple are on the other side of the road. I take a picture of them. Again, I feel an incredible connection with mankind's past.

Chris Woolf

The photo doesn't do the image justice. This is possibly one of the most beautiful images I've seen in my life. The combination of brilliant colors and history. The golden stubble of the wheat field. The brilliant blue of the sky. A line of Muj cavalry. Breathtaking. Maybe the hazards of being in a war zone do have their rewards?

It's not all beauty. The war has not consumed everything, like it has along the Salang Valley. Many villages have people. But some are desolate, bomb-damaged and abandoned. It's impossible to know who, when, where or how. Or why. But there are people somewhere for whom this place is everything—who know the answers to all those questions, all too vividly. It was their home. It is perhaps still their home, in their hearts. People who know the fields and families of the village intimately. All their stories. Now they are gone. I feel for them.

꽃꽃꽃   꽃꽃꽃   꽃꽃꽃

The checkpoints are familiar. I still can't tell which ones are manned by pro-government militia and which ones belong to the Mujahidin. But at some point in the 20 miles (32 km) between Pul-i-Khumri and the city of Baghlan, we enter uncontested rebel-held territory. Baghlan city is not to be confused with Baghlan province, a much wider territory.

Baghlan is the first city I see that is being run by the rebels. It's teeming with life. The streets are bustling with cars, horse carts, donkeys and foot traffic. Pul-i-Khumri—just 20 miles away—looked

Photo: WikiCommons

bleak and empty by comparison. Maybe it's market day, I don't know. But the most glaring difference is the women.

Every woman I see in Baghlan is covered from head to toe in a *burqa*. Most are black, a few are light blue or olive green. But mostly black. There is no *niqab*, the head covering that exposes the eyes. Instead the *burqa* is one

129

piece, covering the whole head and the rest of the body. There is a small, translucent section over the eyes, to allow the woman to see.

It is a striking and unsettling change. I understand that many Muslim women embrace the *burqa* as a symbol of their modesty, and as a sign of confidence in their faith, and I respect that. But I also know that not every woman does. My mind automatically goes back to Masum's friend whom I had met on the bridge over the Kabul River; the woman in the business suit, her hair uncovered, makeup on her face. There is no place for her in an Afghanistan controlled by the Mujahidin. It's unsettling because the Muj are supposed to be our allies and yet their values are so different, as exemplified here by the treatment of women.

I also heard that the *burqa* was not that common in Afghanistan traditionally. Apparently, you did not see many women wearing one prior to the upheavals of the 1970s and 80s, even in the countryside. Women dressed modestly, covered their hair, and often their faces, and were often sheltered from contact with strangers. But the clothes were often brightly coloured and attractive. I saw some myself in other rural areas. The shapeless black *burqa* was a relatively new import. Or so I was told. In conversation with Afghans and Western aid workers, I was told the *burqa* was a habit picked up by many Afghans while living in refugee camps in Pakistan, where Saudi-funded Wahabist "missionaries" took control of food distribution and education. Or in camps in the Islamic republic of Iran, where Shi'ite fundamentalists have a puritanical view of women's dress, like their Sunni rivals across the Persian Gulf. A generation of young Mujahid came of age in these camps, attended those madrassas, or Islamic schools, and brought those Saudi values with them when they conquered districts in Afghanistan from the communists. It's no coincidence that the word "Taliban" is derived from the Arabic word for students.

I did not have enough cultural knowledge to evaluate what I was being told. It seemed plausible, and not a little unsettling. The image I was left with was of a diverse and colourful culture being changed and hardened not just by war, but by foreign influence. It didn't help to know that these Saudi initiatives were in part facilitated by the CIA, together with British and other Western intelligence agencies. It was also common knowledge that the Saudis had stepped up their efforts since the Soviet withdrawal in 1989, when the US and the West began scaling back their own efforts to aid and influence the Mujahidin.

After Baghlan, I can't recall exactly the route we took. I'm fairly sure we continued north to the city of Kunduz to make a drop-off of supplies, as I know we separated from the HALO Trust truck and my Gurkha companion, Alex Shaw, somewhere along the road. It's one of the few blank spots in my recollections and notes. I have some photos tagged as being taken "near Kunduz," including one with Alex. Kunduz is much bigger than Baghlan. I had actually heard of it.

Kunduz at this time, in November 1991, is still in government-held hands, but only just. It had been the scene of a spectacular battle in 1988. A Soviet mechanized infantry division withdrew in August of that year without waiting to be properly relieved by Afghan government forces. The Mujahidin used the error to seize Kunduz. It was the first major Afghan city ever to fall to the rebels. The Soviets had to return to help the communist Afghan forces recapture it.[19] The violence and looting gave a foretaste of what would come after the regime collapsed in 1992.

The road takes us through plains. Some fertile. Some barren. Khaki is the universal colour. The foothills of the Hindu Kush are always present in the distance. Small rivers struggle to wind their course deeper into central Asia. The river beds seem ludicrously wide, as do the long flat bridges that cross them. Water lies only in small channels here and there. The land is thirsty, waiting for winter.

It looks like you could walk across the river beds at this time of year, just hopping over the water channels, or wading where needed. Most precipitation up here falls as snow in the winter. The floods in spring more than fill these river beds. But now, at the end of autumn, the water levels are as low as they get.

Here and there are little herds of goats, with their little solitary human guardians. These boys usually look as thin and hungry as their four-footed charges. The boys might be only 12 or 14 years of

---

[19]See "In Taliban-held Kunduz, echoes of 1 1988 guerrilla assault after the Soviets withdrew," by Dan Lamothe in the Washington Post, September 30th 2015. [washingtonpost.com/news/checkpoint/wp/2015/09/30/in-taliban-held-kunduz-echoes-of-a-1988-guerilla-assault-after-the-soviets-withdrew/]

age, but some have AKs slung over their backs. It seems to be the mark of a male, north of the Hindu Kush, to be carrying an AK.

8◈3 8◈3 8◈3

At some point on the journey, Fred decides we need to have a break. We are deep in rebel territory. He pulls up to a solitary building that seems indistinguishable from others along the road. It's a *chaikhana*, or teahouse. It's welcoming and menacing at the same time. Think Star Wars cantina.

In this particular Mos Eisley, there is no alien band playing loudly, but there is Afghan music playing on the radio in a quiet, understated way in the background.

We push through the beads that pass for a door, and enter a large, dimly lit room. Through the gloom I can see a series of broad tables, some covered in colourful rugs. There are no chairs. The *chaikhana* is crowded with men. No women. Everyone is sitting on the tables, some cross-legged, some with one knee up. Every which way.

The men are mostly young. Most are bearded, and dressed in traditional clothes: sandals, baggy pants, *kurtahs* (the long shirts), waistcoats, flat round caps known as *pakols,* or colourful skull caps. Most seem ragged and dirty. All are polite and dignified. Some sport green US-Army-style cotton jackets, not the dirty brown woolen ones of the Afghan army. They look like vintage US Army M-65 jackets, although I can't be certain.

We hop onto one of the tables ourselves and I find myself staring into the barrel of an AK-47. I can still see it now, mounted on a beautiful wooden stock. The barrel is well worn but clean. No one is threatening me. It's just hanging there, off the back of its owner.

Everyone is packing heat. AKs and RPGs are lying everywhere. Some are slung on their owners' backs, like the one staring at me. Some are leaning against the walls. Most are just placed carelessly on the tables besides their owners.

I look around me. Besides the AK-47 muzzle in my face, there are at least three other weapons pointing in my direction, including an RPG-7.

My only experience with firearms had been in the military, where muzzle discipline is instilled from a very early age. Never point a weapon at anyone unless you intend to kill them. Never leave a weapon lying around. Any weapons not in use must be stored carefully in the armoury and a full accounting made of rounds and even empty casings.

There are no such niceties in northern Afghanistan.

One holy warrior senses my discomfort, smiles politely and moves his weapon, lying on the table beside him. He doesn't alter the barrel's direction, he just pulls it a little closer to him, to give me more leg room. The muzzle is still pointing at me, only now it's six inches further away.

I flashback to my army days. When I was the platoon radio operator, I carried a Sterling sub-machine gun (SMG). I don't think I was ever issued ammo, as the weapon was considered so dangerous. I heard stories about SMGs going off by accident all the time, from small impacts like jumping off a truck. Now I'm looking at an ancient Soviet automatic rifle that might well be homemade. I can only assume it's loaded. I hope it's safer than the SMG. I pray the safety catch is working.

It is not a super-comfortable experience, but it's more amusing than frightening. One could joke that this is apparently where holy warriors take their tea-breaks, in-between waging jihad. Some of them may indeed be doing just that, but it's more likely these men are farmers and artisans from the surrounding villages, just hanging out. It's impossible to tell. Of course, even the farmers may be Mujahid as well. Some serve part-time to supplement their income, or when it's necessary to defend their home turf. The main lesson is that no self-respecting man hereabouts goes abroad without his weapon. Whether for self-defence or simply for honour, I do not know.

We are served tea in delicate little cups, only a bit larger than an espresso cup. The tea is extremely strong, and served black with enough sugar to allow you to stand up a spoon, if you had one. I must make a face as I taste it, as there is a round of chuckles. I laugh with them. The tea is hot, so I nurse it. Sip by sip, it starts to grow on me.

Fred shows me why we're sitting on the tables, and not the floor. As soon as he's done with his tea, he flicks his wrist and the tea leaves scatter across the floor. I try to emulate him and make a mess, eliciting more gentle chuckles from my fellow tea-drinkers.

ε◊3　ε◊3　ε◊3

Finally, our convoy reaches its destination. A city called Taloqan. It's a place I have never heard of before today, the capital of a province I'd never heard of, called Takhar. I will spend more time here than anywhere else in Afghanistan.

Taloqan is firmly under Mujahidin control. But the temper of the city seems to be different to Baghlan. It seems lighter, more colorful, more ordered. Burqas are universal, but bright blues and olive greens are much more frequent than the black burqas of Baghlan. The carts and donkeys are decorated with flowers and tassels and colourful pieces of cloth.

Our first impression of the order in the city comes from a traffic cop. He stands on a little podium in the middle of a busy four-way intersection. We hear him before we see him, from the shrill blast of the whistle pursed between his lips. Then we see his immaculate white cap. His shirt and trousers are neatly pressed. He wears immaculate white gloves on his hands which give point to the arm signals he uses with brutal precision to control the traffic of cars, trucks, bicycles, donkeys, horses and carts. His black mustache is equally well-disciplined.

I can't stop smiling, even now, at just how incongruous he looks. Not the authority figure I had expected to see in a city run by the Mujahidin—men we had stereotyped as bearded, ragged, and possibly lawless, mountaineers.

The image was created by design. Taloqan is Exhibit A in the case being made by Ahmed Shah Massoud—the local Mujahidin strong-man—to show the world that the rebels can be trusted to administer the affairs of a country.

Over the next couple of days, Chris and I will go about the city to test out that claim.

But first, our convoy has to deliver the humanitarian supplies we've carried all this way from Kabul. We look for the "international" section of town. There is no permanent United Nations office in Taloqan, so we head over to a clinic run by the International Committee of the Red Cross / Red Crescent on the edge of town.

It's run by a charming Afghan called Doctor Haidar. He has a full black beard and an irrepressible grin. He wears the large tinted glasses fashionable in the 1980s, and he seems to be always wearing a *pakol*—the flat round woolen cap popular among the Tajiks of Afghanistan. Indoors and outdoors, the *pakol* is inseparable from Dr Haidar. He's a little shorter than me, and looks to be in his 40s or early 50s. It's hard to judge age in Afghanistan, where the rigors of life can quickly wear you down.

Doctor Haidar

I do not recall his full name, but Dr Haidar's warmth and hospitality and sincere selflessness helped define my experience of the Afghan people. I've tried searching for him online without success. I did find the name of one Dr Gholam Haidar on a government death list dating from 1989, where he is listed as a physician from Panjshir. The list was found, verified and published by a Dutch human rights group. It consists of Afghans to be executed without trial if captured. Hundreds of them. I don't know if it's the same Dr Haidar, but it's a chilling indication of life, and death, under a real police state.

If it is the same Dr Haidar, his crime, according to the government's death list, was being an *Ikhwani*. The closest equivalent in English is "Muslim Brother." The Ikhwan al-Muslimin was a movement founded in 1969 by the future warlord, Gulbuddin Hekmatyar, together with future president, Burhanuddin Rabbani, in an effort to create a more Islamic society in Afghanistan. There were two main Muj groups in this part of Afghanistan in 1991, one under this same Hekmatyar, and one under Ahmed Shah Massoud, and both were nominally still subservient to Rabbani. So that makes it plausible that the Dr Haidar on the death list is the same Dr Haidar as the gentleman I met in Taloqan. I can't be certain.

My Dr Haidar is indeed firmly attached to the Mujahidin cause. He makes no secret about it. I am a little shocked by this, as Red Cross/Red Crescent officials are supposed to be strictly neutral and impartial. However, I don't recall ever seeing him pray or showing any other indication that he was especially devout.

The flat, round, woolen *pakol* cap that Dr Haidar is so fond of is another clue to his affiliations. Wearing one suggests support for the Mujahidin commander, Ahmed Shah Massoud. The cap is widely known today, and is assumed to be a universal Afghan fashion. It is not. Until the Soviet invasion, its use was largely confined to the isolated region of Nuristan. But then Massoud adopted it as part of his branding. Allegedly he favoured it to help him cover a mutilated ear that was injured while he was a fugitive in the 1970s. He made it part of the uniform of his guerrilla army and the rest, as they say, is fashion history.

Dr Haidar lives in the clinic, and he opens his home to us. There's a room that functions as a reception by day and living room by night. It is to be our home for the next few days.

The walls are bare except for a thin coat of yellow paint. The floor is covered by a large red rug. There's no furniture except for long red cushions that line the wall, and a miniature table just big enough to hold an oil lamp. The cushions provide somewhere to sit during the day, and are big enough to sleep on at night.

No rest for the wicked, though. While Fred and the other UN guys deliver the supplies, Dr Haidar offers to help Chris and me explore Taloqan and learn about the splendid rebel administration of the city. He provides us with a car and driver, and offers his services as translator. More usefully, he seems to know everybody, and makes all the introductions. I tag along to watch and learn.

The driver is a pleasant young chap with a thin beard. His baggy pants are light purple, and match his *kurtah*. He sports a *pakol* on his head and keeps warm with one of those green cotton jackets that look like they're from a US Army surplus store.

The next two days are a tiring round of interviews with officials and tours of public projects and buildings. Taloqan, as I mentioned, is under the control of the famed guerrilla commander, Ahmed Shah Massoud. But he isn't just a talented general. There is a civil administration hereabouts: the Shura-e-Nazar. This Shura functions like any local government anywhere in the world. It raises taxes, and appoints local officials who run the utilities, maintain the roads, administer the schools, the hospitals, the police and the courts. I did not appreciate at the time how fully it was Massoud's organization.

None of the interviews are in an office. Most are outdoors, or where work is being done. You can feel the pride of the officials involved, whether it's the man in charge of the grain depot, making sure it's distributed fairly, or the teacher with his classroom of eager schoolboys, slates and chalk in hand.

The school is a little heartbreaking. It's a fairly modern structure, but quite badly damaged, with many broken windows. The mayor shows us around, along with the principal. They are worried how they will keep classes going. Winter is coming. The heating will not work with so many windows out.

The classes are huge. The teachers earnest. Afghanistan has a huge literacy problem. Even before the political violence began in the 1970s, only about one in ten Afghan adults could read and write. The kids are clearly thrilled to be in class. There is some kind of capacity problem; either the school isn't physically big enough, or there aren't enough teachers. The kids come on alternate days, or maybe it's that some come in the morning and some in the afternoon. I can't remember for sure. But I am impressed how seriously everyone takes the problem: teachers, kids, officials.

The mayor of Taloqan is a man called Muhammad Omar. He is hard-working and keen to show us how well his town functions.

When Chris challenges him about the apparent absence of girls in the school, the mayor rises to the defense of his chief, and the right of girls to be educated. He says there simply hasn't been time to restore and open that side of the school yet. We aren't sure if we believe him. Taloqan has been in rebel hands, more or less, for several years. My hunch is that the officials are well-briefed to say the right things to Western reporters, so as not to alienate public opinion overseas, while slow-rolling the opening of a girls' school to placate religious hardliners.

Mayor Omar is a Pashtun and this fact is used to demonstrate the argument that Massoud's movement is not ethnically sectarian. Massoud's supporters are overwhelmingly Tajik, so some critics say this "tribalism" disqualifies him from being a potential leader of all

Afghanistan. Giving a high profile role to a Pashtun like Omar helps Massoud appear more inclusive.

Muhammad Omar will continue to rise through a variety of different positions in support of Ahmed Shah Massoud and his successors, until becoming Governor of Kunduz province in 2004. He was killed by a bomb here in Taloqan in 2010. Assassinated by the Taliban.

Chris starts every interview with the same question. What's the population of the city? After we get a very confident answer from the first official we meet, I'm surprised he puts the question again to the next official. Surely we have the information we need? I am more surprised to hear an equally confident answer that's very different from the answer from the first official. Over the course of several days I think we hear everything from 10,000 to 200,000. It's an interesting lesson to me about how fluid facts can be. Confidence and authority can be scams. Chris is using it as a warm-up question to establish a baseline of his interviewee's credibility. Very smart. I'm learning a lot.

Despite the obvious PR, things do seem to run pretty well in Taloqan. But there are limits. Not long after we start reporting, we're out a-walking downtown, not far from the traffic cop in the white gloves on his podium. I jump when I suddenly hear the loud *brrrttt* of gunfire not too far away: a burst from an automatic rifle like an AK. The street is noisy but the roar of bullets drowns out the traffic and the hubbub. A small convoy of trucks is coming up the road. A wedding party. Riding in army-style four-tonners, crowded on the benches in the back or standing. I see a gent sitting on a bench in one of the trucks raise his AK in one hand and let rip with a burst of a dozen rounds straight into the air, just as he's passing us.

The street is crowded with people going about their business. No one seems to flinch. I back up slowly into the doorframe of a store. What goes up must come down, I think. Even a spent round can kill you.

No one else seems to care, least of all the traffic cop. Just folks having a good time.

There are plenty more bursts as the convoy progresses through town.

I am shocked by the carelessness of the shooters. I now know this is a common practice across the Middle East and Central Asia, wherever men carry arms. To shoot in celebration. But until this moment in Taloqan I had never seen or heard of such a thing. This was before I visited New Hampshire and other parts of rural America, where letting rip with a firearm can be a common part of a celebration, although usually on private property.

Weddings! Now I knew why Alex and the other de-miners with the HALO Trust in Pul-i-Khumri had said that weddings were the only time they hit the deck. To take cover from stray rounds.

Chris and I become tourist attractions in our own right. Whenever we stop for an interview, crowds of children and curious onlookers gather around to gawk at the clumsy, oddly dressed foreigners. I wonder how many assume we're Russian?

Children seem to be everywhere. Most of them are hard at work. Girls carrying baskets. Boys stooped under heavy loads at the granary. Many of these children have a look of mature confidence. I guess it's something that comes from a life of hard work and self-reliance from an early age. The girls, I'm told, remain unveiled until they reach puberty.

Taloqan is not a loud place. There's the noise of chatter and laughter, of motorized and the clip-clop of horse drawn vehicles, as

well as the occasional burst of gunfire. I assume it's the celebratory kind, although I'm told the war is not far away.

At night we can hear explosions in the distance.

ᏋᏬᏋ   ᏋᏬᏋ   ᏋᏬᏋ

The city of Taloqan is not exclusively the preserve of Ahmed Shah Massoud's Jamiat-e-Islami movement. We are taken to the edge of town to see a recently captured BTR-60, the same kind of armoured personnel carrier that we had seen blown up on the outskirts of Kabul. It's on display as a sort of trophy of war.

It had been taken by a rival Mujahidin group, called the Hezbe-e-Islami, led by the notorious warlord, Gulbuddin Hekmatyar. Hekmatyar has a remarkable physical resemblance to the British actor, Christopher Lee. At the time of my visit, he was allied with Massoud. But they had occasionally fought each other, including quite recently. The two warlords had been in a bizarre, almost symbiotic, relationship since the 1970s, alternately working together and then trying to kill each other. The accounts I've read, and the stories I've heard, suggest that Hekmatyar was the more treacherous and unprincipled of the two. In 1994, the BBCs Mirwais Jalil interviewed him up here in northern Afghanistan. On the way back to Kabul, Mirwais was ambushed and killed. Murdered. It's widely assumed, although never proven, that Hekmatyar changed his mind about some of the things he'd told our reporter.

Sitting on top of the BTR-60, guarding the prize, is a young Hezbe-e-Islami Mujahid. His look seems a little different to the other Mujahid about town. He's wearing a camouflage-pattern battle dress —jacket and pants. His jacket is open. His AK is on his leg, with the barrel pointing to the sky. He has a neat mustache, rather than a beard. But the most distinctive feature about this sentry is his headgear. I can't tell if it's a turban or a giant wool cap, but it points up as well as hangs down behind his neck. I'd seen something similar worn by some of the militia we had seen on the road. Hekmatyar's supporters are mostly Pashtun but this hat looks more central Asian.

The man is a puzzle, but I'm even more curious about how the Muj had figured out how to move the armoured personnel carrier. Obviously it has been brought here from the battlefield where it had been taken. I'm curious how illiterate farmers learned to move and operate armoured vehicles and heavy weapons. I'm told first that the Soviets build things pretty idiot-proof, so the controls are simple and intuitive. Like the AKs and the RPGs. But then I'm told that sometimes their crews come with them.

It's a hard concept for modern Westerners to understand, brought up as we are on notions of total war and national loyalty. Switching sides and working for the enemy is inconceivable: the worst kind of disloyalty and treachery. Anyone who does so would likely face the necessity of having to kill their former comrades. It's unthinkable to our modern minds. But in fact, for most of human history, desertion has been quite thinkable. In civil conflicts, especially here in

Afghanistan, it's still quite common. The alternative is usually worse: you don't hear of any prisoner-of-war camps.

The side benefit for the captors is this transfer of technological knowledge. So the old crew of this BTR-60 may well have driven it here from the battlefield, and perhaps were now teaching others how to operate the vehicle and its weapons.

The rivalry between Hekmatyar and Massoud intensified in the 1990s, with serious fighting at times, followed by renewed alliances. After the rise of the Taliban in the mid-1990s, Massoud became the champion of Afghans fighting their puritanical madness, while Hekmatyar made common cause with the Taliban after the US invasion. He continued fighting the US and coalition forces, until he cut a deal in 2016 and returned to Kabul. His name is despised by many Afghans. One of my Afghan friends calls Hekmatyar a monster.

In the market of Taloqan, we are introduced to a relic of another war. An old man sits with his son, cross-legged, on a table in their clothing store. The son looks to be in his 40s or 50s. The old man has a white beard, and on his face are those age spots that hit some of us in our 80s. Despite his age, he looks spry. We are told they are Tajiks, and that the old man is originally from what is now Soviet Central Asia. He had fought the Red Army there in the 1920s, and fled south to Afghanistan to escape the Soviet conquest. His sons and grandsons had fought Soviet imperialism themselves in the 1980s here in Afghanistan. I was confused, as I thought they said he was from

Bukhara, which is in Uzbekistan, but I have since learned that many ethnic Tajiks did indeed live in Bukhara until purged by the Soviets in the 1920s. We did not get any more details, but it would have made for another interesting story. Apparently, Tajiks in the Russian empire first rebelled in 1916, against conscription into the Tsarist army, during the First World War. The fight continued, against the Reds, down to 1920, when the Soviets made concessions on Islam. But guerrilla war flared up again in 1927 as Moscow enforced collectivization of farms, even out in deepest central Asia.

Late that afternoon, we are introduced to another Afghan who speaks English, like Dr Haidar. Chris is very excited. Initially, I assume it's just because he can record a different voice. He's an official, like the others we've met, and appears to have a couple of armed men who follow him around.

He's a tall young man, with a neatly trimmed black beard over a strong jaw. He has a big playful face, and an impish grin. He's quite energetic, but relaxed and confident. I take an instant liking to him, and he seems to enjoy our company.

Little did we know that in 2014 this charming man would become Afghanistan's chief executive.

His name is Dr Abdullah.

Chapter 12

Dinner and Home Movies with the Mujahidin

Dr Abdullah is the head of the Shura-e-Nazar Reconstruction Committee, the Mujahidin's local government.

More importantly, Abdullah has some sort of connection with the great man himself, the Lion of the Panjshir, Ahmed Shah Massoud. That's the real reason Chris is excited. I learn for the first time that we might have a chance to meet the great man himself. I feel a frisson of excitement at the mere thought that he might be in the vicinity. Massoud was known to me as one of the greatest generals of the 20th century, on a par with Erwin Rommel, who helped pioneer tank warfare, or Vo Nguyen Giap, who led North Vietnam to victory against the French, the Americans and South Vietnam. A pioneer in a new way of warfare. A hero who defied the odds and turned history in his favour. As a history buff, I had read about such people since I was old enough to pick up a book. Now one of these makers of history is close by.

At the time, I was not clear what Abdullah's connection with Massoud actually was. I assumed the Shura-e-Nazar Reconstruction Committee was an autonomous body that impartially helped administer rebel-held areas. I did not appreciate how intimately it was intertwined with one particular rebel group: Massoud's Jamiat-e-Islami. In reality, Abdullah was Massoud's right-hand man, one of several young intellectuals he had gathered around him to run the parts of the country that he occupied. Abdullah, as young as he was, had spent much of the 1980s running Massoud's health department, overseeing medical aid to injured Mujahid as well as providing health services to the people. At the time I met Abdullah, I was under the impression he just happened to know Massoud, as they operated in the same vicinity.

I also learn this is the real reason that we are here in the north of Afghanistan. My buddy Chris had received a tip in Kabul that we might be able to see Massoud. Securing an interview with him would be a tremendous scoop for Chris and the BBC. The aid convoy was a lucky coincidence. Or maybe it wasn't. The UN wanted a response from Massoud to their peace plan. Maybe we were just pawns in a bigger game. I don't know.

Chris had hoped all along that we would meet with this leader of the Mujahidin, this Lion of the Panjshir. And that we would be entering the Lion's den.

Abdullah is to be our connection.

Chris had kept the tip quiet for obvious security reasons. Massoud is a wanted man. Perhaps "Enemy Number One" for the regime in Kabul. He has already survived repeated assassination attempts. His security is good. He has learned how to avoid getting trailed and targeted by hostile military forces. Chris didn't want me blurting anything out, as I might well have done, given how green I am.

This, apparently, is also the real reason we had left behind Chris' fixer, Masum, in Kabul. Chris explains that Masum probably has to tell the government where he's going and who he's meeting. If we were to meet up with such a high-value target as Ahmed Shah Massoud, we could not take the risk that we could be compromised. There's a lot going on that I don't know about.

This is all hard to accept. Chris's fixer, Masum, is the embodiment of kindness. But as many have since told me, it's a fact of life for people in a civil war that they have to make compromises to stay safe and survive.

Chris interviews Dr Abdullah like the other officials, but this time without an interpreter. Afterwards, he agrees to stay for dinner. It's a promising sign for our developing relationship, and our goal of getting access to Massoud.

We spread out on the red cushions in Dr Haidar's reception room, and I take a moment to scrutinize our guest.

Dr Abdullah's clothes straddle two worlds. He has a European style striped shirt, neatly pressed. But it's hanging untucked over traditional white baggy pants. He has a white cargo vest, of the kind you could find at Old Navy in the 1990s, but also a *pakol* cap on his head and a *shemagh* around his neck.

I'd seen these *shemaghs* everywhere. They are different from the woolen or heavy cotton *keffiyehs* of the Palestinians, which are so fashionable among Western intellectuals. Shemaghs are made from a very fine cotton, or occasionally silk, and are generally much more colourful than *keffiyehs*. Dr Abdullah shows me how useful they can be, as a scarf to keep draughts off your neck and chest; as a belt if you need somewhere to tuck a dagger or wallet; as a bag, or as a facecloth in a sandstorm. Chris and I both pick one up in the market the next day. They cost us less than a dollar. I get the sense that the seller thinks he's robbed us blind.

Shemaghs are also known as *chadars,* or more simply "Panjshiri bandannas." Ahmed Shah Massoud's home province is Panjshir. It's another of his fashion innovations—part of his brand, like the *pakol* cap.

Dinner would be familiar to anyone who's traveled in Afghanistan. Everyone sits cross-legged or splayed out on the long cushions along the walls of the room. The meal is served by the boys of the house. No women are to be seen. The boys place platters and boards and bowls containing different dishes on the rug in the center of the room. Lamb, rice and flatbread, assorted dried fruits, almonds. We diners peck with our hands. The food is all delicate and flavorful. I love it, but eat sparingly to avoid appearing greedy. I'm also still clumsy, eating with my fingers. I'm the source of much entertainment.

I don't know who prepared this food. It just seemed to appear as if by magic on most days of our trip. I don't know who paid for it. Dr Haidar would not take any payment for his hospitality. Looking back, it could well have been an in-kind gift from the Mujahidin. I'll never know. When you're this tired and hungry, your ethics can be quickly put on the back burner.

Dr Abdullah is an interesting chap. "So just to be clear, what is your name?" asks Chris. "I hear Abdullah and I hear Abdullah Abdullah. Which is correct?"

"Well, like many Afghans, Chris, I only have one name. Abdullah. My parents only gave me one name. It's something you foreign journalists seem to find hard to understand. So when they ask me what is my first name, I say 'Abdullah,' and when they ask me what is my last name, I say 'Abdullah.' So they call me Abdullah Abdullah. But my parents only called me Abdullah."

He sighs, and continues, "I've learned to go with the flow, as you say in England. But please, if you can, just call me Abdullah."

"Speaking of which, where did you learn to speak such good English?" I ask.

"Ahhh, well. You see, Chris, I was not a very good Mujahid." He shakes his head as he speaks, grinning all the while. His voice has a wonderful lilting quality. And I was one, once, like everyone. We were going over the mountains to Pakistan. I was riding on a donkey, going up a very steep slope. And I fell off, and broke my leg. And so, like other injured Mujahids, I was taken to a hospital in London to get better. Wimbledon, actually. It's a beautiful town. Have you been there?"

"As a matter of fact, I haven't," I reply, a little dumbstruck.

"It's so nice. So green," he continues. "As soon as I could, I went out to explore and talk to people, and that's how I learned English."

I have no idea if any of that story is true, and no way of verifying it. But that's what Abdullah told me while we were sitting cross-legged, breaking bread, in Dr Haidar's living room. And his English was near perfect. I have to say, I love the image of convalescent Afghan warriors—who might otherwise never have left the mountains of their homeland—wandering the streets of Wimbledon, a leafy middle-class neighborhood in south London, home to the famous tennis tournament. Or the image of wounded Mujahidin rambling over the neatly mown green parkland of Wimbledon Common. We knew western governments were providing material aid and support to the Mujahidin, and this kind of non-lethal assistance would be less controversial for the UK government, if discovered.

"You're from Kabul," starts Chris. "But you live up here. Are you Pashtun or Tajik or something else?"

"I am Afghan," Abdullah replies sternly. "Maybe the only one," he softens, with an impish grin in the corner of his mouth. "You see, my father was Pashtun and my mother Tajik. So I am neither. And both."

"I am mixed, too," I add sympathetically, half-joking. "At least that's the way I was seen at school. I am English, Scottish, *and* Welsh, which was very unusual where I grew up."

"Yes," he nods. "It can sometimes be hard to know where you fit in."

"You go by the title of doctor. Is that academic or medical? Or honorary?" one of us asks.

"Medical. I was an eye doctor," he points to an eye. "I was in the health field for a time. But I haven't practiced for long while." He's far too modest. He had in fact been in charge of health services for Massoud for some years.

"And how old are you?"

"I'm 31 or 32," replies Abdullah.

"You're not sure?" I ask, incredulous.

"No. One thing you must learn is that Afghans don't count time like you in the West. We don't really keep track of birthdays. What's the point, we say?"

"To celebrate yourself, I guess." I suddenly feel that's a very selfish concept.

"We do not. We are here as long as God wills it, and are just thankful for every day, *alhamdulillah*." Alhamdulillah means "thanks be to God." You often hear it added to the end of any sentence describing anything in your life. It's a little prayer.

"But what about official records, and documents? Don't you need a birthday for that?"

"I think I myself have a piece of paper somewhere," he explains. "But that's unusual. You forget that nine out of ten Afghans cannot yet read or write. They have no need of records. They have no use for documents."

For a Westerner, these are all pretty mind-blowing concepts. I mean, the truth of Abdullah's words immediately seem obvious in context. But we carry our assumptions everywhere we go. It was a good lesson in unconscious bias.

I look for more comfortable topics.

"Are you married? Do you have a family?"

"No." He seems to blush slightly. "How about you Chris, are you married?"

"Why, yes." I answer. "I've been married three years."

"Any children?"

"No. Not yet," I say.

Abdullah smiles approvingly. The "not yet" is a little turn of phrase I picked up in Kenya and Tanzania: countries with cultures that prize big families, like Afghans.

I felt like we'd established a rapport.

"So I have another question, and it's a little sensitive, so forgive me for asking," says I. It's now clear Abdullah is a *bone fide* representative of the Mujahidin. He's a former Mujahid; now an official helping to run a rebel-held territory. The Mujahidin are the allies of the West in this war against our common Soviet enemies. But I'm a journalist and a historian, with a passion for truth, however uncomfortable, and I feel the moment has arrived to ask a question that truly bothers me.

"The Russians say you mutilate prisoners and kill them.[20] The British used to say the same thing, back in Kipling's day. Why do you do that?"

Specifically, bodies are found naked, bound, badly cut, and the penis cut off and stuffed into the mouth. The British imperial poet, Rudyard Kipling warned soldiers in danger of getting captured on the Frontier to save the last round for themselves, rather than fall into the hands of the Afghans and their long knives.

"Well, Chris. It happens sometimes. It's mostly just to send a message to the people who find them," explained Abdullah. "But you shouldn't worry, they're usually dead first."

It was difficult to come up with a follow up question to such a frank admission. Usually dead first. The implication was chilling.

---

[20]See partially redacted CIA document on execution of captured Soviets in Afghanistan, 1985; CIA-RDP85T00287R0013011000001-8. [www.cia.gov/library/readingroom/docs/CIA-RDP85T00287R001301000001-8.pdf]

"But it's simply not true that we kill everyone,[21]" he adds quickly. "Especially Ahmed Shah Massoud." Abdullah's charming smile returns. "He is a merciful man. In fact, there are many prisoners who are Muslim, or who convert to Islam, and stay with us. Many become Mujahid themselves."

I must have stared in disbelief, so after a pause he says: "Yes, in fact, there is one man who has become a trusted bodyguard for Ahmed Shah Massoud himself. And there's another near here. I'll see if we can bring them over to meet you."

葳 葳 葳

It's not until late the next day that Abdullah returns with a larger than usual posse of men, most of them armed. He introduces two of them to us. He says they are both former Soviet soldiers, missing in action. MIAs. Captives of the Mujahidin. Prisoners of war.

I am stunned. It's almost three years since the last Soviet combat troops withdrew across the Peace and Friendship bridge. This would be a discovery on a par with finding American POW/MIA servicemen in the jungles of Vietnam, years after the withdrawal of US troops. In say, 1978. It's the plot of several B-list action movies. You almost expect a Russian Rambo to come over the hill to rescue them.

I know that the Soviets are anxious about their MIAs in Afghanistan. There are several hundred soldiers unaccounted for, maybe as many as 1,500. I know from the news that Soviet leader, Mikhail Gorbachev, has been conducting some personal shuttle diplomacy to try to find them and bring them home. Many in Russia and abroad scoff at his efforts, stating baldly that the Mujahidin do not take prisoners. The murder of captives is documented, and even acknowledged by Mujahidin leaders, as I had just heard myself, the day before. But as Abdullah had said, it is not universal. Clearly there are exceptions.

We are skeptical at first. How can we know this is not some elaborate propaganda stunt? Well, the two men are dressed as

---

[21]See "The Russians' Lot in Afghan Hands," New York Times, November 2nd 1985. [nytimes.com/1985/11/02/world/the-russians-lot-in-afghan-hands.html

Afghans but their faces look very European; their Russian sounds natural; and their back stories sound plausible.

The two men are not restrained. In fact, one is armed. The tall one with the AK is introduced as Islam-ud-Din, the bodyguard to Ahmed Shah Massoud. I'm intrigued. If he's a bodyguard then that must mean the Big Guy himself might be in the vicinity. The other is a guy who is introduced to us as Nek Muhammad.

Nikolai Bystrov, also known as Islam-ud-Din

Both men have a sad, world-weary air about them. Both have black beards. Both wear Afghan clothes. Both have converted to Islam.

Ahh, so maybe that's how you survive becoming a prisoner of the Mujahidin in Afghanistan? You submit to Allah and maybe espouse the cause of your captors.

Abdullah says many of the POWs who remain are Muslims, from the central Asian republics of the Soviet Union. Some speak Uzbek, Turkmen and Tajik like their kinfolk here in Afghanistan. Most of the other POWs have converted to Islam, we are told, like these two gentlemen. Abdullah is a little hazy on the timeline of when exactly these captives submitted to Allah. My suspicion is that it was very early on in their detention. We're told some captives have not converted to Islam, but we are not offered any proof, nor have I since found any. I am told Nek Muhammad is no longer a Mujahid, that he had stopped fighting after the Soviets left. Again, it's impossible to verify.

I instantly realize this is a good story, and I pitch it to Chris. He says I should do it, since I thought of it, and he lends me his recording kit. Abdullah pitches the idea to the men, and it is agreed.

But first, we must eat.

ണ്ട ണ്ട ണ്ട

I've dined in eclectic company before and since, but I don't think I've ever broken bread in a stranger crowd. Here I am, a young British journalist, sitting down to eat with a Red Cross official who is working with the rebels; a Mujahidin official who learned English while convalescing in Wimbledon; two former soldiers of the Red Army, both POW/MIAs, who have now joined the Holy War; and a bunch of Jamiat-e-Islami guerrillas.

The room is crowded for dinner. Men sit cross-legged, jostling for room on the long red cushions that line the walls. For once the AKs and RPGs have been left outside the room.

The dinner is similar to yesterday's, only larger in scale. Young men and boys bring in the platters and lay them on the floor. Everyone eats with their hands, taking whatever they fancy. I'm still not sure of the customs so again I pick sparingly, not wishing to be seen as abusing the hospitality. I'm also still clumsy at eating by hand, but I'm getting better.

Dinner is finished. Coffee is coming. It's getting dark. Now may I record my interviews?

"Later, later," says Abdullah. "First let's watch some movies."

Wait, what?

The night is getting more surreal. Here we were in the wilds of northern Afghanistan. Electricity is hard to access. And yet a big TV is now being wheeled out, complete with a VCR player. I can't remember the brand but the TV is big, Japanese, and modern-looking. I've no idea where it came from. My pre-trip research had suggested TVs were almost unknown in Afghanistan, but evidently I was quite wrong.

The mood in the room becomes more boisterous. There are maybe 12 young men, mostly Muj foot soldiers, jostling for a good view and exchanging the sort of cheeky banter I recognized from my own army days, even if I could not understand the words. There was definitely some teasing going on.

Abdullah and his mates pull out some VCR tapes. I have no idea what they will be. Hollywood? Bollywood? Home movies? In my army days, the only videos were training films or pornos.

Abdullah attempts to silence the room with a word. Like a teacher with a rowdy class, he repeats himself more loudly and adds a very stern look. It's a new view of him. Until now he has been all sweetness and self-effacing charm. The men obey.

The tape starts. There's some fuzz and static, then loud, dramatic Middle Eastern music. Too loud; it's distorting slightly. Okay, this is some sort of home movie, I think. Or at least an amateur local production. Credits roll, in Dari. There's polite applause when the title comes up. I'm told it's a kind of celebration of the combat achievements of the Mujahidin, and the lives of individual martyrs.

One sequence really sticks in my mind. There's this one big fellow operating a heavy machine gun, firing downhill. A red bandanna is tightly wrapped round his shaved head. A murmur of approval goes round the room. The film slickly goes into slow motion, so you can see individual casings ejected from the chamber, as the music becomes more dramatic and intense. A caption comes up in Dari, which I'm told says these images were shot just moments before this particular hero was martyred. *"Allahu akbar"* murmurs across the room. "God is great." You can tell the respect and reverence is sincere. Thankfully, the martyrdom itself is edited out.

The movies are pretty slick. Each one is short, maybe 20-30 minutes. As I said, they are well-edited, with music and graphics. The sound is a little distorted—over-modulated as we would say in the audio business. But otherwise very well-produced.

Everyone has seen this style of movie since, as a staple of Islamic militant propaganda on social media. I couldn't help wondering where the Muj had got the equipment and training to produce these. I'd put money on some of it coming from Langley, the CIA head-quarters.

ε◇϶ ε◇϶ ε◇϶

Can I do my interviews now? Former POW Nek Muhammad appears to have cold feet. He's polite but firm. He says he must leave. I'm disappointed. Islam-ud-Din, the bodyguard, is getting ready to leave as well. Chris and I plead with Abdullah and Dr Haidar to intervene, and he reluctantly agrees to stay. Nek Muhammad disappears into the night. I'll hear no more of him until he pops up in a news story a couple of years after the US invasion of Afghanistan, still living in Kunduz. Married, with a family of his own. He was interviewed and profiled by Carlotta Gall of the New York Times in 2003.[22]

Islam-ud-Din seems sad. His gaze is often off in the distance, as though his mind is somewhere else. Not in this body. Even while speaking, he rarely makes eye contact. But when he does, the effect is piercing.

A *pakol* cap is perched on the back of his head, a black and white *shemagh* scarf curls leisurely around his neck. He's wearing a very

---

[22]See "A Stranger in Afghanistan, Too Torn to Go Home," by Carlotta Gall, New York Times, July 31st 2003. [nytimes.com/2003/07/31/world/a-stranger-in-afghanistan-too-torn-to-go-home.html]

European looking thick wool sweater. It's clean and new. Patterned. Over the sweater is a vest, in disruptive-pattern camouflage. He wears the traditional local baggy pants, in dark blue.

He does not look like much of a warrior, although later press reports describe his military prowess as legendary. In fact, I'd say he looks calm and gentle.

He is ready. We move into a small room, isolated from the hubbub. It feels like a closet. It's too small for us to sit, so we stand. Islam-ud-Din speaks alternately in Dari and Russian. Dr Haidar will translate—apparently his Russian is as excellent as his English.

The POW is a full head taller than me, while Dr Haidar is shorter. So this will take some deft work with my single microphone. Haidar's presence will make it hard for the former POW to speak freely. The doctor is a known Mujahidin sympathizer, if not outright supporter. The room next door is full of rebels. But it's all we have. I make a mental note to add a caveat to the story.

I check my sound levels, and roll tape.

The tape is no longer in my possession, but these are the highlights as best as I can recall.

"What is your name?"

"Nikolai Nikolaievitch," is the name he gives me. "My name here is Islam-ud-Din."

I ask him again, as it doesn't sound complete to me. I am no expert in Russian naming customs, but I am pretty sure a patronymic like Nikolaievitch, "son of Nikolai," is not the family name.

"Nikolai Nikolaievitch," he repeats. "My name here is Islam-ud-Din."

I guess that he doesn't want to make himself completely identifiable. He's savvy enough to know the interview could be heard back home. I move on.

"Where are you from?"

"I was born and grew up in a place called Krasnodar. My father is Russian and my mother is Ukrainian."

"I've heard of it. That's near Crimea, right?"

"Yes."

"In Ukraine?"

"No, southern Russia," he clarifies.

"When and how did you get captured?"

"It was 1982," says Nikolai. "I was a new conscript." I do a quick calculation. As a new draftee he would have been 18 or 19. That would make him my age, or a year older at most. He looks much older than Chris or me.

"I was at Bagram," he continues. Bagram was the main Soviet base near Kabul. We'd driven past it on the way up. "I was outside the wire. And I just got caught."

I assumed he was out on patrol. In 2013, he told Russian blogger and writer, Natalia Konradova, that he and two comrades were sent out by the veterans in his platoon to forage for food, without proper orders.[23] So technically he was absent without leave.

"How did you survive?"

Nikolai lets out a little snort, half-laugh, half-grunt. "I was lucky. My comrades died. But I was taken to Massoud. He does not kill prisoners. Some wanted to kill me, but he did not allow it."

"Is that when you became a Muslim?"

"No, that was later, after I had seen and learned more about Islam, which was quite foreign to me. It was some time before I submitted to God. There is no God but God, and Muhammad is his prophet. And now I serve God and Massoud."

"Do you think you could have survived if you had not converted?"

"It's hard to say." It is hard to say. With a pro-Muj translator, it would be hard to say anything else. "But how else would I find a wife?" Nikolai smiles broadly.

"Oh!" I'm not sure if he's joking. "Have you found one?"

"Not yet." His face is serious again.

"Do you know any POWs who have not converted to Islam?"

"I do not."

"Did you join the Mujahidin?"

"You have to do what you have to do. My hair is fair, so I dye it black, along with my beard." He gives a shallow laugh and his bright

---

[23] «Жена разбирается в компьютерах, а я только убивать умею», "My wife understands computers, but I only know how to kill," by Natalia Konradova, May 14th 2015, published in Alex Dars' blog, 'Journal A.' [alex-dars.livejournal.com/405334.html]

blue eyes twinkle as he deflects the question. "I can't hide my eyes, though."

"It's been what, nine years since you were captured and converted to Islam? Did you ever have to fight against your former comrades?"

"I have served, but I have not fired my rifle," replies Nikolai. I'm not sure I believe him, at least in terms of not opening fire. I'm not sure how you could serve for so long as a Mujahid in such a war-torn country, and not open fire. On the other hand, studies of US soldiers in the wars of the mid-20th century show that a significant proportion of troops never open fire, even in close combat.[24] So anything is possible.

"Besides, I soon became a bodyguard," he adds.

"Yes, speaking of that—how did Massoud come to trust you so much that he would make you one of his bodyguards?"

Unfortunately, I can't recall Nikolai's answer to this exactly. I have a vague impression of him saying Massoud liked to have a Russian close to him. I presumed it was for the public relations value, to show the world his magnanimity and discipline.

"Do you ever think of home?"

"Of course. I miss it terribly. Especially my mother. She must be so worried."

"Does she know you're alive?"

"Actually, yes. In fact, I have been able to exchange letters with my mother." He is grateful to Ahmed Shah Massoud personally, he explains, for arranging for his letter to be taken across the border and mailed from there. One had even come back from his mother through the same circuitous route. One of the Soviet republics to the north of Afghanistan is Tajikistan. Massoud himself and most of his army is ethnically Tajik, and many Tajiks in Afghanistan have family on the other side of the river that marks the frontier—the legendary Oxus river of Alexander the Great's time, now the Amu-Darya. Presumably Massoud's people had used one of these connections.

"Do you think you'll go back?"

"Maybe," he answers wistfully. He adds *"Inshallah"* after a pause—the universal Muslim phrase for "God willing." "Of course, I could not

---

[24]See S.L.A. Marshall, "Men Against Fire," 1947. [books.google.com/books/about/Men_Against_Fire.html?id=rzLxoITDhQQC]

158

go while the war was on. I saw the homeland across the river, but I was not allowed to cross myself." I am intrigued by the notion that the "war" ended with the Soviet withdrawal. I had heard that a few times by now. The war seemed to be very much alive and kicking, to my mind. Maybe it was just the intensity of the conflict, I don't know. Maybe it was because the enemy was no longer a foreigner.

"But the Russians left more than two years ago. Why not now?"

"Massoud has said I may go. But not yet. I don't know if I'm ready. And even if I could, it would not be easy, now that I have served with the Mujahidin." His honesty is refreshing. "Anyway, I serve Massoud now. Thanks be to God."

"What's it like living here?"

"It's hard." He's about my age, but his face is already much older, already wrinkled by worry. "But maybe I'll find a wife and stay here." He grins slightly, and the wrinkles crackle with life.

"I work for the BBC World Service, so there's a chance this interview might be heard in Russia. What message do you have for your family?"

The gentle warrior's face has been mostly impassive through the interview, but now he's taken aback. He makes eye contact, glowering directly at me, teeth clenching. He switches from Dari to Russian.

"For my family?"

A fierceness wells up. He looms forward. But then the tension is released. His shoulders sag. He drops the stare, with a gentle sigh, and his gaze again turns into the distance.

"I want my mother and family to know I'm okay. I will see you again. I love you."

His eyes are wistful again for a moment, before the poker face returns.

I think I recorded about 40 minutes in all. It's exhausting, peering into another person's tragedy.

ઠ◈ક ઠ◈ક ઠ◈ક

Nikolai and Abdullah leave to spend the night elsewhere.

For years I tried to make a more positive identification of this young man. To try to learn what might have happened to him. For a long time I mixed him up in my memory with Nek Muhammad, who —as I mentioned—came into the media spotlight in 2003. That left me confused, as my notes clearly stated this was Islam-ud-Din, or Nikolai Nikolaievitch. There was a long period where I assumed he had lied about his name.

It was only in 2020 that I finally connected the dots, by translating various articles in Russian media containing his picture. My Nikolai was being truthful about his Russian name, his Islamic name, and his hometown, of Krasnodar, near Crimea. Even the fact that his parents were mixed Russian and Ukrainian. I learned that I was right to be skeptical about the patronymic Nikolaievitch not being his surname. His proper family name is actually Bystrov. Nikolai Bystrov. Apparently he was always careful about his name while in Afghanistan.

In these interviews with Russian media he describes how he and two fellow foragers were ambushed in a village near Bagram. They were all wounded and captured, after running out of ammo. One comrade who could not walk was killed on the spot, as the rebels needed to bug out quickly. Right in front of Nikolai. Their assailants were a mix of Massoud's Jamiat-e-Islami and Hekmatyar's Hezbe-e-Islami. They split their prisoners. Nikolai was taken by Massoud's people. His comrade was taken by Hezbe. He was never seen again.

Bystrov really was Massoud's bodyguard. Massoud really did save his life personally after he was captured, and won his loyalty. He gave him purpose, and faith.

Massoud's death in 2001 was the biggest tragedy of Nikolai's life, he is quoted as saying in a 2013 article by blogger, Natalia Konradova. Nikolai told her he believes he could have prevented his assassination, had he still been there. He would have died for his chief.

But Nikolai—Islam-ud-Din Bystrov—returned to Russia in 1995, with Massoud's help. According to Konradova's essay, he did not want to go, but his wife faced a complicated childbirth and they needed better medical attention than they could get in Kabul. Massoud helped get their papers in order. Bystrov returned to southern Russia. The birth was successful. But before they could return to Kabul, the Taliban defeated Massoud and his allies and drove them back into the mountains. The Bystrovs were then stranded in Russia, and had to make a new life for themselves there.

According to Konradova, Islam-ud-Din's wife, Odilia, is an interesting character herself. She is not one of those stereotypical, sequestered, rural Afghan women. Instead, she is an educated, professional woman, and a feisty communist. They met in Kabul after the overthrow of the communist regime in 1992. He protected her from Mujahidin bullies who did not like the way she dressed. She stabbed one assailant herself, she told Konradova. Nikolai also helped nurse his wife back to health after she was severely injured in a bomb blast. They make an interesting couple, a Russian soldier who became a devout Muslim, and an Afghan Marxist. They now have three children.

Islam-ud-Din Bystrov returns frequently to Afghanistan. He works part-time with a veterans group, trying to locate former prisoners of war, alive or dead, and bring them home. His knowledge of Dari and Pashto, and his local connections, make him invaluable. The war is not over for Russia while one man remains, he told one reporter.

There's an interview with him on the Russian TV channel, Russia Today, from 2014, with Sophie Shevardnadze.[25] Bystrov's eyes still seem sad. But it was deeply satisfying for me personally to finally hear—after all these years of doubt in my mind—that his loyalty to Massoud and his new faith were sincere, not coerced. There was nothing to stop him being honest in these interviews in Russia, decades after leaving Afghanistan, his second homeland.

The final line of Konradova's article is telling. When the reporter asks him to send her a photo, Bystrov replies by telling her to ask his wife. "She understands computers better than I do. I only know how to kill."

8◊3   8◊3   8◊3

---

[25]You can see the interview online. [rt.com/shows/sophieco/174260-afghanistan-war-taliban-pow/ Follow @SophieCo_RT]

Nikolai's comrade Nek Muhammad followed a different path. As I mentioned, he popped up in a New York Times article by Carlotta Gall in 2003. I learned from this that his original name was Gennadi Tseuma, or Tsevma, from Ukraine.

By the latest accounts I can find at the time of writing, he is still living in Afghanistan, near Kunduz, with a growing family. He's actually a year younger than me but his face looks 20 years older. He keeps getting profiled by journalists, so it's not hard to follow him. In particular, he was the subject of a profile by the BBC's Lyse Doucet in 2009, and by Andrew Kramer of the New York Times in 2018. He seems to tell every interviewer a different story about how he was captured, how he survived, and his subsequent role in the wars. He was either captured on a patrol or he was a deserter, depending on his audience.

I found a two-hour documentary about him on YouTube, from "Russia Today." They actually took Gennadi to visit his home town of Amvrosiivka, Ukraine, in about 2011, to be reunited with his mother and siblings.

In that film, he denied he was ever a Mujahid, let alone that he had ever fought against his former comrades. I guess that's what you tell a Russian and Ukrainian audience. I guess you don't survive three decades in such a hostile environment without knowing how to massage your message for your audience.

At one point in the Russia Today documentary, Gennadi attends a meeting with a few local "Afghantsi"—men who had served in the Soviet army in Afghanistan. They were not welcoming. They did not believe his argument that he did not serve with the Mujahidin. How could they have let you live if you had not converted to Islam and promised to join them? They have a point.

Gennadi contemplated staying in Ukraine. The government has long offered full pardon and relocation assistance. But in the end, he decided to return to Kunduz. He could not imagine a life in Ukraine for himself, let alone his Afghan wife and children.

Ironically, staying in Afghanistan was probably safer for them. In 2014, war came to his home village in Ukraine. Ethnic Russians, supported by Moscow, rebelled against the government in Kiev.

Several of Gennadi's family were killed by the fighting, and the village remains under Russian occupation at the time of writing.

8◈3 8◈3 8◈3

It's been a long evening, and it's relatively late when our guests leave. We turn in for the night. The red cushions we'd been sitting on for dinner become our mattresses. It isn't very cold.

Sometime in the middle of the night I awake to the crump of artillery fire. I listen carefully to confirm my first instinct. The explosions are clear, every 20 or 30 seconds. I need to take a dump, so I head outside to the facility. It's a cloudless night. The moon is bright enough to show me the way. The artillery fire is much louder outdoors. The facility consists of a little wooden shelter over a big deep hole in the ground. The structure is half open to the elements. There are only two walls, made of thin shingles. Being the doctor's home and clinic, there is a pile of lime and a shovel, so you can lime your waste after defecating. The lime glows in the moonlight. The hole is pretty full and also glowing.

The artillery fire is getting louder, and rounds are landing every few seconds now. So I'm squatting doing my business, perched over the hole, and I realize the artillery fire is getting closer and closer. I can't see flashes but I can guess from the sound it's probably only half a mile away now. And so I start to think about where I can take cover if the fire becomes effective. I had not made a note of where the other shelters were. I make a mental note never to neglect that again. There is only one place to take cover in a hurry. Beneath me.

I knew an old sergeant in the army, who had served with British special forces in Borneo, fighting communist insurgents in the 1960s. He told a story of how they used to go about camp naked when off-duty, because of the heat. He was using the latrine when there was a surprise attack from the commies. He had been obliged to take cover in the shit pit, bare-arse naked. At least I had clothes.

Artillery is a terrible thing. In the army, I had been trained to dig in as soon as we stopped moving, even if we were only going to be somewhere for a few minutes. It's to protect yourself from the blast and flying metal unleashed by a shell. I also knew that artillery shells were powerful enough to collapse a slit trench, if they land within 100 feet or so. The blast creates something like a miniature earthquake.

So I focus on finishing my business. I close my eyes, and say a little prayer, hoping the shells would not come so close that I would have to dive into the shit pit. I was more concerned about the danger of burns from the lime than the waste. Still, that's better than shrapnel, I calculate. My second prayer is that if I do have to jump in, that the shells wouldn't be so close that they collapse the pit.

I amuse myself and chuckle a little when a stupid pun pops into my head. I won't take this artillery strike lime down. A pun on lying down. And the lime. Not really funny, but you do what you must to take your mind off the risk.

Anyway. Business done. The shelling drifts away again. Back to bed. Another artillery lullaby.

Chapter 13

Meeting a Legend: My Time with Ahmed Shah Massoud

A cock crows. Sunday 10th November 1991 dawns over Taloqan blue and clear, like most days on our trip. The air feels a little cooler and crisper. We wake from our beds, those red cushions lining the walls. We sit cross-legged and wait for tea to be served and breakfast to be brought in by Dr Haidar's people.

The day's plan is uncertain. The UN aid workers led by Fred need to get their vehicles back to Kabul before the snows close the passes, but Chris is still hopeful Abdullah can secure us an interview with Ahmed Shah Massoud. Fred himself has pressing business in Mazar-i-Sharif. He decides he can afford to leave the heaviest truck, the four-tonner, for another day, with its driver, Osman. But he has to go. We say our farewells.

Then we wait.

Dr Haidar helps pass the time by describing how regime warplanes attacked the city recently. His clinic sits slightly apart from the town, across a flat open space. This, he says, is the market square. On market day, this hard, dusty plain is filled with stalls and traders of all kinds, farmers selling their produce, and artisans their crafts. Beyond the clinic, going away from town, the ground slopes away downhill. He describes how, on market day just two months ago, Communist jets surprised the town. They had been flying low, down in the valley, beyond the clinic. They then roared up, as if from nowhere, and immediately poured death into the crowded marketplace with rockets, bombs and machine guns. They flew right over his head, here in his clinic.

We must have sounded skeptical, because he immediately takes us to the children's hospital, a short drive away. Hospital is too kind a word. It's a large but damaged two-story house, maybe the size of a large suburban house in the US. Outside, the ground is just dirt, like almost everywhere in Afghanistan. The building seems dark and dingy, despite the bright day. Through a broken window I can hear children crying.

We go inside. It's dark. It smells faintly of bleach. In one room there's maybe a dozen kids, of all ages, on makeshift beds. They are not sick. They all seem to have injuries, with splints and bandages. Dr Haidar says they are still recovering from the air raid.

It seemed hard to square the injuries with an air raid two months prior. But even if some had been hurt more recently by landmines or combat, it is a heart-rending sight.

This is one of the places being helped by the aid in the UN convoy that we had ridden up in. Word had reached a UN official in Kabul that people up here needed medical supplies, or some might not make it through the winter. So supplies had been collected and men had risked their lives to bring it up. We had traveled with them, risking mines and crossfire. You hear a lot of conversation critical of aid programs and aid workers. Some of it may be justified. But when you look into the frightened eyes of small children, with scarred faces and bloody clothes, it's hard not think these aid workers are some of the finest human beings on the planet.

As final proof of the air raid, we are taken to see a section of town that had allegedly been hit by a bomb. The damage certainly looks like an upward blast from a bomb hitting the ground. A crater lies where the center of a two-story mud-brick house used to be. It looks like one of those images from the fighting in Normandy in World War II. Entire walls missing, blasted away, so you can clearly see the interior of the upstairs rooms. Houses around the blast site have been repaired, but this one remains abandoned. A sprinkling of auburn leaves lends an almost rustic charm to the site, despite the apparent violence.

The evidence of the air raid is good but not convincing enough to the point where we can report it. Most of the children's injuries seem too fresh. The damage to the house is clearly from an explosion, but we can't say for sure what caused it. All we really have is the word of known rebel sympathizers with an interest in making the regime look bad. In the days before smartphones, one wonders how many atrocities and war crimes went entirely unknown by the outside world.

That's not to say we don't empathize or worry for ourselves. I make sure to find out when the next market day is scheduled, so we can avoid it.

We still have time to kill. We stop for tea at another *chaikhana*, and are introduced to a man who seems very old—incredibly old by Afghan standards. He has a wispy white beard and white turban. A wristwatch denotes he is somebody of consequence. He's introduced to us an old warrior. I have a note of his name as Sufijan, but I don't recall any of the stories told about him. I only mention this chance encounter because at every turn in Afghanistan you meet extraordinary people.

Suddenly word comes from Dr Haidar. Abdullah is back, with good news.

ॐॐॐ ॐॐॐ ॐॐॐ

Ahmed Shah Massoud—the Lion of the Panjshir—has agreed to meet us. But he can't come to us. We must go to him.

"Where is he?" we ask.

"I can't tell you that, of course," says Dr Abdullah. "But it's not far." I've been in-country long enough to know that's often code for something else.

Chris is gung-ho. I have a million anxieties. Osman—the UN driver—is scheduled to leave tomorrow, with or without us. If he's gone, how would we get back to Kabul? Abdullah says he knows ways over the mountains without going through the Salang, assuming the snows don't close the passes, *inshallah*. He smiles broadly. Given Abdullah's story about breaking all those bones on a previous climb over the mountains, I am hardly filled with confidence.

"And what about government attack? Massoud is a priority target, surely?"

"There are no government troops where we are going," Abdullah assures us.

"Okay, but what about air attacks? Scud missiles?" A shrug and another broad grin.

"They haven't found us yet."

We still don't know where we're heading, but we are told to bring our backpacks, so possibly overnight. We grab our kit and pile into Abdullah's jeep. It's a soft top. Abdullah drives, with a guard riding shotgun (literally). Chris and I are in the back.

We head out of town, passing through a green fertile area, with rich looking orchards. Abdullah drives fast. He's always smiling and laughing.

Here and there we see groups of armed men. Abdullah waves. We are not challenged.

We pass one group of Mujahidin near a walled compound, with trees shading the road.

Suddenly, shots ring out. Deafening. Bursts from a couple of AKs.

The men had looked friendly and I assume it's just celebratory gunfire, like at the wedding. But Abdullah slams on the brakes, and backs up. He bolts out of the car, and starts yelling at the armed men.

They seem visibly shaken and cowed. I can see them now in their green jackets and flat *pakol* caps.

I start to suspect Abdullah is not just an official with the regional reconstruction council. Maybe his Mujahid days are not quite over, as he had been suggesting.

Yes, they had been fooling around, but it was undisciplined and unnecessary, Abdullah explains as we drive off. He clearly wants us to think that the rebels around here are disciplined soldiers, not wild militia.

Abdullah adds that the only Europeans those men have seen are Russians, and again we are warned that Chris and I could well be mistaken for Russian agents or advisers.

The road continues through an open plain. Dusty again. We stop outside a large compound. Looking back, it reminds me of one of those compounds anywhere in the Middle East and Central Asia— ones that Americans are only familiar with by seeing them in news footage, usually through night vision goggles. The compound is the home of a large landowner hereabouts, and Abdullah needs to pay his respects. Up to this point, I had not conceived that Afghanistan still had landowners, and in some areas, a semi-feudal society. I had somehow assumed the communist revolution had driven them all away. Maybe it had. But here at least, they're back, and clearly they are persons to be reckoned with. Abdullah is a man of consequence himself, so if he needs to pay his respects, then evidently this landowner is significant. We never learn his name.

We still don't know where we are, or where we're going. From the sun, I reckon we are going east, or southeast.

We leave the orchards and fields behind. The land is once again brown and dry. The car kicks up dust. I'm glad I have my shiny new *shemagh*, the colourful cotton neckcloth. Abdullah had shown us how to wear it in so many useful ways. Now it makes a useful face covering to keep out the dust.

The hills start rising either side of us. The plain becomes a valley. We are soon running beside a river. Its shallow gray-blue water exposes multiple sandbanks. Some of these sandbanks are substantial enough to have scrubby bushes growing on them. The brush and the

landscape are all khaki brown. In the distance, the snow-covered peaks of the Hindu Kush appear again, like old unwelcome friends.

There aren't many people or buildings. The valley seems emptier than any other landscape we have passed through, even the Salang, which for all the devastation had been full of soldiers.

Finally we learn this is the Farkhar Valley, and we are heading to Massoud's headquarters somewhere in the mountains.

I review the geography of Afghanistan in my head. I've never heard of the Farkhar valley, but if it slopes southeast to a pass over the Hindu Kush, then the other side of that should be the Panjshir Valley, which had always been Massoud's stronghold. It made sense that he had extended his control in this direction. It would also be safer from government attack as it's further away from the government's strongholds and pretty inaccessible. I put this theory to Abdullah, who congratulates me. Yes, this was the first territory that Massoud captured outside the Panjshir, he tells us. He says that happened as long ago as 1982. I have not been able to verify that.

The journey is long and the day is fast drawing on. There's no way we'll be back to Taloqan today. A worry starts to gnaw in the pit of my stomach that I will be late back to Kabul, and then late to get back to work in London. I can't afford to lose this job. My flight out of Kabul is supposed to be on Tuesday. It's going to be tight.

But there's nothing I can do. I try to relax and enjoy the ride. There is no gunfire to be heard, which is pleasant. I'd forgotten what that was like. The air is cool but the sun warms our faces.

Massoud's Chancellor of the Exchequer

Somewhere along the way, another vehicle joins us. Mujahid for sure, all AKs and RPGs. But they're driving a UN jeep. That's most irregular, and quite bad form. Use of humanitarian vehicles by a warring party can of course lead to those humanitarian agencies being targeted by the other side.

Seeing this is all quite an education for me. Add it to the knowledge that Dr Haidar of the International Red Cross/Red Crescent was such a transparent supporter of the Muj, then I was getting a much clearer picture of how insurgencies are fought.

The new arrivals greet Abdullah and his guard like brothers. Some are wearing blankets to keep off the chill. Most are wearing the flat *pakol* caps fashionable among supporters of Ahmed Shah Massoud.

One of them is introduced to us. He's young, with a young man's wispy beard. But an intelligent face. We are told he is Massoud's Chancellor of the Exchequer, or Treasury Secretary, an economics graduate from Kabul university. Except for the youthful skin on his face, he looks and acts like any other Mujahid. He must be good at what he does, as Massoud appears to run an efficient operation, where bills and wages get paid on time. Its part of his popularity.

It occurs to me now, decades later, that its quite likely that some of Massoud's revenue came from poppies. Opium production was, and is, Afghanistan's most lucrative crop. In fact, it's the biggest producer in the world. The climate is perfect, and so is the lawlessness. Yes, other plants can be grown, but the profits are incomparably greater from opium poppies. In a profile after his death, the New York Times reported that Massoud allowed poppy production to continue in the areas he controlled, at a time when the Taliban was shutting it down elsewhere in Afghanistan.[26]

Our little convoy climbs a hill, just as the sun starts to go down. The view is spectacular, with golden sunlight bouncing off the valley walls below us. We pull off to the side of the road.

"Time to pray," explains Abdullah.

The Qu'ran, the holy book of Islam, mandates prayers five times a day for those who submit to the will of God. The word "Muslim" literally means "those who submit." Islamic custom allows those on jihad, or holy struggle, an exemption from prayers and other duties of the faithful. But these Mujahidin decide to pray anyway.

They take their blankets, and make a rough row, near the cliff, looking down over the valley toward the setting sun in the west. Toward Mecca. The sun's orange glow lights up the scene and the faces of the faithful. As one, they brush their faces, kneel and bow their foreheads to the ground, their lips reciting a prayer.

As you know, dear reader, I was a man of faith myself at this time: a committed Episcopalian. So to witness such an act of faith in wartime left a powerful impression on me. It was this faith that had sustained the rebellion against the godless Communists, despite years of unconstrained violence and brutal oppression. Simple men, yearning to be free—willing to fight and die for their faith, their land, their families, their way of life. These had been our allies. While we in the West had enjoyed our comforts, these men had been risking their all to bring down our common enemy. I was not here in Afghanistan to fight, of course. But I had been a soldier once, whose only real

---

[26]"Rebel Chief Who Fought the Taliban is Buried," by Barry Bearak, New York Times, September 17th 2001. [nytimes.com/2001/09/17/world/rebel-chief-who-fought-the-taliban-is-buried.html]

purpose had been to defend against a potential invasion by the same Red Army that had devastated this land.

My mind also wandered back to other Westerners who had made common cause with Muslim warriors over the centuries, and I began to have a sense of how those bonds developed. They must have gazed on similar scenes countless times.

While they pray, I use the time and the fading light to read a chapter of my little Gideon Bible, to bear witness to my faith. Abdullah sees and nods.

❦❧ ❦❧ ❦❧

The sun goes down fast. Pretty soon it is dark. Isn't this a dangerous time to be out? Abdullah reassures us this road is quite safe, as it is so strictly under the control of Massoud's people. The guards at the checkpoints are therefore not so jumpy. I think he throws in a dig against the government forces, suggesting Massoud's troops are better disciplined.

The drive has taken hours. But finally we arrive. It's now pitch black. And freezing cold. We learn we are at rebel training base in the foothills on the north side of the Hindu Kush. We can't make out much in the darkness. A blackout helps prevent government planes finding it, but it also means we're mostly blundering about in the dark. It feels like all the buildings are made of stone.[27]

We're shown to a barrack block carved into the mountain. Chris and I are the only occupants. I can't recall with any certainty, but I want to say we had beds, rather than just sleeping on the floor. Metal framed beds. I can't be sure.

The barrack block is largely under the mountain, so that means we are protected from air raids, should they come. However, Abdullah warns us that we must be alert to the danger of earthquakes, which are common in these parts. In which case, get out fast. If we weren't so exhausted from travel, that warning could well have kept us awake.

---

[27]This is the exact same base where Ahmed Shah Massoud was assassinated by al-Qaeda on 9 September 2001, just two days before the al-Qaeda attack on the US. He was blown up by terrorists posing as journalists.

Maybe we'll see Massoud tomorrow, *inshallah*. He's not here at the moment. Maybe we'll go to him.

Being good travelers, Chris and I both have flashlights, so we can organize our kit in the dark.

I don't recall what if anything we ate, but wherever we went in Afghanistan, our hosts were kind and shared whatever they had. So I'm guessing we were given food.

Then we crash, keeping half an ear out for air raids and earthquakes.

8◆3   8◆3   8◆3

It's still dark when Abdullah appears.

"It's time," he says unhelpfully. "Grab your tape recorder. Come with me."

Chris and I look at each other. "Massoud is here?"

We go out into the night. We're too excited to care about the bitter cold.

Abdullah leads us across the compound toward another darkened building. The interior is deceptively bright after the dark outside. Blackout curtains prevent the light seeping out to be seen by enemy bombers.

The building is otherwise surprisingly cozy and homelike. The walls are neatly painted. There's a couch and a pair of armchairs. A nice coffee table. Even the curtains are patterned, like something you'd find in a 1970s department store.

We wait for a while and have tea. Abdullah explains Massoud has never given an interview to any journalists coming from Kabul. Our presence is remarkable because we have successfully made that journey, the first since the Soviet invasion in 1979. This is a huge scoop for Chris and the BBC.

Dawn breaks, and the chintzy blackout curtains are opened.

In walks the great man.

Ahmed Shah Massoud ranks as one of the great generals of the twentieth century, if one defines great generalship as being able to understand the great currents of history and technology, and to make

the best of limited resources to impose your will on the enemy. Massoud had mobilized, trained and equipped an army of peasant farmers, shepherds and displaced intellectuals, and prepared them to confront and withstand the might of the Red Army. He had used the rugged terrain for full tactical and strategic advantage. He knew how to keep the population behind his cause. He knew his enemy's weaknesses and fully exploited them, in particular their doctrinal rigidity. He knew how to use the media to gain international attention and support.

Massoud had also—up to that point—conducted himself with honour. He was respected by both sides in a war more commonly led by cutthroats.

So yes, in my mind, it was a privilege for me to meet someone who had made history, and was still making history.

Physically, he was impressive, too. His most distinctive feature was a big aquiline nose. His black beard was combed into a point as well, like a mirror of the nose. He wore his Tajik flat cap, the *pakol*, at an impossibly jaunty angle. I learn later this is allegedly to cover the damage to his right ear, injured long ago. His shoulders were exaggeratedly broad from the traditional Tajik brown robe he was wearing, made of fine heavy wool. He was only 38, but his face was old and care-worn.

Chris and I are introduced and we shake hands with the Lion of the Panjshir. He looks me squarely in the eye when Abdullah says I've come from London. Looking back, I wonder if he thought I was representing something other than the BBC. Maybe Her Majesty's Government? Speaking through Abdullah, he asks where I went to university. Cambridge, I say. Cambridge, of course, is famous for its spies.

His sharp brown eyes speak of a formidable intelligence, and strength. Through much of the interview, he avoids eye contact. His gaze is downward, or off into space.

Massoud sits at one end of the couch. Chris is motioned to sit at the other end but he wants to be closer to Massoud for the recording, so he plops himself on the coffee table. Abdullah sits at the other end of the couch to act as interpreter. Massoud understands a little English but not nearly enough to give an interview. He does better in French, apparently.

Chris asks him all the usual questions one would expect. How's the war going? What are your goals, given the stalemate? What are your forces trying to do in this place or that place? What negotiations are taking place? Which political factions are you finding it difficult to cooperate with? That sort of thing.

I don't realize this is actually a historic moment. The United Nations had been pushing a peace deal hard. All the parties had responded except for perhaps the most critical player, Massoud. His response to the UN's diplomatic feelers had been to say, if you want to know where I stand, come and talk to me. It was a power play, but one in keeping with Afghan culture, of showing respect for power. If you want an audience with the area strongman, you come to him. Then you wait, maybe he'll see you, maybe he won't. Anyway, there was no way anyone senior enough in the UN could get to Taloqan. It was too dangerous. But perhaps if you drop heavy hints to a couple of BBC journalists, maybe that would do the trick? With their global audience, maybe these BBC guys would be sufficiently powerful enough for Massoud to share his take on the peace process?

It works. Chris gets the answers the UN is seeking. A conditional acceptance of the peace process.

It's all very good. Topical. Newsworthy. Looking back, I wish I could have asked a big picture question about how he saw his place in history or something of that nature. What kind of Afghanistan do you dream of? What are your own ambitions?

In the moment, of course, when it comes to my turn to ask a question, I can only think of one thing.

"If and when the Mujahidin come to power, will you respect the Durand Line?" I ask.

Abdullah translates and the Lion of the Panjshir lifts up his head, looks at Abdullah, slightly startled, and then brings those piercing eyes directly into my soul, searching for my true meaning. Am I really just a curious journalist, or am I a representative of the West, come to see if we can count on him not to destabilize the Indian subcontinent?

The Durand Line, you see, is the border between Pakistan and Afghanistan. As its name implies, it is an arbitrary line that was drawn through the mountains by a British civil servant called Mortimer Durand during a visit to Kabul in 1893.

The Durand Line literally divides the homeland of Pashto-speaking people in two. Families, clans and princedoms are divided by this artificial imaginary international frontier. Many Pashtuns refuse to recognize it to this day. In the 1970s, President Muhammad Daoud Khan denounced it. Anxiety over Afghan claims to the northwest part of Pakistan helps fuel that nation's efforts to keep Afghanistan weak and divided.

If the Muj came to power in Kabul, a new battle-hardened regime could turn its eyes, and guns, towards the Durand Line. So it seems like a good, big-picture question to me. And I'm pretty sure Ahmed Shah Massoud left the interview thinking I was indeed a spook. After all, why would the BBC send two journalists?

Massoud did not equivocate, as I recall. Of course he respects the international boundary. He may have added a rider about keeping an eye on Pakistani conduct, but I don't recall exactly. I was slightly surprised, as I know the Durand Line was a passionate issue among Pashtuns. Massoud was a Tajik, so he needed to work hard to win support from Pashtuns, the biggest single ethnic group in Afghanistan. If he spoke too much in favour of it, then he risked alienating them. But he was a much better strategist than I, so I'm sure he'd thought it through.

ᔕ◈ᔐ   ᔕ◈ᔐ   ᔕ◈ᔐ

After the interview, we can finally look around the compound, and discreetly snap a few photos. The first thing I notice is that there are only a handful of people here. If this is a training camp, then this must be the off-season. Security is loose. We can wander around at our pleasure, with occasional glances from scattered sentries. The sentries all seem to be wearing similar light green combat jackets, and the flat, round *pakol* hats. The ubiquitous AK is slung over their shoulders. I notice they're not openly

carrying extra magazines, and there are no heavy weapons in sight, so they must feel very secure in this location.

Two ancient round towers, made of stone, guard the entrance to the camp. They are about two stories high, well made and maintained. Small loopholes ring them at musket height. So at least part of this compound is old: militarily, these defensive towers became obsolete centuries ago. A black flag hangs limp from a pole atop one of the towers. Straight stone walls stretch from each tower to the sides of the valley. They are not very tall or thick. More like boundary walls. Probably good for keeping stray animals at bay, but they wouldn't do much to stop a tank. However, they have been maintained: I can see they have been recently topped off or repaired with cement.

Most of the rest of the compound comprises much more modern buildings. Some with traditional flat roofs. Some with western style roofs. All in dull khaki.

Looking north—down the valley up which we had driven the night before—the dirt road is flanked by New-England-style stone walls. The road zig-zags down the valley, following the contours carved by the river. The hills and mountains are bare as usual, but in the flat narrow plain, there are fields and bushes, all brown. And more grey stone walls.

Looking south—up the valley—the Hindu Kush should have loomed before us. But the peaks are obscured by clouds and a big foothill a couple of miles away. Hiking over that one would be a challenge, let alone the high passes beyond, above 12,000 feet. And that is what we might face, if we can't get motorized transport back to Kabul.

The author at Massoud's camp, 11 Nov 1991.

It has been a tremendous rush, coming to a secret rebel base in the mountains and meeting such a historic personage as Ahmed Shah Massoud, but there's a good chance we have lost our ride home as a result. A UN truck had been left for us in Taloqan for 24 hours, but that time is now up, and we are still a long way from there. Without it, there is no safe option to get back through the frontlines to government-held territory by road. If the truck is gone, we would be facing the alternative suggested by Abdullah, of hiking over the Hindu Kush.

I reckon I could cope with a multi-day hike, but I would infinitely prefer going back to Kabul by road, back through the Salang. I had done plenty of "tabbing" in the army; what the US military calls ruck-marching. In fact, I had competed for, and won a place on the

Regimental team sent to participate in the Nijmegen Vierdaagse—a 100 mile march in the Netherlands—in 1983. But that was eight years ago.

I am fit and could probably manage hiking through the Hindu Kush, but the prospect is daunting, especially with the winter coming on. Did I have enough warm clothing? Probably not. I wish I had proper boots not just my brogues. Plus there is the risk of landmines, air attack, ambush, robbery. The usual.

A more likely scenario, if we fail to hitch a ride back to Kabul, is that we'll be stuck here in northern Afghanistan for the winter, as the snows will soon close the passes to foot traffic. That prospect is dreadful. Not only is this a dangerous place, I would almost certainly lose my job in London or be placed on unpaid leave. That would be such a hardship for my wife, trying to make our new mortgage payments on just her income.

There's no point dwelling on it. I just have to pray that the UN truck is still there in Taloqan.

As we explore the base, suddenly there's a hustle and bustle. Massoud is there, walking through the compound with a walkie-talkie. Out come a couple of lads with giant radios on their backs, like I used to carry in the army. They scurry back and forth trying to keep up with Massoud as he paces back and forth. He towers over them. He has changed out of his big cloth robe into a green combat jacket like his sentries. We're ordered to put our cameras away.

We hear there's a battle taking place, near Golbahar or Jabal-os-Saraj, at the entrance to the Panjshir Valley. We had heard that there was fighting there last week. We had passed through the defensive line at Jabal on our journey up to the Salang. We watch the great man barking orders in rapid succession. His face scrunching as he gets reports. At one point he consults a map.

As a military history nerd, it's just astounding to me to watch history being made. Here is one of the greatest military commanders of the twentieth century, directing a battle right before my eyes. Probably only a minor skirmish, or some minor manouvers. But I am seeing it happen in real time. Sadly, I never find out what the outcome of the day's action might have been.

Then we're told it's time to go. Later it would occur to me that Massoud's enemies could have been trying to triangulate his position.

Triangulation is a technique used by the military to locate enemy command posts. A listening post can tell which direction a signal is coming from. If a second listening post identifies the same signal, then you can draw those two lines on a map, and the point where they intersect is where the enemy radio is located. In the army, we were told that the Soviets were pretty good at triangulation, and under optimal conditions, could bring heavy artillery down on your position in three minutes. These things stick with you when you yourself are the radio operator, as I was for part of my military service.

Of course, we are not in artillery range of any known government forces, but there is always the danger of air or missile strikes.

None of this occurs to me in the moment. Thankfully. But we understand the urgency in our hosts. We grab our packs and are hustled back into Abdullah's jeep to head back to Taloqan.

Compared to elsewhere, that Muj compound up the Farkhar valley has been a place of relative peace and quiet on our bumbling journey. There had only been the anxiety about possible air strikes or missile attacks, or earthquakes. We faced much more danger elsewhere. But for some reason this camp would haunt me for years to come. The dream of getting stuck there or somewhere like it, or of struggling to get to safety from there, would become a recurring nightmare.

੩◉੩ ੩◉੩ ੩◉੩

The drive down the Farkhar valley, back to Taloqan, seems much faster than the drive up. There is no shooting this time, and no stops to pay respects to local "big men."

As we move down the valley the clouds lift and the sun returns.

Finally, we're back in town. The traffic cop is standing on the island again at the intersection, with his whistle and his immaculate white gloves and cap. We cross the empty market square and arrive back at Dr Haidar's Red Cross clinic.

Bad news. The UN truck has gone.

For the moment, we are lost for ideas about how to get home. I shudder at the thought of getting stuck here for the winter. Besides the danger, there is a good chance I would lose my job at Bush House —the job I had struggled so hard to obtain.

More immediately, I am now definitely going to miss my flight out of Kabul tomorrow.

Chris is just as keen to get back to Kabul, to break the story of his interview with Ahmed Shah Massoud and his response to the UN peace initiative. That kind of scoop can make the career of a young reporter.

The prospect of hiking over the Hindu Kush starts to seem more attractive. We'd have to figure out a route. Abdullah suggests going back up the Farkhar Valley and crossing over the mountains near a place called Anjoman. He promises a guide and an escort. But there's no safe way to get from rebel-held Anjoman, high in the Panjshir Valley, back to government-held Kabul. Anyone coming from there would have no legitimate business, as far as the Afghan government is concerned. But we have to go soon, before winter closes the pass. We only have a few minutes to think about it, because Abdullah can't stay.

We decide to roll the dice and stay in Taloqan and try to scrounge up a ride from here. It's a gamble, but it must be safer than trying to cross the lines from the Panjshir. We are the first journalists to have crossed the lines safely into rebel territory since the war began, but that was thanks to being able to piggy back on the UN convoy. There would be no such escort on the other side if we followed Abdullah's trail to the Panjshir.

We say a fond farewell to Dr Abdullah. He has been kind, funny, informative, and extremely helpful in keeping us safe and, of course, in making the connection with Ahmed Shah Massoud and intro-ducing us to the Russian POWs. We couldn't know at the time, but Abdullah has a long career ahead of him as a leading figure in Afghanistan, culminating in becoming its chief executive in 2014 and leader of the peace talks with the Taliban in 2020.

As he drives away, he takes with him our immediate opportunity for attempting to cross the high country. We face the real prospect of being stuck here for the winter.

Chapter 14

The Shepherd Boy

Our prospects for getting out of Dodge City may be grim, but I have a more immediate concern. I need to get word of our dilemma back to my office in London, so I don't get in trouble when I don't show up for work. I'm scheduled to be in the office on Thursday. Today is Monday.

I can still remember the shift I was scheduled for: the "HUBs cross-shift." That was the desk in the Bush House news room that wrote and prepared the news for the Hindi, Urdu and Bengali sections. It seemed such a silly job when faced with the realities of war and peace, and life and death. All those artificial constructs of jobs and mortgages and rules seem so petty and irrelevant when you're in a combat zone.

And my poor wife! She needs to know that I am okay, at least for now, and that I am trying my best to figure out how to get home.

This is 1991, remember. There are no cell phones. It's Afghanistan, in war time, and so there are no telephone landlines between here and Kabul.

What if I never make it home? How would she ever know? Your mind can wander in these situations, when you have time, as I now do. And you start to contemplate small matters like whether she can claim my life insurance if there's no proof of death. How would Mum take it?

The worst thing about these situations in which I keep finding myself in Afghanistan is this feeling of helplessness. Powerful things are happening around me, and *to* me, and there's nothing much I can do to influence the outcome. I don't speak the language; I don't have an interpreter; I can't negotiate for a car or anything; I don't even have any money. I can't call for help; I don't have a radio or even a phone; I don't know anyone to call, even if I did have the means.

Dr Haidar hears Chris and me talking about my communications dilemma and offers to help. He has a radio in his van. He'll try to get a message to his bosses at the Red Cross in Kabul. Maybe they can get a message through to my bosses at Bush House.

The radio crackles into life. Dr Haidar shouts out his Red Cross call-sign. There's no answer. He climbs onto the roof of the van and stands up, in the hope of getting more of a signal. "It usually helps," he says.

I can see him now in my mind's eye, standing on the van, clutching the radio's handset. The blue sky behind him. His tinted glasses. His short black beard. Headphones over his *pakol* cap. The worry lines in his face.

Finally a response. He's reached someone who knows us. I'm not sure if it is the Red Cross or the UN or someone else. But someone we'd met during my brief stay in Kabul.

It's an open line, so he chooses his words carefully.

"Please be informed that Charlie," he starts, looking at Chris. Charlie is the phonetic alphabet code word for the letter C. In radio usage, when you want to be discreet you might identify someone or something by their first initial. "Please be informed that Charlie—and the other Charlie"—he looked at me, "are stuck here for now while looking for transport back to Kabul."

I look at Chris and say, "We're a right pair of Charlies, all right!" And we both start cracking up. In British-English someone who is a "right Charlie" is a bit of wally, a doofus, a plonka, a chump. In other words, a little bit foolish. Here we are, stuck behind rebel lines, on the wrong side of the mountains, without any idea how we are going to get home. Oh, I felt foolish all right. The words and the moment seemed perfect. We laugh our faces off.

Dr Haidar looks on bewildered. He is oblivious to the joke.

"The other Charlie will not make his connection. Please to notify Bravo Bravo Charlie and ask them to notify next-of-kin . . . Roger. Out."

After the call, we try to explain the joke to Dr Haidar between our fits of laughter. But it's useless.

Our situation is hopeless. All we can do is laugh.

Dr Haidar says his contact in Kabul will try to get word to London. Hopefully my bosses will pass the word on to my wife. *Inshallah!* I assume the chances of word actually getting through are pretty slim. All I can do is hope that we can get going as soon as possible. We drop our packs in our old room at the clinic. We take a quick nap on those big red floor cushions, and eat another meal courtesy of our host.

I can't say enough about how generous the Afghan people are whenever they have guests. They will share whatever they have, and go without if necessary. I am grateful and awed.

After lunch, Chris does some more reporting around town. I tag along as usual, trying to keep busy. I don't remember much except for seeing some remarkable ancient irrigation systems. Water is a precious commodity in much of Afghanistan. Rain is often in short supply, so water is used carefully, especially by farmers. Just outside Taloqan I see, for the first time, an "Archimedes screw" in operation. This is a water screw or screw pump that's used for moving water uphill and particularly into irrigation ditches. The water is scooped up and rotated around a clever system of spirals till it gets to where it needs to be. It was allegedly invented by the ancient Greek scientist and mathematician, Archimedes, hero of the siege of Syracuse in 213 BCE. But archeologists have plenty of evidence that they had been used by the ancient Egyptians for centuries before that. I thought it was absolute genius.

It's also a nice distraction. But I think it will get old pretty quickly if this is all we can do through the winter.

⌘⌘⌘   ⌘⌘⌘   ⌘⌘⌘

When we get back to the clinic, late in the afternoon, out of the blue we suddenly hear that a vehicle will be coming to town. Tomorrow. We're not sure how it happened. We assume that the folks that Dr Haidar had reached in Kabul on the radio had in turn mentioned something to the UN, and that Chris' friends there had called around to see if they could find a vehicle for us.

We get an early night. There are explosions in the distance again, to lull us to sleep.

Early to bed, early to rise. In the old English saying that's supposed to make you healthy, wealthy and wise. But here in Taloqan it made for a long, tedious and frustrating morning as we waited for our ride. Hurry up and wait, as we used to say in the army.

It's after lunch by the time the white four-ton truck of the United Nations rolls into town. The letters "UN" are painted loudly in blue on the side and front. It's a comforting sight. Maybe we will be able to get back to Kabul before the snows close the mountain passes.

The driver pulls up to us. The dust settles. It's Osman. And he's clearly unhappy. I'm not sure if he's been on private business or what, but I get the impression he has been tasked with coming back to Taloqan to pick us up against his will. We're unable to communicate. He speaks no English, and we don't speak enough Dari. There's no interpreter to help us clear the air.

I can feel the tension, but I'm not sure of its source. I know it will make for an uncomfortable ride. Two days or more. I could be wrong, but it feels like the trust between us is breaking down.

There's no time to worry about it. It's already late and we're a long way from our destination. We can't be on the road at night. Far too dangerous.

But first of course we must wait some more. Osman couldn't come this way empty-handed, so we must wait for his cargo to be unloaded across town at the granary, and then wait a little longer for him to scrounge up some fuel. He works quickly and efficiently. He's as keen as we are to be on his way, it seems.

Finally it's time to go. We say our farewells to Dr Haidar, and thank him for his incredible help and hospitality. Then we grab our packs and climb into the cab of the truck, next to Osman. Chris gets in first and sits in the middle. I follow and take my place by the door.

It's already late so we probably won't make it to Kabul today, but we hope we can at least make it to Pul-i-Khumri before it gets dark. I definitely won't be making my scheduled flight tomorrow, but at least we won't be stuck north of the Hindu Kush for the winter.

Once again, I don't know exactly where we are, or the route we'll be taking. We have no paper maps and of course Google maps are a thing of the future. We just have to trust Osman.

Looking at a map today, it seems obvious. We traveled west out of Taloqan on the main road toward the city of Kunduz. I don't recall passing through that city on the way back, so it's fair to assume we turned off at a place called Khanabad, taking the shortcut across country toward a place called Aliabad, where we rejoined the main road south to Baghlan and Pul-i-Khumri.

This matters to me now as I try to identify the locations of the most terrifying moments of our trip.

As we drive out of town, I can't help thinking how different I feel now, compared to the beginning of our road trip just a week ago. I have lost my innocence and sense of wonder. I've seen so much blood, and felt a degree of fear and helplessness that I have never felt before.

I am anxious to get back. At the back of my mind, I am a little concerned for my safety, thinking how Mum would take any bad news. Or whether anyone would ever even know if something happened to us out here, in the violent heart of central Asia. At the front of my mind, I'm feeling more pressure to get back to work in

London on time, and to simply reassure my wife and family that I'm still alive. Add to all that this new unexplained tension with Osman.

Despite all these unspoken anxieties, there is a tremendous sense of relief that we've finally begun the journey home. I push the dark thoughts away, and concentrate on the scenery.

The snow-capped mountains of the Hindu Kush lie on the horizon. In front of us, and all around us is a giant dusty plain.

This part of Afghanistan looks like the Star Wars desert planet, Tatooine—at least at this season of the year. I have traveled a fair deal in Europe, Africa and India, but this looks and feels thoroughly alien to everything I have ever experienced. You can see fields and meadows that might bloom green after the spring floods. But now, on the eve of winter, green is just a memory. Everything is dusty, dry, brown or khaki. The homes, made from adobe, are the same. Their flat roofs and small windows evoke images from childhood Bible stories, or of Tusken raiders. There are few people to be seen. Not much life at all, besides the occasional herd of goats. The only signs of modernity are long, flat concrete bridges over empty river beds. It's other-worldly. It's captivating.

The rebel checkpoints come and go. If the armed men wave us down, we slow to a crawl, and lean out of the window, shouting *"Moolee-mata-heed! Moolee-mata-heed!"*—"United Nations! United Nations!" in Dari. Usually it works, but sometimes we have to show our papers. We are traveling alone, not in a convoy, so we seem to be getting flagged down more often than not. I'm grateful that we're in a UN truck, with *bona fide* papers. I can't imagine how we'd get through without them.

For our driver, Osman, the checkpoints are clearly getting tiresome. He starts to tsk and mutter and curse at the delays.

Up ahead we see a kid.

A goat herder.

My guess is he's 13 or 14. His clothes are a little ragged. His sandaled feet are caked white with dust. His unkempt mop of black hair is also speckled with dust. He has life and death in his hands, in the form of an ancient looking AK-47.

He is flagging us down, but he seems to be alone. There is no roadblock; his goats are off to the side of the road. Osman tsks. My buddy Chris urges him to slow down. But Osman has had enough of delays. I get the sense he thinks this is one "checkpoint" we can afford to ignore. He curses and pushes down on the accelerator. I gasp.

As we fly by, I can see the kid pulling the weapon up to his shoulder.

He opens fire.

ε◇϶ ε◇϶ ε◇϶

Getting shot at is an awful feeling, especially at close range. The sound rips open your stomach with an intensity you cannot imagine. It's worse than being on one of those terrifying old wooden rollercoasters which feels like it's about to come off the rails and hurl you to your death. I can feel it again now as I write; my gut is clenched. My head feels giddy, almost intoxicated. Time slows down to the point where life feels like it's in slow motion.

Chris and I have seen death on our trip. We have heard gunfire and heavy weapons every day for a week. We've been among landmines. Heard artillery exploding. Seen the aftermath of air strikes. But as journalists, among aid workers, we have felt a degree of immunity. Nobody actually wants to kill us, right? There is always the chance of accidents, of simply being in the wrong place at the wrong time. But we don't think anybody wants us dead.

That small corner of our minds, where we had preserved a sense of safety, suddenly vanishes. At the hands of scrawny, dirty little shepherd boy.

It is only a single shot. Rounds are probably expensive to him. But we cannot afford to risk another. None of us are hit, but it will only take our assailant a moment longer to fire a burst. Osman slams on the brakes, shaking up a huge cloud of dust as we stop and wait to hear the judgement of the shepherd boy.

Again, I have no control over that decision. My instinct is to keep going, knowing how inaccurate these homemade ancient AKs are, thinking that we could outrun him. I later learn that's the worst thing you can do if you come under fire in a vehicle. Combat psychologists will tell you that a shooter will keep firing at a vehicle until it stops moving. Something compels them.-

The kid of course decides to approach our vehicle on my side. He emerges from the dust cloud. I open the window and shout the obligatory *"Moolee-mata-heed! Moolee-mata-heed!"* but I doubt the kid has ever heard of the United Nations. There isn't even any guarantee that he understands Dari. He is definitely not impressed.

The kid is yelling and waving his gun around. Osman leans over us and speaks with him briefly through the window. Then he looks at us and says *"baksheesh"* quietly and tips his head toward the kid.

"What's that?" I whisper.

"The kid wants a bribe to let us pass," says Chris.

I do a double-take. "What?" I whisper again. In a sense, the goat herder has become his own tollbooth. I have no money so I'm at a loss what to do or say.

"No fucking way," mutters Chris while smiling at the boy. He leans over toward our would-be robber and repeats the words *"Moolee-mata-heed! Moolee-mata-heed!"* and gestures as if pulling at empty pockets.

I join in the chorus, and add in my best BBC English that I'm awfully sorry but we have no money to give you, hoping quiet charm and confidence will do the trick. My mind flashes to the image of the British paratrooper, Major Carlyle, in the movie *A Bridge Too Far*, carrying his umbrella into combat. Hopelessly genteel.

I look around at the bleak, drought-ridden, hardscrabble landscape. What a miserable place to die.

Pleading poverty seems like a desperate strategy. How could we ever be so poor as not to spare something for a penniless goat herder? But somehow it works. The kid lowers his gun and allows us to leave, without paying him anything. He waves us on dismissively, yelling what I suspect is a rich vein of curses. It cost him a bullet to get our attention, for no gain. We waste no time, and speed off before he can change his mind, our hearts still pounding.

I have to give credit to Chris and Osman. Osman may have caused the trouble but he helped get us out of it, too.

I came away learning the lesson that no hazard is too small to be overlooked in a combat zone. Normal rules are little help. Guns are power. They make the rules. On the other hand, bluster can help, too. Sometimes.

Of course, we do not stop to see if there is any damage to the truck. We double check to make sure none of us are hit—I know how shock can sometimes mask the pain of wounds. We're all okay

After coming under fire for the first time, while working as a reporter in Cuba in 1895, Winston Churchill observed: "There is nothing more exhilarating than to be shot at with no result." I have felt that exhilaration grip my stomach, that surge of adrenaline that brings the giddiness. The high. Some people find it addictive. But not me. I do like having a story, and being able to say that I've been shot at— and that they missed. But it's not something I would ever want to feel again. To be honest, I feel pretty foolish. I did not need to be in this situation, and now I just want it to be over.

Unfortunately, our troubles are just beginning.

$$\text{🙰} \quad \text{🙰} \quad \text{🙰}$$

The truck is quiet. The mood is still pretty sour. Osman may have been angry about having to come get us, but now I'm a little angry that he just put us in danger unnecessarily. The trust between us is now definitely even thinner than when we started. Chris seems unflappable as usual. It's impossible to tell how anxious he might be. I never want to play poker against him.

We all now keep a much more careful eye out for roadblocks, check-points and innocent-looking shepherd boys. We start hearing occasional explosions in the distance.

At one checkpoint, we see more men than usual. The mood is tense. Osman is talking with them a long time. He and they seem to be gesturing up the road a lot.

Osman sinks back in his seat with a sigh. Through sign language and insistent talking, Osman manages to convey to us that there is heavy fighting ahead and the road is closed.

Chris and I are skeptical. We have been hearing artillery period-ically for a while now, but it does not seem to be any heavier at the moment. Chris tries to tell Osman we have to keep going, waving his arm down the road, saying "Pully! Pully!" and pointing at his watch. But Osman will not budge.

Last week, I had seen Fred—the Kiwi with the United Nations— stop a battle with pure *chutzpah* and a radio. Now, though, there is no Fred and no radio.

I do not understand the geography perfectly, but we are now back in an openly contested zone. Baghlan is Muj-controlled. Kunduz to the north and Pul-i-Khumri to the south still belong to the government. Everything in between is contested.

I still to this day have no idea exactly where we were, or where we went next.

Osman fires up the engine, and simply turns off the highway onto a dirt road. Where the hell are we going?

I have no idea if we can fully trust Osman. He is angry. We've just had the fright of our lives. What is he up to?

The normally irrepressible Chris finally looks concerned. There's the smallest of furrows in his brow. With his handful of Dari phrases, he tries to find out what's going on.

I just have a sinking feeling. Of peril. Of isolation. Of anxiety about ever getting back to Kabul, let alone home to London. Of helplessness. I wonder if maybe I'm starting to get paranoid.

"I think he's saying he knows people up this way," explains Chris. "I think he wants us to stay with them until the road is clear."

"Do you trust him?" I ask quietly.

"We don't have a choice," replies Chris.

Osman may not have known it, but we are heading straight into no man's land—the killing zone between rival armies.

$$\text{8◊3} \quad \text{8◊3} \quad \text{8◊3}$$

We seem to be driving forever on this dirt road. My mind is full of concern. When will we ever get back to Kabul, if we make it out at all? We can hear shelling. How close is the fighting? What is Osman up to? Can we trust him? As Chris says, we don't have much choice.

Eventually we pull up to a respectable looking farmhouse. Respectable meaning it has a walled compound and multiple buildings, part stone and part adobe. We pull up to a pair of wide, heavy-looking gates. There's a man outside. He's armed, as we've come to expect for this part of the world: an AK slung on his back.

Osman gets out to speak with the guard. He doesn't seem to recognize Osman, but he shouts and the gates open. Osman climbs back into the cab and we drive forward into a central dirt courtyard. We are immediately greeted by curious children who run up to see us, as we get out of the truck. In the shadows, we see women scurrying away into the buildings.

Several men appear. They are unarmed, thankfully. The kids are sternly shooed away. A short, slender man in the center greets Osman cordially but without warmth. They talk. Osman waves his arm at us. We smile at our host but only receive a brusque nod in exchange. The conversation seems heated, but it's hard to tell.

We are clueless and helpless. None of the Afghans can speak any English or French, and Chris and I have almost no Dari. All we can do is smile and try to look harmless.

I have no idea if we are welcome or not. I have no idea what their real relationship is with Osman. We are totally at their mercy. They could do anything to us. No one would ever know.

An explosion in the distance seems to seal whatever deal is being discussed. Osman gestures for us to get our kit and we are ushered into one of the buildings. But then Osman disappears.

The room looks a lot like our living and sleeping quarters at Dr Haidar's clinic in Taloqan. The walls are plastered, painted and clean, but otherwise undecorated, except for maybe a rug on the wall. Rugs also cover much of the floor. Just as in Taloqan, there is no furniture, only the familiar long cushions lining the edge of the room, doubling as seating during the day and beds at night.

We are asked to sit down. We can hear gunfire in the distance. Heavy machine guns now, as well as artillery.

Chris and I attempt to ask how long we will be staying, but it's impossible to get an answer. There's still time to get to Pul-i-Khumri before dark, if we can leave soon. Hope gives you delusions. We can only sit and twiddle our thumbs, waiting for clues as to whether our hosts are hostile or not.

After what seems like an eternity, our host and a couple of other men enter the room and stand over us. Behind them, more men follow. Scruffy looking men. In the dim light I think they are carrying weapons.

My heart stops.

I couldn't be more wrong. It's a tea service. Our hosts take a seat on the cushions across from us. The scruffy fellows appear to be servants and older boys, who serve us our tea.

It's a relief. But the tea break is not very relaxing. Our hosts remain stiff and serious. For example, I don't recall being introduced formally, as I thought was customary. To this day I have no knowledge of any of their names. Chris and I are still anxious to get going. Clearly that will have to wait till after tea. There's still no sign of Osman.

At least we now get a chance to examine our host in detail.

He is a short, serious but gentle-looking man, probably in his mid-30s. He is slender. His face is shaved, except for a well-trimmed moustache, indicating he has more business with the government than the rebels. His skin is not weatherbeaten like so many Afghans, so he must be a man of some substance. He has a colourful skull cap, worn at a jaunty angle on the back of his head, a traditional long Tajik off-white shirt, untucked, over baggy off-white pants, and a colourful waistcoat, which he wears open. But the most striking thing about his appearance is his face. He has short fair hair, blue eyes and what, to me, looks like a very English face. I remember thinking he would not look at all out of place if you picked him up and plopped him in one of England's home counties like Surrey or Bucks. But he is, of course, very much an Afghan.

I was genuinely surprised by just how "European" many Afghans look, especially in the north. On this night, I wonder how they could have "ended up here," recalling the attempt at colonization by Alexander the Great. Of course, that was an absurd Euro-centric way of thinking. Modern scholarship and DNA evidence has shown that what we now think of as white Europeans originated here on the steppes of central Asia, before migrating west about 5,000 years ago.

Our host seems polite. But he remains dour and serious, as do his companions. I don't think I once saw him smile.

After Chris and I have exchanged all the platitudes we can in Dari, there is no more conversation, except for attempts to communicate in sign language. We can convey where we've come from and where we are trying to go. But we can't convey who we are or what we do. He doesn't recognize the BBC brand, so it's likely he is not a listener to the BBC's Dari and Pashto news broadcasts. We have no idea what Osman has told them.

After tea, we are left to our own devices again. There's nothing to do except listen to the fighting in the distance. The sounds of battle now appear to be coming from all directions.

As the afternoon fades, it becomes apparent we are going to be stuck here for the night. No one would drive in darkness, especially with combat taking place so close by.

After a couple of hours of darkness, our host and his companions re-enter the room and spread out on the cushions. An oil lamp is lit. Heavy curtains black out the windows. The boys bring in dinner. Plates of rice, bread, vegetables, and lamb are placed on the floor and we eat with our hands. After a week of dining like this, it's a comfortable and familiar routine.

The conversation is again muted, and heads are always turning to listen to the increasing volume of the battle outside. It dawns on me that several families live here in this compound and yet we haven't met a single woman, only young girls. So the residents are traditional in that respect.

After supper the din of battle becomes a roar. Small arms now, as well as heavy machine guns, artillery and rockets. Some of it quite close. What if the compound is targeted? What if hostile forces come in? We'd seen earlier that day what one shepherd boy could do; what about undisciplined, battle-hardened angry militants? It doesn't matter which side. We'd been told how the government folks assumed we were American spies, while the Muj thought we were Russian agents and advisers. Our attempts to find out if there are any bomb shelters are futile.

I go outside to use the bathroom and pause in the courtyard to listen. I can hear shells and gunfire, some of it whizzing overhead. I duck involuntarily, and scurry off to go do my business in the outhouse. I pause on the way back, astonished, trying to make sure I'm hearing it right. Yes, some of that fire is passing directly overhead.

I never thought I'd one day find myself stuck in no man's land.

There's a vibrato quality to the rapid cracking of rounds overhead, followed by what sounds like an echo immediately afterwards. Of course, it's not an echo but the thumping sound of the weapon being fired. CRACK-CRACK-CRACK-THUMP-THUMP-THUMP. The rounds travel faster than the speed of sound, so they crack as they pass by, before you hear the sound of them being fired. It's disorienting, and has never been captured properly by Hollywood.

It's pitch black. Blackout curtains prevent light getting out from the farmhouse. The walls are high enough that I can't see any muzzle flashes, there's just a flickering in the distance.

There's a knot in my stomach, but I'm not frightened. Only curious. I can tell that nothing is being directed toward our location at present, only over it. Our hosts seem to know the same thing and show no signs of panic, only an occasional furrowed brow, or an eye cocked toward the sky.

Of course, that sense of relative safety could change in an instant, if an artillery round drops short, or a rocket goes astray. But for now, we seem to be in as good a place as any. Am I happy here? No. But it's better than the alternative. That's one thing you will hear from anyone who's been in a war zone. You create circles of relative safety.

I've mentioned before how—when confronting real life and death issues—I become serene. Perhaps this is one of those moments. We have no body armour, and no real cover, so there isn't much we could do anyway. Helpless again.

The roar of battle intensifies. I decide I want to record this for posterity, so I go inside to grab Chris's tape recorder. It's dark, despite the oil lamp, so I fumble around in the backpack to find it, then fumble around some more, plugging in the mic and headset. I then go back out into the courtyard.

It's deafening.

I kneel down to lower my profile, just in case any rounds start to drop lower, and I hold the mic up into the night sky. On both knees, for stability, with my arse resting on my heels. I record the constant rattle and thud and bang, with an occasional whiz and screech directly overhead. I roll tape for several minutes.

I wish I still had the tape. I kept it for years, but I must have lost it when I moved to America.

Like many civilians in war time, I have no idea who is fighting whom, or for what. There are a lot of heavy weapons in play, which would suggest it's government forces doing most of the shooting. But why? I cannot tell you. I don't even know where we are, or what the strategic or tactical situation is. We are just in the wrong place at the wrong time. Or given that it is passing overhead, maybe it is the right place?

I am anxious. But my concern has surprisingly less to do with the battle and more to do with our hosts. In my head, I feel the battle is somewhat controlled for now, and that the fire is not directed at us. But for some reason, I become convinced our hosts mean to harm us.

I cannot explain it. Yes, they have opened their home to us, and shared their food. But there remains this tension. Osman is nowhere to be seen. Our hosts are stiff and wooden.

I become quite paranoid.

It is probably the combination of Osman being pissy all day; his foolishness trying to outrun the shepherd boy; my sense that our trust with him was broken. Then there is our frustration at the road being closed, and my anxiety about ever getting a flight out of Kabul. And while I don't feel terrified by the battle outside, there must be fear at a subconscious level. Add to that the inability to communicate with anyone. The isolation. The vulnerability. The helplessness. The inability to know what is happening.

Then there is sheer physical exhaustion—we have been on the road, sleeping rough for a week now. Getting shot at earlier in the day doesn't help, of course, especially when it came as such a surprise, from a little goat herder. But whatever the cause, for no logical reason, I become thoroughly paranoid. I expect to be betrayed.

Late in the evening, our hosts extinguish the little oil lamp. Clearly we are being told to sleep, despite the fighting. By the time I lie down, I have convinced myself our hosts will likely cut our throats and rape us in the night. In which order, I am not really sure. I am not thinking logically. If they don't do it themselves, then it will be their guerrilla or militia associates.

The rape thing sounds a little dramatic, but if you don't know, dear reader, Afghanistan is home to a charming tradition known as the *bacha bazi*. Young, poor, beardless boys are somehow attached to military and police units as servants, to clean shoes and kit, carry water and fuel, prepare meals, dance, and provide sexual services. Receiving or taking pleasure from a *bacha bazi* is not gay, it's just, well, customary. In my book, it's rape. It's child sex abuse. It's illegal, but widely tolerated. When the boy becomes a man, he is released from service and is expected to resume normal life. *Bacha bazi* continues to this day. US forces have, as policy, turned a blind eye, despite complaints from the Pentagon's own Inspector General for Afghanistan, and even lawsuits from US veterans. It's not universal, but it happens on quite a wide scale.[28]

As for myself, I am both blessed and cursed by youthful good looks. Looking young is a treat now, in my 50s, but for much of my early professional life it was often hard to be taken seriously. Anyway, in Afghanistan, at 27, I look much younger. Beardless. And I already felt like I had got some creepy looks from a few Afghans, like those on Chicken Street in Kabul. It's pretty unsettling.

I'm too ashamed of my thoughts to share them with Chris. It couldn't change anything, anyway.

I try to stay awake but cannot, and as consciousness fades, I can only hope my paranoid fears do not come true.

As Chris said, what choice do we have?

---

[28]See "Bacha Bazi: Afghanistan's Darkest Secret," by the Bright Blue human rights organization in the UK, August 18th 2017. [humanrights.brightblue.org.uk/blog-1/2017/8/18/bacha-bazi-afghanistans-darkest-secret]

Chapter 15

Taxi!

I wake up around daybreak, never more glad to be alive. It's quiet. The battle has ceased. But then the memory of my fear washes over me again. I feel no pain, but I check my neck and body for any injury. All well. Chris is also fine. I feel foolish for being so afraid.

It's so quiet I have a hard time believing there was so much fighting last night. I listen back to the tapes just to prove to myself that it had happened. I thank my lucky stars we are okay.

I find a quiet spot, and pull my little Gideon Bible out of my backpack. Today's reading is the first chapter of Saint Peter's second letter, where he teaches the faithful to add goodness to their faith; to goodness, knowledge; to knowledge, self-control; and to self-control, perseverance.

We didn't know it yet, but we would need a lot of perseverance to get through the coming day.

Our hosts bring us breakfast, and by sign language inform us that, yes, the battle is over and that the warring factions have moved apart. No one seems to know or care who had won or lost. The only thing that matters to civilians in wartime is that the fighting has gone away. The property is undamaged and its people unhurt. Nothing else matters.

We sit cross-legged as usual on the long cushions, and eat with our fingers. I am getting used to it now, but I have little appetite. I feel foolish again. I'm enjoying their generosity and kindness, after having misjudged their intentions so profoundly. They refuse any kind of payment.

Then I remembered the Pakhtunwali. The Afghan code of honour. It mandates hospitality. But I then remember the story of how the hospitality ends at the property line, and that we could be betrayed once we are over it. Fear swings back into my soul.

The pit of my stomach is filled with anxiety. A physical thing.

It wasn't until years later that I learned that the Tajiks do not follow the Pakhtunwali. That's just a traditional Pashtun thing. My cultural bias as a Brit is now clear. Most of what we, as Brits, learned about Afghanistan was from the imperial poet, Rudyard Kipling, and military historians, who were obsessed with the Pashtuns, or Pathans as the Brits used to say.

I wish I could have been more grateful to our hosts. I gave them a cursory thank you. It was not enough. But during life in wartime you can never go back. It's the same with Osman: his contacts and local knowledge had helped keep us safe through a nasty little action, and yet I had succumbed to irrational fear and paranoia.

It's shameful now to recollect my resentment and fear of these people, our hosts, sharing their home and food, and possibly putting themselves at risk of retaliation for sheltering foreigners. But in the worst of times, the worst of fears can creep into your mind, and it takes a strong person to shake them off and move on.

I was weak that day.

ɛ◈ɜ ɛ◈ɜ ɛ◈ɜ

Wednesday 13th November is another beautiful sunny day in northern Afghanistan, with blue skies contrasting the khaki country-side. We board the UN truck, and head back across country towards the highway.

The war appears to have vanished as quickly as it appeared yesterday afternoon.

Within a couple of hours we pull into the now familiar streets of Pul-i-Khumri, and meet up with our friends from the HALO Trust de-mining charity.

But this is not to be a simple pit stop. Through an interpreter, our driver Osman informs us this is the end of the road for him. He is now under UN orders to take the truck elsewhere, and not back to Kabul.

Crap. We are still more than 140 miles (225 km) from Kabul, with the rugged Hindu Kush mountains still ahead. The anxiety returns, about when or whether we can get back to the relative safety of the capital.

To make matters worse, as of today, my visa has expired. I was only legally entitled to be in Afghanistan for a week. I'd picked up my accreditation after arrival last Tuesday, so I might have been able to argue that I was still legit yesterday. But now it's Wednesday, and, if challenged, I would not have a leg to stand on. So I could be arrested for just being here, let alone working as a journalist. I know how the government was always on the lookout for western "spies." At best, my arrest could create embarrassment, difficulty and expense for my employer and the UK government. At worst, I could disappear into a ditch.

More practically, my flight out of Kabul was scheduled for yesterday, and I am supposed to be back at my desk in London on Thursday. Tomorrow! There is still no way to communicate with the outside world. I have no way of knowing if the Red Cross message got through to London. If I don't show up for work, and can't get them a message, then I could be disciplined or fired. How would I then pay the mortgage? That seems trivial compared to the thought of being tortured and killed. But try as I might to ignore these thoughts, they keep popping into my head.

My feeling of helplessness returns. I was trained by the army to adapt, improvise, overcome. But there is nothing much I can do to help, with no language skill and no money. Chris works with the HALO guys to try to find alternative transport. No other UN convoy is scheduled. No other aid vehicles are going that way. Everything seems to be winding down as winter approaches. There are no cars or trucks to rent. Chris even asks about buying one.

𐆌◈𐆎   𐆌◈𐆎   𐆌◈𐆎

Then out of nowhere, Chris appears and says he's found us a ride. Today!

Our saviour is a taxi driver that Chris has managed to persuade to take the risk of driving the five hours to Kabul. The HALO guys apparently use taxis occasionally to transport handwritten letters to their head office in Kabul, so they probably suggested the idea and made the introductions.

I'm sorry, again, that I cannot recollect the driver's name, but I remain forever in his debt.

You see, this is to be no ordinary long-haul taxi ride. The dangers of cliff roads, ice and snow are obvious. But then there is the small matter of the war.

Remember, this road is thick with checkpoints, both rebel and government-controlled. Each one is manned by poorly trained kids with itchy trigger fingers. We'd had a pass up until now, as we'd been hitching a ride with recognizable UN aid vehicles. Our taxi would have no such pass. If the rebels thought our driver un-Islamic, he could be killed on the spot. Not having a beard could be enough. If your beard is too long, then government forces might assume you are a rebel, with equally lethal consequences. Our driver thinks he'll be okay, as he happens to be sporting three days of stubble.

Then there's a risk that our driver could be recognized or targeted by someone with a grudge. Maybe someone would think he was a former rebel or government soldier. Or maybe we'd just run into someone who needed vengeance against his clan.

Our experience with the shepherd boy yesterday was a stark warning that you might also just run afoul of someone who wants to rob you, or demand *baksheesh* under arms. Or steal your car.

There is also danger from the nature of his passengers. Us. We are foreigners. Infidels. I am getting tired of the Muj mistaking us for Russian advisers, and the Commies mistaking us for American spies.

And, of course, there is always the danger of landmines.

War is not like a movie, or a military history book. It is not scripted. There is no predictable outcome. There is no benefit of hindsight. People try to do things, and shit happens. It's obvious, but it's hard to understand at the same time. You start to live by probabilities; you measure things by the odds of them happening and trust your gut. You have to try to put aside the fears.

Our driver exacts a good price. A round trip fee. Plus danger money. Half up-front. I am almost out of money, but Chris thankfully has enough, and says he can expense it. The driver speaks no English, so Chris has to get help from the aid workers to translate the negotiations.

We grab our bags and say our goodbyes to the de-miners. But before we take off, our driver has to run some errands.

First he preps the car. He takes down the pictures from the visor of his car, and hangs up some prayer beads on the rear-view mirror. Pictures, even of your family, can be used as evidence of idolatry by Islamic extremists. The worshipping of idols is forbidden in Islam, and when taken to extreme, can mean a prohibition on all images of the human form or even of animals.

Then he drives home to say goodbye to his wife and children. Just in case. We tag along, as he is also going to give her our up-front money for the fare. Just in case. She is veiled with a red *niqab*. They hug. She cries. The kids are silent, hopefully too young to be really aware of the danger.

Next we drive up to the military depot on the edge of town. Not to the front gate, but to a hole in the chicken-wire fence. I see money change hands and a jerrycan of fuel is passed through by a soldier in the usual dirty brown uniform. The driver fills up the car and passes the empty can back. I've never seen a black market operate so brazenly.

All seems well, and we have plenty of time to get to Kabul before dark.

We start to leave town. We climb up a hill and get to the last government checkpoint on the road south out of Pul-i-Khumri, heading for Kabul. Finally!

Not so fast.

8◊3   8◊3   8◊3

We pull up to the checkpoint, and at first it just seems like one of the dozens of others we've been through before. But this is our first time traveling without the protection of a United Nations vehicle or a Mujahidin leader.

I can't visualize it now in my mind's eye. Most of the checkpoints we went through were very informal. You'd see armed men on the side of the road and they'd wave you down. Occasionally there was a flimsy barrier, like you'd see in a parking lot. If there was a defensive position, it was usually off to the side. There were rarely the sandbag walls and concrete jersey barriers that readers may be familiar with from the US occupation in Iraq.

All I remember of this checkpoint is the greasy brown uniforms of the regular soldiers, mostly very young, and others—older men—in clean, olive green, cotton shirts. The soldiers mostly carry AKs. The olive green men mostly sport pistols in holsters on their belts.

There's a delay. That's unusual, I think to myself. They ask for papers. They're peppering the driver with questions. They argue amongst themselves.

More delay.

Quiet.

Our driver opens the door and gestures for us to get out. The soldiers shepherd us into a hut and we're told to sit down on some boxes. Our guards continue debating among themselves, before deciding to take it outside.

None of the guards speak English, and we have no interpreter. The driver's face is unreadable; maybe there's a hint of resignation. The mood of the guards is not hostile, but there is no question: we cannot leave just yet.

We wait nervously. I'm more concerned about getting to Kabul before nightfall, and feel frustrated with the delay. Our papers show we're not US spies so what's the holdup?

But wait! My papers are no good. My visa has expired. Plus, we just witnessed our driver buying gas on the black market, from the hole in the fence of the army base. Oh boy. Where's this going?

Politely but firmly we're told to get up. The guards have guns at the ready now. Our taxi driver is separated from us. One of the men in olive green uniform gets into the driver's seat of the taxi and drives off. Chris and I are guided to an army truck and told to get into the cab.

I take a moment to sigh and glance down the hill toward the city of Pul-i-Khumri. Then I look up. There is a slight haze of dust or smoke—like Colorado in wildfire season. But the sky is blue and cloudless. It's a beautiful day. Then slowly I climb into the truck.

We have been detained by the secret police—the infamous KHAD.

Chapter 16

Guests of the Secret Police

We are driven back into town, passing through a couple of checkpoints. Our man in the neatly pressed olive green uniform then parks on the street next to some modern-looking government buildings. The buildings are well-guarded and semi-fortified, meaning there are lots of fences, barbed wire, and some sandbag emplacements.

One large Soviet-style building has barbed wire facing inward, as if to stop people getting out. There are no civilians on the street, which —looking back—makes me think this street had restricted access, for security reasons. Maybe this was Pul-i-Khumri's miniature "Green Zone."

"Bugger," says Chris. "It's the KHAD building."

My heart sinks. Anxiety fills the pit of my stomach again, and I feel giddy—I guess from the adrenaline. You see, the KHAD has a reputation like the Gestapo of Nazi Germany, or Stalin's NKVD. Their job is to find traitors, government opponents and terrorists; to torture them to confess; then deal with them summarily. Usually a bullet in the back of the head. I start to wonder what it would be like to have one's nails removed and whether losing a toenail would hurt more than a fingernail.

KHAD is an acronym—just like Gestapo is an acronym for *Geheime Staatspolizei* (Secret State Police). Likewise, KGB stands for *Komitet Gosudarstvennoy Bezopasnosti*, or "Committee for State Security." The KHAD's proper name is *Khadamat-e Aetla'at-e Dawlati*, which translates as "State Intelligence Agency" or "State Information

Services." It was first set up after the violent communist seizure of power in April 1978, and was trained by the KGB. If you know nothing about totalitarian states, the first thing you need to learn is that every such regime has one of these secret police forces, and that no laws apply to them. These are the guys watching you and waiting for you to show disrespect for the regime. Then they pounce. If you're considered a serious offender, maybe they'll round up your family and friends for good measure. If you're lucky you'll just get a beating and be released. If you're unlucky, you and your family might end up in front of a firing squad or in some sort of concentration camp, with hard labour. Maybe there'll be a show trial. But sometimes those are held after sentence has been executed. There are no safe spaces here.

I was telling my wife this story recently, and after she picked her jaw up off the floor, she asked "How did it feel to be completely and utterly fucked?"

It took me a moment, then I described to her what I call the circles of ridiculous hope. An Iraq veteran friend described to me how being stateside is better than being in-country. Being in the Green Zone is better than being on a Forward Operating Base (FOB). Being on a FOB is better than being in a combat outpost (COP). Being in a COP is better than being out on patrol. A quiet patrol is better than combat. In combat, having a decent rock to hide behind is better than being out in the open. Safety becomes relative. Each situation might suck, but it could always be worse. People cling to hope in the worst of situations. You negotiate hope with yourself. It's a phenomenon I noticed when my father was sick. He's in remission; the cancer is back; let's hope it's months, not weeks. Let's hope it's weeks, not days. Let's hope it's days, not hours. Not today, please. For God's sake not today. Please.

My first circle of defensive hope is built when they take our taxi driver into the KHAD building first, not Chris or me. It seems a bit ruthless to hope your taxi driver—someone putting their life on the line for you—is the sacrificial lamb in this situation. But that's one of the central moral dilemmas of anyone who's lived, worked or served in a war zone. Better him than me. It's uncomfortable and unpleasant, but that's the way it is.

Hopefully he is the focus of their concern, not us. Hopefully they won't find out about his black market gassing up of the car. Hopefully he won't be tortured, and can live to see his family again. Hopefully, somehow, we can get back on the road.

Then I remember again that my visa has expired. I realize I have photos of military positions on my camera—that's the definition of spying. Plus there are pictures of Ahmed Shah Massoud and other Mujahidin, so clearly we have been in close contact with the enemy.

So how do you feel in a situation like this? It's a roller coaster of positive and negative thoughts and emotions. One minute you're focused on minutiae like which way the wire is facing; do the guards have their guns at the ready, or are they slung on their backs? The next minute you wonder how your wife or mother will feel if they never know what happened to you. Time is the real stressor. When stuff is happening you are often too distracted to fret. With time on your hands you can dwell on the enormity of your problems. We have time, while we wait.

Chris and I are still sitting in the cab of the truck. The driver's seat is empty. The keys gone. A very young soldier watches over us nervously on the street in front of us. His AK is slung over his shoulder. Others are milling about, but paying no attention to us.

"Hang on a minute," says Chris. "I know this place. That building there . . ." He gestures with his thumb behind us. "That's the governor's palace. I was there a couple of months ago. We got drunk together. If I can get to him, he should able to vouch for us."

"How can you do that? That guy is watching us," I nod toward our guard.

"There's no guarantee, but it's better than sitting here," says Chris.

There's a brief pause. "I know," he says. "You distract him!"

I snort out a half-laugh. "That's like something from the movies."

"Yeah. That's it. You distract him and I'll do a runner." Chris's face is serious. My smile fades. I swallow.

"How?" I ask.

"Hmm. You'll have to get out and get the other side of him, so he turns around. Then I can slip out, when his back is to the truck."

"Oh," says I. Thinking of a million ways this could go wrong. "You're not serious? He has a gun."

"Totally serious," says Chris.

"But what if he sees you?" I ask. "What if you can't get through the other guards?"

"Got to be worth a try. What choice do we have?" It made sense. I sighed. The day had escalated so quickly; it was hard to keep up with how grave the stakes had suddenly become.

So this is it. The moment one has to break cover and do something ridiculously dangerous, because the alternative is worse.

I grumble assent. "Let's hope the doors aren't locked."

Chris is sitting by the passenger door. I'm in the middle seat. I slide over to the driver's seat, and give our guard a polite smile and wave. I make a hand signal like I have to talk. I try the door. It's open.

The guard seems stunned. I walk slowly, with my hands up. I use the two or three words I've picked up as local greetings. *"Hubastay"* may have been one. But mostly I'm talking in my politest Cambridge University/BBC English gentleman pleasantries, hoping to sound charming and unthreatening. "How do you do? Lovely day, isn't it? Come here often?"

The guard braces up. His right hand lets go of the sling of his AK and he grabs the butt. But he doesn't bring it down.

I don't walk directly toward him, but try to move in a half-circle, drifting into the center of the street, and aiming to come around behind the guard. He turns to keep his face to me; he's still baffled by my behaviour. It feels like an eternity, but it's probably only a few seconds, and soon the guard's back is to the cab of the truck. My eyes are locked with his, so I have no idea if Chris has made his attempt to slip away.

The guard's patience snaps. The gun comes down off his shoulder into his hands, he starts yelling, pointing the gun at me and then at the truck. While I can't understand him, it's pretty clear from the sign language he wants me back in the vehicle, pronto. I have no idea where Chris is. I can't afford to break eye contact with the guard. If I glance over, I'll tip him off that something is up in that direction.

I try to buy time, by playing dumb. I'm smiling and saying sweet nonsense. My hands are still up, palms facing our custodian. But there's only so much I can do. I slowly make my way back to the truck and climb back in.

Now I see Chris is gone. His door is closed. The guard does not notice that Chris has slipped away. I can't believe our luck. The whole episode seems surreal.

But now I am alone. I have no other plan. Now it's time to wait and see, and hope for the best. Again, it feels like forever and I honestly have no idea if it was five minutes or fifty. It's so quiet.

Suddenly there's a hubbub. Men are shouting. The truck door opens and Chris hops back in. Our guard looks dumbfounded and then relieved, as he checks around to see if his commander realizes that he temporarily lost one of his charges.

Chris is beaming.

"Well?" I ask.

"Good news and bad news," says Chris. "I got in."

"Great!"

"But the chief wasn't there."

"Fuck," says I.

"But I did run into his son. I don't know him as well but he says he remembers me from the booze-up, and says he'll vouch for us. Funny fellow. He speaks good English—went to school in Birmingham."

"England?"

"Yeah. I'll tell you more later."

My spirits lift.

Now we wait. This man I don't know, and will never meet, is now advocating for us with the secret police, based on my buddy's story of a drunken binge with his father.

We have done all we can. Now we have to wait again.

It works.

We see our taxi driver coming out of the KHAD headquarters. His face still unreadable. With the language barrier, we will never know his emotions and thoughts while a prisoner of the KHAD. If Chris did not have a relationship of sorts with the governor, who knows what might have happened.

We wait again to get our passports and other documents back. I'm relieved no one appears to have checked the date on my visa too closely.

So there were no explosions or dramatic chases, but somehow, with courage and Chris' ingenuity, we have all managed to escape the clutches of the Afghan secret police.

Looking back, that young guard watching us reminded me of myself, back when I was on sentry duty outside our Territorial Army drill hall, protecting it against the IRA. I had a uniform and a gun, but no real idea of what I was supposed to do; no clear rules of engagement; no orders about when to open fire. I suspect that the young sentry outside the KHAD headquarters didn't know what to do with us, either.

Finally we're off. It's 140 miles by road to Kabul, or five hours, given the roads and the mountains. How many more fucking checkpoints will we have to pass through, and how much crap will we get? The stress is getting to me.

ଽ◈ଽ   ଽ◈ଽ   ଽ◈ଽ

"So what happened back there?" I ask Chris. "After you hopped out of the cab and did a runner?"

"Not much of a runner," Chris snorted. "I didn't run. Which was hard. Didn't want to attract attention. I just walked up to the guard at the gate of the governor's palace and introduced myself. I have just enough Dari to manage that. Then I tried to say I had an appointment to see the Big Man. I got past the first bloke and into the lobby, but got stuck there. It was tough. I wasn't really getting anywhere, when all of a sudden the son walks by."

"That was lucky. The chap who went to school in England?"

"Yes! Jeff."

"Jeff?"

"Sayed Jafar Naderi. Sayed is a title. Naderi is the family name. So his first name is Jafar. And Jafar became Jeff in America."[29]

"In America?"

"Yeah. Allentown, Pennsylvania, if I recall correctly. He was a bit of a handful so he was sent to a different set of cousins by the ones in

---

[29]Our saviour "Jeff"—Sayed Jafar Naderi—was the subject of a documentary in 1989 called "Warlord of Kayan" by legendary US war reporter, Jeff B. Harmon. Kayan is where Jeff was born, in 1965, at the Naderi palace, located up a remote side valley off the Salang. He was also the subject of an article by Howard Witt of the Chicago Tribune in the same year (June 25th 1989). Both highlight "Jeff's" love of motorbikes and his big red Mercedes sports car, which he loved to race around Pul-i-Khumri and the rest of his territory. My buddy Chris was treated to a ride in the Mercedes "at breakneck speed" on a subsequent trip.

England. He's hysterical. Speaks perfect English, of course—which was how he was able to help."

"What the hell is he doing here?"

"He's the son of the Big Man in town, Sayed Mansur Naderi. That's the gent I got hammered with, a few weeks back, up in the mountains where he has another palace and a stud ranch, of all things —with these amazing appaloosa horses.[30] But, anyway, Jeff is a bit of hell-raiser himself by all accounts. Fast cars, motorbikes, booze. He was even in a heavy metal band—when he wasn't working at McDonalds, that is."

"No way?"

"Yeah! Anyway, Jeff was getting out of hand in America, so they brought him back. Had to teach him Dari all over, he'd been away so long. He'd been sent away when his dad—Mansur, the patriarch— was arrested way back in the 1970s. But Dad was released a few years ago, when he cut a deal with the government. So Jeff comes back and he's made a general."

"Seriously? This heavy metal kid? What is he, our age?"

"He's about that, yeah," says Chris. "26 or 27."

"And he's a general?"

"Yep. And technically he's the governor, too, of Baghlan province. But I think his dad is the one who's really in charge. Dad was the one I thought I needed to see just now."

"But this lad—Jeff—was able to sort us out. What did you say to him?"

"I acted kind of cocky. You have to in these situations. I told him my press credentials had no restrictions on travel, and whether you say it or not, I know you have no desire to detain or arrest a BBC correspondent. You know that will cause trouble for you."

"And that was it?"

---

[30] In 2020, after we reconnected, Chris Bowers gave me more details of that boozy trip to the horse ranch in the mountains of Kayan: "I had one extraordinary trip where I was taken to see SJN's father Sayed Mansur Naderi up in the mountains. He had some wonderful appaloosa horses—the only ones in Afghanistan—mostly used for *buzkashi* [an Afghan form of polo]. I was allowed to ride one of the tamer ones but told not to kick it otherwise it would gallop for a day without stopping. I remember watching some horsemen training for *buzkashi* which involved them hurtling along on the horses, hooking their knee round the wooden pummel and swooping down with their hands to pick up rocks from the ground while the horse was still moving, then raising their hand with the stones above their heads while back in the saddle."

"Not quite." Chris grimaced. "I let slip we'd been to see Massoud."
"Oops!"

"So then I had to say we needed to get back to Kabul with his answer to the peace plan. He wasn't happy, so then he calls Kabul and asks me to wait. But I said, do you want to be the one responsible for stopping us getting through? I reminded him about my credentials and that I didn't need permission. He told me off, but laughed and said I'd have to wait in the truck."

"So he gave us a pass? He has the power to do that?"

"Yeah. Nothing in writing. But he commands the 80th division—those are his lads up ahead in the Salang. So hopefully they'll leave us alone," says Chris. "It's ironic really."

"What is?"

"Jeff's favourite band is AC/DC, and his favourite song is "Highway to Hell." And the Salang is surely that."

I laugh, but I'm still confused.

"The funniest thing is Jeff is a dead-ringer for John Belushi."

"The actor?"

"Yep. You know—the Blues Brothers, Animal House. Jeff looks like Bluto."

"Blimey," I say. "So this place is like Animal House meets Mad Max, with an AC/DC soundtrack?"

"Ha, yes!"

"Insane," I say. "So let me get this straight. Dad is the powerhouse who rules this area, pretty much. And his boy is a general and governor, on behalf of the communist government. But I thought you said they were religious leaders? I thought all the good Muslims were against the communists? And I thought you said they both like to party?"

"Yeah. Remember I said they're like the Aga Khan?"

"Remind me?"

"They're Ismailis—that's a sect—I think it's more Shia than Sunni. So they're not seen as good Muslims by the Muj-types. But their people are very loyal to them. They're like medieval barons—but also part pope, part warlord."

"And part playboy?" I add.

"Well," Chris screws up his face. "Not sure I'd go that far. But they drink like fish. I should know," he grins. "I remember Sayed Mansur—the dad—taking me for a picnic and ordering his servants to bring, 'a bottle of whisky, a bottle of brandy, a bottle of vodka . . . oh, and some meat!' " Chris shakes his head, like someone regretting an over-indulgence. "Anyway, their position is inherited so they can pretty much do whatever they want. Their followers still worship them and pay them tithes."

"So that's why the government co-opted them? Because of all that local power, and money?"

"Pretty much," says Chris.

"Well, thank God you knew them, or God knows what we'd have been looking at back there."

"I know, right? They have no love for the KHAD, so I think he enjoyed dicking them over."

"And what about our friend here?" I gesture towards our gallant taxi driver.

"He should be okay, too. Fingers crossed."

"Inshallah," I add.

❧❀❧   ❧❀❧   ❧❀❧

After finally leaving Pul-i-Khumri and the KHAD secret police, we head out on the "Highway to Hell."

Our sense of relief about escaping the clutches of the KHAD is short-lived. Our conversation about Jeff and his dad provides a distraction for a few minutes. But we have a long way to go.

Ahead of us lies the Salang Valley. As we have already seen, it's some of the most bitterly fought-over real estate of the war.

In case you've forgotten already, the Salang was critically vital terrain for the Afghan government, which depended on truck convoys from the Soviet Union for pretty much all the fuel and ammo needed in the eastern half of the country.

Needless to say, these convoys were under constant attack from the Muj, hoping to deprive the government of resources and also to pin down the regime's forces, to garrison the pass. It was a relatively

easy way to wage jihad. Find a good spot and wait to fire a rocket-propelled grenade (RPG) into a defenceless fuel truck.-

The defence industry has a euphemism for this kind of warfare. Interdicting supply routes. It sounds very clean and clinical when used in a briefing paper from a Washington think-tank, or in a West Point classroom. The reality is a poor man (usually), desperate for money, taking the ridiculously dangerous job of driving a truck laden with fuel or explosives on an icy mountain road, never knowing when a rocket or landmine is going to blow you to kingdom come or burn you beyond recognition.

Our drive is hard and fast. In my note on the back of a photo I call it the "dash" back to Kabul from Pul-i-Khumri.

And it sucks. That's the only way to describe it. I think by this stage of the trip I am in some sort of shock. We've seen death up close. We've seen the aftermath of air strikes and met wounded children. We've been almost constantly in earshot of gunfire and explosions. There's the constant and ubiquitous threat of landmines. I've heard artillery creeping closer and closer to my perch in the night. We were stuck in no man's land for a night while bullets and shells passed overhead. I'd fallen asleep expecting to have my throat cut in the night. We've been shot at during an attempted robbery. We've seen such casual abuse of firearms. We've been mistaken repeatedly for spies, by both sides. We've been detained by the secret police and escaped. Quite often I've felt helpless, at the mercy of forces and actors way beyond my control. It is just so overwhelming. And worse seems yet to come.

Now we have to go through hotly contested terrain, over the icy mountains, littered with the detritus of war, and landmines, and countless checkpoints, all the while carrying defective papers.

I feel numb.

"How do you cope with all this?" I ask.

"All what?"

"All this getting shot at, and arrested, and never knowing what's round the corner. Landmines and goodness knows what?"

"Ahh," he says, pausing thoughtfully. I think Chris can tell I am close to the edge.

"I keep busy, so I can't dwell on it. Just get through the moment. Worrying about it won't change anything."

He takes a moment to describe how he finds it useful at times like these to do what he calls "mind games." He means basically doing anything to keep your mind busy, so you don't ruminate on the stresses.

Immediately south of Pul-i-Khumri we enter the northern approaches of the Salang, with the valley narrowing and the mountains rising beside us. Chris suggests we count, as a way to keep our minds busy. We had seen how the Salang was littered with destroyed and damaged vehicles. So we decide to count the wrecks. Counting death through the pass.

Only military armoured vehicles, mind you. Not the trucks, cars, buses. They are everywhere. Very quickly we realize there are too many. So one of us counts only tanks, and one of us counts the other armoured vehicles, mostly armoured personnel carriers, with the occasional self-propelled gun. Chris does the tanks and I do the others, since my army training perhaps makes me better at recognizing them. We call them as they come up, and correct each other if we make any mistakes.

It works. We follow the zig-zag road up, through the tunnel, and down the other side. Yes, we pause at checkpoints, and occasionally have to get out. But my mind focusses on the count.

I can't remember the precise breakdown, but I'm pretty sure I recollect the total being 126, split more or less evenly between tanks and other armoured fighting vehicles. About 60 each. That's enough armour for two full Soviet tank battalions.

We make it to the Salang Tunnel. Snow now lies thick all around, but the tunnel is open, and luckily today is a north-to-south day for the traffic flow.

It's icy. Fresh-looking 18-wheelers can be seen tumbled halfway down the mountainside.

There's a picture of me during one of the many stops at checkpoints. White clouds or fog are beside and below us, down the valley. I have one foot on the road, one foot resting on snow piled a couple of feet deep. You can see fresh tank tracks in the snow. My hands are thrust into my jean pockets for warmth. I'm wearing my *shemagh*—the colourful cotton neckcloth—over an aran sweater. My face is tight and drawn and serious. I feel like I've aged a lot in the past week. I don't look at all like the innocent nerdy kid you can see in the photo at Heathrow just ten days ago.

There's also a pic of Chris in the same spot, with one foot buried up to his knee in the snow; his face beaming with a smile. The contrast in our faces is so stark. How differently we seem to be experiencing the day.

We dash down the valley. The road hairpins down the mountainside and slowly broadens into a valley. The gun emplacements and miniature forts are still on every corner. The villages are still desolate and deserted. I didn't know those endless zig-zags would be such frequent visitors to my dreams in the years ahead.

As the valley straightens, so does the road, and our speed. Eventually there's room enough for traffic to move quickly in both directions.

This part of the road is one of the most dangerous. It's close to the mouth of the Panjshir Valley, controlled by the Mujahidin of our friend, Ahmed Shah Massoud. So it's a scene of frequent ambushes and skirmishes.

Then we run into a convoy. One of those huge government convoys of fuel tankers and ammo trucks coming down from Soviet Central Asia. As we crest a hill we can see it stretching away below us for miles. It seems endless.

We and our driver are impatient. We start overtaking them one by one.

They're going at top speed. Ambush could happen any time. Chris describes how a few weeks ago he was on this road and saw an RPG (rocket propelled grenade) go into a fuel tanker right in front of him, exploding spectacularly.

Chris Woolf

This picture is from 2011 but looks no different than a fuel convoy in 1991.
Photo: US Dept. of Defense/Sgt. Rachael Moore

Should we hang back? That could make us late into Kabul. Should we rush past? Suppose there was an ambush? It doesn't matter what I think. I don't have much say. I am a powerless witness again.

Our driver is aggressive. Visibility is not easy when you're in a little Soviet-made car, and you're behind an oil tanker or a four-ton truck. Each attempt to overtake feels like a roll of the dice.

And yet, we pass the convoy without incident. No ambush. No head-on collision.

It was about this time I acknowledge to myself that I might not be cut out for this life, as a foreign correspondent in a conflict zone. There is no direct threat; we are not targets *per se*. No one wants us dead. It was not like the more recent conflicts in Iraq and Syria. And yet death is always around us. Danger is always around us. Maybe my imagination is too strong, but there are always ways to die or be horribly injured, all the time. It's a constant battle of calculating odds to assess which is the best and safest course of action. And yet for much of the time there is absolutely nothing you can do to affect the odds, or change course. The helplessness is perhaps the most overwhelming part. I don't know. There is excitement. There is a thrill. There is an adrenaline rush. There's an important public service to perform. But I'm starting to question if those are enough to outweigh the negatives, for me.

These pictures in the snow are my last pictures from my trip to Afghanistan. I am spent. I want no more mementoes. I am ready to go home.

Chapter 17

Sandbagged in Kabul

We get back to Kabul early in the afternoon. We are joyfully reunited with Masum. We pick up cash and send our gallant taxi driver on his way.

In the week or so that we've been away, Kabul has changed.

We stop by the residence of our friend, the Bulgarian ambassador, Valentin Gatsinski. Ominously, there are now protective sandbags reinforcing the walls of his home. It's the first building to get this level of protection in the city's diplomatic/government quarter. The ambassador is supposedly the best-informed man in Kabul. He represents the Warsaw Pact, and has contacts at the highest levels of government. What he does speaks volumes. He must have good enough intelligence to know that fighting could be here soon, and that he needs to step up his security, with the sandbags, even though it is visibly bad for public relations.

We also see different-looking men on patrol in the city, with baggy pants and turbans. The ambassador tells us they are Jowzjanis, an ethnic Uzbek militia. They have been brought down from the north as it was thought they could be depended on more than the regular army. Chris tells me they have a fearsome reputation for toughness and brutality. They are led by a ruthless, self-made warlord called Abdul Rashid Dostum.

Looking back, the government of Comrade Najibullah was clearly feeling under pressure from the rebels, although we did not realize the extent of it at the time. We were not aware that Washington and

Moscow had secretly agreed to cut aid to their respective proxies in the New Year.

Whatever the big picture, like anyone in a war zone, I have to focus on my own affairs. Now that we're back in Kabul, the first article of business is to get my papers in order. I don't want any more run-ins with the KHAD, and we have no idea how long it will be before I can catch a flight to Delhi. Masum takes me back to the Interior Ministry. Luckily, they're still open, and I'm granted a three-day extension, stamped into my passport. Hopefully that's enough.

We go back to Chris' place for tea. Masum disappears for a little while then suddenly comes rushing back. He announces that something extraordinary is taking place.

A demonstration.

More than thirteen years ago, the communist regime in Afghanistan brutally crushed all dissent immediately upon seizing power. Tens of thousands of Afghans had been executed for just criticizing the government. There has not been an anti-government protest in the country in all those years.

It's my chance to do some real reporting. Chris wants to focus on writing and getting his tape ready for his big piece on Ahmed Shah Massoud. Snagging that interview and getting the rebel leader's take on the UN peace initiative was a real scoop. So Chris asks me to cover the demo. It's a gift.

I head out with Masum in his beat-up old taxi to a square in a newer part of the city. The protest is pretty much over by the time we get there. No one is chancing their luck. We see some protesters who are dispersing and speak to some witnesses. There had only been about 200 people at the demonstration, quietly making mild demands for reform.

Looking back, I can recognize the courage these people must have had—to go out and protest against one of the most violent and arbitrary police states of the era. But since nothing much had happened, and no heads got cracked, I'm not too excited about it. I write up some news copy and experience the pleasure of trying to send it on a telex machine. Of course, I include the context of it being the first demonstration in Kabul in thirteen years, but I don't over-hype it. The story is sent, and the demonstration becomes a minor news item, a footnote in history.

Taken together, all these signs—the increased personal security for the Bulgarian ambassador, the Jowzjanis on the streets, the demonstration—should have been interpreted as the regime further weakening, but we didn't understand how quickly the end would come. We could not know that in just a few weeks, the Soviet Union would disintegrate, and all those supply convoys would simply stop coming across the Hindu Kush from Soviet central Asia. We could not have known that within six months, the Jowzjani warlord, Abdul Rashid Dostum, would see the writing on the wall, betray his communist masters and make an alliance with Ahmed Shah Massoud. The regime would fall in April 1992. President Najibullah himself would eventually be swinging from a lamppost.

I am more focused on getting out.

I have to re-book my flights, with Masum's help. I am pleased to learn I can get on a flight out to Delhi, India, the very next day, Thursday 14th November. There's no financial penalty, even though I'd missed my flight a couple of days before. It seems that getting trapped by the war is an acceptable excuse for the airline of the Democratic Republic of Afghanistan.

That evening we try to relax, and we all behave as if everything is normal. In many ways, it is. For those expats living and working in a war zone, our experience on the road had been nothing unusual. I don't know how they do it. I honestly don't.

As I recall, we have dinner with Valentin, the Bulgarian ambassador and his assistant, Ana. Then we go for a final drink in the expat club. I think I see Fred and buy him a well-deserved pint. I also see Anil—my saviour from the airport terminal—and pay my respects. It's all a bit of a blur. I think I'm still in a state of shock.

६⊙३   ६⊙३   ६⊙३

The next day is my last in Afghanistan. The sky is blue and clear again, with that wonderful light from the altitude.

I am pleased to be leaving.

Chris has to work, so we say our farewells at the house. Masum drives me to the airport. The signs at the airport are still illegible to me, but Masum points me in the right direction. We hug and part ways. Masum has been nothing but a delight. An asset. A friend. In some ways, he symbolizes all Afghans for me: funny, kind, hospitable, despite the horror of living in a land of such hardship and violence.

At the appointed time, I join the dash across the runway and board the plane as fast as possible. Thankfully, there is no incoming rocket or mortar fire today. I don't see any ammo crates on this flight. At the back of my mind is the sight I saw from the streets of Kabul the week before: of the plane dropping flares to decoy heat-seeking missiles. I am praying today is not the day that the Muj will try to bring down an airliner.

One of the pleasures of air travel in a war zone is that you don't waste time. Before everyone is seated, the plane is moving. There is no safety briefing. We are up in the air after the briefest of taxiings. I'm grateful there's no hostile fire. No Stinger missiles.

I have a window seat again, and watch the snow-capped mountains slowly disappear behind us.

My days of bumbling through the Hindu Kush are behind me.

I am relieved to be getting away. But my heart goes out to those who do not have that luxury: the Afghan people. So many good, kind, generous souls, still stuck in the minefields of modern war.

It's only a two-hour flight, but it takes us over Pakistan, then as now hostile to Afghanistan and India. There is no incident. But I don't think I relax fully till I feel us starting the descent into Delhi. I pass the time writing the first draft of my notes about the trip. I know it has been an adventure that I will one day want to document properly.

Joy of joys in Delhi—I am able to get on a flight back to London the same day! As you may remember, I have a standby ticket, so again there is no financial penalty.

In Delhi I am finally able to call home and let my wife know I am okay and on my way back. We have not been able to speak since I left her at Heathrow, and I wasn't sure that the BBC had relayed the message that I would be late. They had.

I have time to kill so I get a bus into the city for a couple of hours of sightseeing and have a meal. Not a bright idea. Whether it's the food, or the drop in adrenaline levels as I start to relax, I do not know. But by the time I am heading for the gate for my flight to London I am struck down with the runs. I dose up on Imodium and eat only plain rice and drink water. It is, needless to say, an unpleasant nine-hour flight.

I give myself no time to reflect on how my life may have changed.

Chapter 18

Welcome Home?

Returning to London, I was immediately struck by the rudeness and coldness of the people, compared to the kindness, warmth and curiosity of Afghans. The indifference.

I also felt the cold hand of the impersonal, machine-like quality of mass transportation in one of the biggest and busiest cities of the world.

I had felt this feeling before, when returning from other trips to the "Third World," but this time there was a new element.

I was angry.

Angry at how these people utterly failed to appreciate their assumption of safety and security. It was just part of their daily lives. A foundation so strong that most people clearly had never even contemplated life without it.

Don't you know? Can't you realize? It's an illusion. I've just come from a world where death can strike at any minute. Why can't you appreciate what you have? Why do you have to be so cold and miserable, when you are so much luckier than so much of humanity?

The feeling got worse over the next few weeks. I wanted to shock them. I wished I had bought more Afghan clothes and one of those $10 AKs, then I could have just walked over Waterloo Bridge trying to startle them out of their cold indifference.

But I did not have the clothing, and in London they were too expensive to acquire. Plus, somewhere at the end of my thought process was something, something, firearm laws, something, something.

An Iraq veteran friend told me something similar, about wanting to dig a battle-trench in his Mom's front yard after he got home. Just to shock people out of their complacency.

He didn't of course. And neither did I try to frighten the good people of London. So I would wear my *shemagh* every day as a scarf, in the hope it would prompt a conversation, at least.

I'm no psychologist, but I suspect this is a symptom of post-traumatic stress. The need to convey just how disturbing and disorienting it is to lose that anchor of safety. The floor of your existence. The everyday, unspoken assumption of personal security.

賏&#x3; 賏&#x3; 賏&#x3;

I don't recall exactly when I went back to work at Bush House—the elegant headquarters of the BBC World Service—but it was pretty quickly. Within a day or two. Thankfully the message from the Red Cross had got through. Dr Haidar of the Red Cross/Red Crescent in Taloqan had radioed his bosses in Kabul; they forwarded the message to the Red Cross headquarters in Geneva. Some kind soul in Geneva had called Bush House.

My manager, the dear departed Val Anderson, enjoyed recounting how Geneva had called to say: "Chris will be late for his shift on Thursday. He's stuck behind rebel lines."

My colleagues at Bush were only mildly interested in my trip. It seemed everyone had done something similar. That made it harder for me to process the events of the last couple of weeks. Maybe it wasn't that special after all? Maybe I was just being soft? Maybe I hadn't articulated it clearly enough?

I tried to put it behind me, and accept that maybe this was something I just needed to get used to, if I was going to pursue this career.

I was still thinking that was the direction my career should go. I didn't want to let on that I had felt scared and helpless, just in case that would prejudice my chances. So I didn't talk about details. I brushed it under the carpet. Mustn't grumble, as we say in England. Worse things happen at sea.

I had no outlet outside of work, either. I chose not to be very honest with my wife or family about the dangers I had faced. Again, I didn't want to create any obstacles to future trips or long-term assignments. I would avoid giving any details and deflect any direct questions. "It was fun," I'd say. "Some hairy moments, but beautiful country. Amazing scenery. And such nice, kind people."

My editors were interested in the stories, though. In particular, my interview with the Soviet POW, Nikolai, caught people's attention. I got help pulling a couple of clips for a short radio story for the World Service in English, which ran that Sunday, 17th November 1991, as I recall. I gave the tapes of the interview to the Russian and Persian language services, who gave it a much fuller treatment than I could provide. I never got the tapes back.

The story had an impact.

The Soviet Union was in turmoil and, although we didn't know it at the time, it was in the process of collapsing for good. The last Soviet leader was Mikhail Gorbachev. He was distinguished by a prominent red birthmark on his bald head, and famous for allowing the people of East Germany in 1989 to "tear down that wall"—the Berlin Wall that had divided the historic German capital for a generation.

Anyway, one of the policies that Gorbachev wanted to achieve most ardently before he left office was to bring home Soviet POW/MIAs from Afghanistan. There were several hundred young men missing over there. Maybe more than a thousand. Gorbachev had ended the Soviet occupation; ended the dying of young Soviet men; and now he wanted to bring home those left behind in enemy captivity. In the past few months, he had sent top officials around the world to try to negotiate their release, even making diplomatic trips and calls himself on their behalf.

That effort appeared to end rather abruptly after my story.

Soviet citizens could hear the voice of one of those POWs, Nikolai Bystrov, saying clearly he was happy where he was. He was a Muslim now. His name was Islam-ud-Din. I filled in the context that he was serving as a bodyguard for none other than Ahmed Shah Massoud, perhaps the most famous anti-Soviet Mujahidin leader.

The story jived with Soviet military prejudices, that the Afghans took no prisoners, except those who converted to Islam and agreed to betray their former comrades and fight against them. The only Soviet soldiers left in Afghanistan were assumed to be dead or traitors.

I now know that Nikolai Bystrov, also known as Islam-ud-Din, became quite well-known in Russia.

I have no idea if my story really made a difference to Moscow's attempts to bring these boys home, or if it was just coincidence. Gorbachev had plenty on his plate, and resigned on Christmas Day, just five weeks later, as the Soviet Union was finally dissolved. But it was an uncomfortable feeling for me.

I felt bad. I had tried to make clear in my story that Nikolai was speaking through an interpreter who was clearly sympathetic to the Mujahidin. So obviously he could not speak freely. He was only one man. We did not get a chance to interview his comrade, Gennadi Tseuma.

My mind was soon taken off such things, as my life changed dramatically and delightfully. My wife and I had been thinking about starting a family for some time, and early in the New Year we discovered we were going to have a child. I was going to be a dad. I had never been happier.

A few days later, I was working at Bush when my boss, Val Anderson, swung by my desk. Appropriately, I was working the south Asian desk, located right in the center of the newsroom. Val squatted down, resting her arms on my desk across from me, her hands folded. She was grinning widely. I can still see her now. She started asking me about my trip, why I went, and probing my knowledge of Afghanistan. Then she got to the rub.

"Chris Bowers is not looking to be extended, so we were wondering if you'd like to apply for the post?"

Return to Kabul? Become a foreign correspondent? I was thrilled and honoured. It was why I had gone to Afghanistan, to see what it was like, establish my name, and open the door to these kinds of opportunities.

Of course, there would have to be a formal application and interview process—the BBC was and is committed to equal opportunities. But it sounded like the job was pretty much mine for the asking.

But my mind was consumed with practical difficulties. My wife was pregnant with our first child. Kabul was simply too dangerous for a family. The spouses and families of the UN and other non-governmental organization workers in Kabul were all in Peshawar, just across the border in Pakistan. That was not a very pleasant place for a young family, and at best I'd only be able to visit once a month. I couldn't bear the thought of being apart from her and my new child that much. Then there was all the danger of working in a war zone. It would be cruel to leave a child without a father at such a tender age. (I was also deterred not a little by the fact that you were never off the clock; a correspondent has to work pretty much 24/7, looking for stories, making contacts. That was not very appealing to someone wanting to spend time with their kids.)

So I did not apply for the job of Kabul correspondent. That honour was taken by my friend and colleague, Susannah (Suzy) Price, who—with help from our friend Masum—distinguished herself immensely with her courage and skill reporting the collapse of the old regime in Afghanistan and the onset of a new civil war.

As for me, I learned to fly a desk, as they say in the Royal Air Force. I had discovered I had a penchant for staying serene and calm in a crisis, which made me very useful in live radio news production: writing, editing and directing under intense pressure. While some people broke down and cried from the strain, I took it in my stride. I was useful and at the same time I was not exposed directly to the horrors of war.

I don't recall thinking about the physical dangers of working in Kabul as a deterrent to applying for the job. I had tried to accept them as an occupational hazard. In time, I have come to realize that perhaps subconsciously my fear did influence the decision.

Anyway, everything happens for a reason. Or rather, there are no mistakes, only experiences. Our experiences, our mistakes, make us who we are.

৪◈৪ ৪◈৪ ৪◈৪

I had no idea what I had been through in Afghanistan. As I said, it didn't seem special or unusual compared to the stories I heard from so many colleagues at the BBC, let alone military veterans, or those heroes at the HALO Trust. So I tried to dismiss it and carry on.

I became irritable, easily frustrated, quickly moved to tears by suffering and joy, and even a little jumpy. Fireworks unsettled me. I couldn't bear to see violence on TV crime dramas. I'd seen too much blood.

A few years later, I started to dream.

The details often change, like who I am with and what is happening. But the theme is pretty constant. I am in peril and in the midst of a difficult, terrifying journey to get to a place of relative safety, to get away from some kind of camp that I've been visiting. The context might vary, but there always seems to be dusty mountains. Then one day I woke up and realized the people in the background, and sometimes in the foreground, are Afghans. Occasionally, Afghans are pursuing me across London. Sometimes I am being taken captive again. Threatened with death. Sometimes I am being executed. Usually just on the run. Sometimes, I wake drenched in sweat. Occasionally I bolt upright, yelling or gasping, at the moment of execution.

It's odd. I've had plenty of traumatic experiences in my life, but my subconscious always takes me back to Afghanistan.

Occasionally I'd be triggered during my wakeful moments. Reading a story, or producing an interview with a victim of trauma, or watching the movie, *Black Hawk Down,* for the first time. Inwardly, I'd get a visceral reaction, and feel like I was back there and vulnerable again. Outwardly, I'd react inappropriately, by saying stupid things or making jokes. Sometimes I'd drink to distract myself.

This went on for a few years. It was never disabling; never so bad as to prevent me from functioning. Only occasionally was I unable to get back to sleep, or back to work. It just became part of my life.

Anyway, one sunny Tuesday in September, a plane flew into the World Trade Center in New York City. I was working in Boston for a US-based BBC co-production called *The World*. I remember asking our researcher to find out how many people worked in the World Trade Center. Fifty thousand, she said. I shared with the newsroom the realization that this could be worse than Pearl Harbor. Then another plane flew into the other tower, live on TV in front of us. We were all in shock. And traumatized. Like the nation, And the rest of the world. Our assumption of safety and security was temporarily shattered. But I had one more problem than everyone else. I was the safety guy for *The World*. Our program relied on my judgment as to whether reporters should go to dangerous places, and how. I would have to decide who went to war, and there was one place for sure that would be first on the list: Afghanistan. The terrorist group responsible for 9/11, al-Qaeda, was based there, sheltered by their allies, the Taliban, who controlled 90% of the country. Ahmed Shah Massoud had controlled the other 10%, until his assassination by al-Qaeda just two days prior to 9/11, at the very same base in the Farkhar Valley where I had met him.

My own life was in turmoil at this time, too. On September 10th 2001, my wife and I had separated. It was our 13th anniversary. I had begun the process of moving out to an apartment the day before 9/11.

My kids were sent home early from school that fateful Tuesday and got home just in time to see people falling from the Twin Towers. Later that week, as I was tucking my 9-year-old son into bed, he asked me if a plane hit the Hancock Tower—the tallest building in Boston—would it fall on our house?

That Friday, I helped fish a young fellow off the rail tracks at Harvard subway station, after he fainted. What a week!

That Sunday I went to church for the first time in a long while and prayed with a priest after the service, to ask for courage and wisdom in sending my people off to war.

On the 19th of September 2001, I wrote to the US Army recruitment folks online, outlining my military experience and knowledge of Afghanistan, and asking to enlist. I'd prefer to go back into the infantry but would serve however and wherever needed. I never heard back. I did not follow up, since it soon became clear just how much my place of work needed me to help keep our correspondents as safe as possible. No one else in our little newsroom had ever been close to anything like the things I had seen in Afghanistan.

I was good at my job, I think. Nobody was killed or wounded on my watch over the two decades that I wore the safety hat. But we had a few scares along the way.

On October 7th 2001, the US began its assault on Taliban-controlled Afghanistan. It unfolded as I predicted, with air strikes and special forces trying to rally a coalition of local forces that could fight against the Taliban and al-Qaeda. We had one reporter in Pakistan trained and ready to cross the border, Jennifer Glasse. She went in over the mountains in mid-November, with a local Afghan strongman and a couple of other journalists.

The next morning I awoke to hear the awful news that an unidentified female journalist had been killed. Jennifer was not responding to calls or any communications. I rushed to the office. The victim had been found on the very same road where I expected Jennifer to be—without any ID. I heard she looked southern European, like Jennifer.

Jennifer's step-mother called me.

I could only assure her that the victim was part of a group that did not fit the profile of the group that Jennifer was traveling with, and that she had been trained to be more cautious. Needless to say, it was an anxious day as we repeatedly tried to get in touch with Jennifer and get more details on the victims. Late in the afternoon, Jenn called in safe and sound. She'd been unable to get access to a satellite phone We learned that the victim was an Italian, Maria Grazia Cutuli. Jenn actually knew Maria from their time reporting from Congo. It was a tragic loss, but I was relieved that my reporter was safe and that I did not have to make that call to her family.

The following year I had all our reporters trained and equipped to cope with nuclear, biological and chemical warfare, in anticipation of the invasion of Iraq. That was long before the rest of the BBC and our competitors. The chem-bio-radiation course was on top of intensive training on surviving in a hostile environment and providing first aid. How things had changed since the days when the only help or advice available to a would-be war correspondent was "wear a pink shirt." Our reporters all had full body armour and ballistic helmets, satellite phones, first aid trauma packs, chem-bio suits and gas masks, communications plans detailing how often they should check in and a reaction plan if they missed a call; plus we had access to the "security" teams hired by the BBC, for emergencies.

I personally had to make the decision whether to leave our reporter in Baghdad when the invasion looked imminent. I was awake all night on that one. Eventually I decided the risks were manageable, and that I myself, as a father of young kids, would be willing to take them. I respected his courage for taking the assignment. He soon after left us for NBC, where he's now a senior correspondent. I was pleased for him, as our managers had not all treated him well. However, I was disappointed by his book in which he states he went to Baghdad alone and unsupported. That was not the case. I still have the documentation.

Earlier in this book, I also related the advice I gave Quil Lawrence, up in the north of Iraq, regarding landmines, during the invasion. I believe that helped keep him safe.

My experience in Afghanistan definitely helped me be better at this part of my job: preparing people for war. In particular, sharing my experience of believing that I was well-prepared for a visit to a conflict zone. Being confident, resourceful and well-informed cannot prepare you for blood and terror.

Anyway, it was around this time, in the mid-2000s that the regular nightmares about my own time in Afghanistan began to recede. Perhaps it was because I'd found a use for the experience. One that I believe helped others stay alive. I don't know.

I apologize for saying "no" so often to reporters who wanted to push the envelope, but safety has to come first. I've been there. I'm proud to say that every reporter that I commissioned came home in one piece, although some still endured trauma.

It's inevitable with war.

☃ ☃ ☃

I was always baffled by US policy in Afghanistan after the invasion in 2001. I thought the opening phase had been handled well. From my experience in 1991 and 1992, I understood that war in Afghanistan is as much about prestige and momentum as it is raw military power. The US quickly created a winning combination with its air power and the local alliances made by the CIA and special forces, including with our old friends, Abdul Rashid Dostum (of the Jowzjanis), Sayed Jafar Naderi (the Belushi-esque governor Baghlan) and Ahmed Shah Massoud's successor, Muhammad Fahim.

One day in early December 2001, my correspondent, Jennifer Glasse, called in with urgent news. A source had seen a mass of abandoned Taliban and Al-Qaeda vehicles, mostly pickup trucks, at the end of a valley. Hundreds of them. Their occupants could go no further by car, and had followed the trails on foot up steep hills to a place called Tora Bora. Tora Bora was well-known as a fortified cave complex used as a focal point for resistance to the Soviets, back in the day. Jennifer and I immediately realized this was going to be the golden opportunity of the campaign, for the US and its allies. Clearly, high value targets had just tried to do a runner toward the famous defensive positions up in the mountains there. It was obvious to me that Tora Bora had to be quickly surrounded, or Osama Bin Laden and his chums would escape to Pakistan. This was not something that could be trusted to local allies or Pakistani border police. My hunch was that a full brigade of US airborne troops would be there by nightfall. They were there in Kandahar, ready to go. It would be a dangerous mission, but surely worth it. They never went. An investigation in 2009 by the US Senate Committee on Foreign Relations backed up my hunch, concluding that the US had failed to commit enough troops to the action at Tora Bora and that Bin Laden's escape had prolonged the war. One suspects that President Bush was too afraid of US casualties.

Once the Taliban and al-Qaeda were chased out of power, I saw no reason for the US to stay in Afghanistan. It was obvious that US troops would only become the targets of wrath for a population opposed to any foreign presence. I knew firsthand how Afghans resented any kind of foreign control. Just support whatever alliance of warlords was necessary to keep the Taliban out, or even just to keep them weak. Use Afghans with skin in the game. Maybe send in the occasional air strike in an emergency, and deploy special forces if a target like Osama bin Laden popped up. It would not be stable, but it's Afghanistan. It must find its own equilibrium. Outsiders can tilt the scale, but maintaining troops and bases there could only end in an expensive failure.

Instead, there was a continued international presence, with no apparent purpose. I understand that Iraq took centre stage for the Bush administration—a colossal blunder in its own right, and still to my mind an unjustified war of choice. But it was a terrible mistake to try to think the US could stay in Afghanistan, or worse still, try to remake Afghanistan in its own image. What hubris?

This was obvious to any serious observer by 2009, when the Obama administration came into office. Vice-President Biden rightly suggested drawing down the military presence to a bare minimum, and using air power and counter-terrorist specialists if necessary. Instead, President Obama chose to double down, and surged troops to Afghanistan. In my analysis, that was a strategy based solely on domestic US politics. The left in the US had been critical of Bush for taking America's eye off the ball in Afghanistan when he invaded Iraq. The right in the US saw Obama as weak. My opinion is that Obama just wanted to give himself political cover for evacuating Iraq. He acted tough in Afghanistan to get out of Baghdad, despite knowing that the Afghan surge was a useless waste. I'm not a real Afghan "expert," but I've heard several agree with me.

So here we are, twenty years after 9/11. Joe Biden is now president and is implementing the policy he proposed in 2009. It might have worked then, when the Taliban was much weaker. But in 2021, it's been a disaster. The government that America had defended for twenty years collapsed like a house of cards.

The decision to withdraw was long overdue. But the manner in which it was executed was a disgrace. It did not need to be this way. The US military footprint had been insignificant since 2014. It was not a problem with Afghan courage either: Afghans have been dying by the tens of thousands every year to fight the Talibs. Kabul had the resources at the start of the campaign in April 2021 to contain the predictable Taliban offensive. So what went wrong?

The defeat was largely psychological. The US made it plain that it had no confidence in the Kabul government, destroying its *izzat*, or prestige, and leaving ordinary Afghan soldiers feeling abandoned. So why die for a hopeless cause?

That's the true parallel with 1992 and 2001—even the British wars of 1841 and 1880. War in Afghanistan is all about prestige and momentum. If you appear to be succeeding, you attract support, which in turn makes success more likely. Loyalty is always malleable in Afghanistan. Desertion is less stigmatized there than in the West.

I'm ashamed that the US government failed to appreciate this—or worse, that they understood this and failed to act to maintain confidence in Kabul. Now the friends I left behind must face a new wave of religious lunacy, murder, rape and robbery.

By contrast, when Moscow decided to pull out in the late 1980s, they did everything possible to help preserve their successor regime. President Najibullah was given a free hand to play Afghan politics, mobilizing local interests to join the fight. If the Soviet Union had not itself collapsed, Afghanistan would have faced a very different path in the 1990s.

But it's not all doom and gloom. Despite their apparently easy victory, the Taliban will not find it easy to rule Afghanistan. The same facts of geography, politics and culture that helped sustain their insurgency will now make it difficult to impose direct control in every corner of the country. One thing has united the Afghan "resistance": hatred of foreign rule. Now that the foreigners are gone, it's easy to foresee new divisions emerging among competing personalities, regions, or interpretations of Islam. The Taliban already have their own war with ISIS.

More importantly, there are huge constituencies within Afghanistan that are repelled by the Taliban's extremism: the cities, the minorities, the educated, and, of course, women. In the long run, these constituencies will likely overwhelm the Taliban, whose power is rooted largely in rural Pashtun areas.

There's no doubt that Afghanistan faces a time of severe testing in the next few years. The Afghan people may continue to suffer from war and instability. But they have to find their own way. My old guide, Dr Abdullah, is involved in talks with the Taliban. I hope and pray that Afghanistan finds an equilibrium sooner rather than later, and ideally, one that is just and tolerant. Afghans deserve it.

My time in Afghanistan definitely changed me.

I grew up.

I lost my naïve excitement when it came to thinking about war and conflict. They're awful and should be avoided at all costs. We all know that; but I *feel* it. Viscerally. I mean, my body shakes with anger when politicians, pundits or activists casually talk about starting a conflict. The physical, mental and moral damage that war and conflict bring to a society far outweighs the temporary excitement of thinking you can be part of history. Starting a conflict—ripping away the illusion of safety from a people—is a crime and should be treated as such.

That trip changed me in other ways, too. It made me realize I would probably have been a terrible soldier, if I had ever been deployed to a combat zone. I'm too emotional. I have too much imagination. Maybe I could have kept calm and done my job for a while, but I think real combat would have messed up my head, big time.

There were benefits. I have some good stories. I wouldn't trade them for the world. And I like to think that my time in Afghanistan made me kinder and more empathetic. I know I became more tolerant, and I discarded what remained of the late imperial mindset that I had been fed in my youth.

I believe my experience gave me insight and empathy for those living through trauma. Sometimes the empathy can be too much, and occasionally after a hard interview, I can't stop myself from crying alone in the studio. Emotional Chris.

I certainly feel for veterans, for people who have lived in war zones, and for survivors of trauma more broadly. I had a stressful time in Afghanistan, but it was only a shadow of what many people endure. Next time you meet a combat veteran or a refugee, understand that they have seen and endured and, perhaps, done things you cannot imagine. Don't pity them. Don't shy away from them. Just understand and accept that they may think, act and react differently. Talking about it can be helpful, or it can trigger the nightmares again. Respect their choice about whether to talk or not.

I've also learned to live a little more in the moment. You have to. You never know how many moments you've got.

I've never regretted my trip. I love having lived. I love the insights I've gained into human nature and the realities of how the world works. But all these things came at the price of enduring that intense stress.

Since the routine nightmares receded, the trauma of my trip to Afghanistan has come back now and then, in different forms. Most recently while writing this book. Over time, I learned to cope when triggered in the daytime. Eventually, with help, I learned to be able to recognize what was happening and found ways to work through it. I learned to allow myself to feel the feelings, accept them and also acknowledge that it's over.

In 2015 my second marriage broke down. As my wife watched somebody die violently on a TV show, the fake blood triggered my old memories. I allowed myself to go back down that road of reprocessing everything I'd seen in Afghanistan. I knew how to work through it. How to accept its existence and get it back in its box. But on this particular night, I consciously allowed myself to dwell on it. It was easier to relive a trauma I could process, than to contemplate the new one caused by the breakdown of my marriage.

Again, in the summer of 2016, I made this journal entry:

"Well, that may not have been too smart. Just on a plane to London and started watching Whiskey Tango Foxtrot, *the Tina Fey action-comedy about reporter Kim Baker's time in Afghanistan. The imagery took me right back, along with the presentation of some of the weirdness of the lives of journalists, and the amazingness of the fixers.*

"What a time it was. Crazy, really, that two weeks could have such an effect on my life. I know I didn't see or suffer much compared to so many people who were there before or since. But this was my experience, and I'm writing it down because my daughter asked me to."

Now it's done. Hopefully I can finally put it to bed. *Inshallah.*

Epilogue: Other Outcomes

About a month after I left Kabul I was surprised to get some mail from Afghanistan. It was a card from **Masum**, wishing me a Merry Christmas and a Happy New Year, and a brief letter saying how much he enjoyed my company. I was deeply touched. I still have them. He may have just been thinking I would apply for the Kabul job, but it felt sincere and caring. He was such a decent guy. Eighteen months later, in May 1993, I was shocked to hear the terrible news that Masum had died. He had survived multiple revolutions, he'd survived military service, he'd navigated all the hazards of working as a journalist in a country in the midst of a civil war, he'd survived the fall of Kabul to the Mujahidin and the bloodbath that followed, only to die in a stupid plane crash. The pilot was apparently flying too low and hit a mountain. So sudden. So arbitrary. So heart-wrenching. Such a decent man. Lost. The BBC did what it could for his family, and those of us who knew him contributed what we could and campaigned for more. It felt insignificant and inadequate. Chris Bowers and Suzy Price both wrote moving tributes to him for the BBC World Service. I have reproduced them in the appendix, with their kind permission.

Chris Bowers left Kabul in the spring of 1992 for a new post in Tashkent, Uzbekistan, the first BBC bureau in former Soviet central Asia. But after a couple of years he left the BBC and we lost touch. He worked for a variety of international humanitarian organizations, including a troubling time during the genocide in Rwanda. Chris later worked for the British government as a diplomat. In 2008, he was serving in the British Embassy in Moscow during a period of tension over the killing in London of Russian dissident, Alexander

Litvinenko. Some media in Moscow alleged Chris was a spy. The British Government as a matter of policy neither confirms nor denies this type of accusation. Chris later served as head of mission in Iraqi Kurdistan and has since been back to Moscow after leaving the Foreign Office. He now lives and works in London as a political adviser to an international corporation. We lost touch until reconnecting in 2020.

The sandbags at the residence of Bulgarian Ambassador in Kabul, **Valentin Gatsinski**, did not prevent him from being wounded in a missile attack on Kabul on 23rd August 1992. He survived, but immediately afterwards Valentin and most other foreign diplomats were withdrawn from Afghanistan. Despite the fall of the communist government in Bulgaria, he remained in the country's diplomatic service, becoming First Deputy Foreign Minister. It was during this time he restructured the Bulgarian foreign ministry along British lines, with a permanent civil service, and an elected politician at the head of the department. Apparently he was inspired by the BBC TV sit-com, "Yes, Minister." Chris Bowers had given him a boxed set. Valentin was later Bulgaria's ambassador to Japan, and then joined the United Nations, serving as humanitarian and security coordinator for the UN in the north Caucasus region of Russia in 2004. I have not been able to determine his current whereabouts.

Fred Estall, the Kiwi bulldog, continued working for the United Nations and other organizations in Afghanistan for many years, mostly in de-mining. His grit and sense of humor were well-known and respected. A few weeks after I left Kabul, Fred made a spectacular appearance at the New Year's Eve Grand Ball at Kabul's Bagh-e-Bala palace, dancing to Swan Lake with some other burly aid workers, all dressed in ballet tutus. He's now retired. I was not able to reconnect with him until after the manuscript for this book was put to bed. We talked about our trip—the "mission" as he called it. I told him how I found the experience "disagreeable" on the whole, and how much respect I had for people like himself who lived and worked there for years. Fred wrote: "I am sure if you had continued, you would have adapted. Just going to see for yourself displays challenge to the norm, and resilience. Don't worry, we all faced the same internal question."

Then this grizzled old vet added: "If that was your first trip, you did well." I was surprised how much those simple words moved me. The sense of relief was intense. If you have never been somewhere like Afghanistan in wartime, I don't think you can appreciate how much that means. In the eyes of a man as experienced as Fred Estall, I did all right.

Alex Shaw, the ex-Gurkha officer and de-mining volunteer, left Afghanistan just a few weeks after me, to set-up a HALO Trust operation in Cambodia, where a ceasefire had just been announced. He says Cambodia was far more intense than Afghanistan. He stayed about a year, but eventually realized that when you're working in minefields every day, you can only be lucky for so long. He went on to enjoy a successful career in business. We reconnected in 2020.

Ahmed Shah Massoud rightfully remains known as one of the greatest military commanders of the 20th century. His reputation was tarnished during the warlord era that followed the collapse of the communist regime, especially when Kabul was shelled heavily. But he was a steadfast opponent of the Taliban and their extremism. He was assassinated by al-Qaeda on 9th September 2001, by terrorists posing as journalists, in the very same camp where we met him. They knew he had a weakness for the media. The bomb was in their TV camera. I went into the newsroom that fateful Tuesday warning that al-Qaeda must be planning something big, thinking they'd make a play in Afghanistan or the region. I had absolutely no idea of what was to come. Massoud's assassination looks like it was part of al-Qaeda's 9/11 plan; they knew the US would try to retaliate in Afghanistan, so they sought to eliminate America's most obvious potential ally. His memory is revered like a saint by many people in the regions he championed in northern and eastern Afghanistan. The day of his martyrdom is now a national holiday.

Our guide, **Abdullah**, became Ahmed Shah Massoud's right-hand man. He was seen as a man of conscience in a world of unprincipled treachery. In some ways he took on Massoud's political mantle after his boss was assassinated by al-Qaeda. He became Minister of Foreign Affairs in the government of Hamid Karzai in December 2001, and later ran for president. After a disputed election he became Afghanistan's "chief executive" from 2014 to 2020, and is now negotiating with the Taliban. I have not been able to contact him since we separated in November 1991. He remains known to the world as Abdullah Abdullah, despite telling me he really only has one name.

I very much regret that I have no idea what became of **Dr Haidar**, our kind host with the Red Cross/Red Crescent in Taloqan, and the man who got the message to my office that I would not be able to make my shift on Thursday as I was stuck behind rebel lines. I hope he is well and has been able to continue to care for the community he loved so well.

I have included in the narrative (Chapter 12) most of the details of the fates of the two Soviet POW/MIAs whom I met. **Islam-ud-Din (Nikolai Bystrov)** continued as Massoud's bodyguard for some years. This devout convert to Islam married an Afghan, a communist. He went home in 1995 with Massoud's help, to Krasnodar in southern Russia, for the birth of their child. They were stranded there when the Taliban seized power. Nikolai remains active in Russian efforts to locate remaining POWs and/or their remains in Afghanistan. **Nek Muhammad (Gennadi Tseuma or Tsevma)**, at the time of writing, remains in Kunduz with his family.

The rocking warlord, **Sayed Jafar Naderi**, who looks like John Belushi, and whose help we needed to escape the secret police, continued as governor of Baghlan despite the collapse of the communist regime. "Jeff," jumped ship when he saw the writing on the wall in 1992 and joined the Muj. He became an ally of Massoud. He later helped fight the Taliban till they drove him from power in 1998. He had to flee on foot over the Hindu Kush in winter. He joined the US side after 9/11, and re-entered politics, allied to Abdul Rashid Dostum. However, a rival is now governor of Baghlan province. This metalhead who grew up in Birmingham, England, and Allentown, Pennsylvania, is still someone to be reckoned with in Afghanistan. He"s still a revered leader of the Ismaili sect.

Sayed Mansur Naderi—the stern head of the Ismaili Shia sect in Afghanistan; father of "Jeff," the fun-loving governor of Baghlan. Now in his mid-80s, at the time of writing, he is still active in politics, the head of a party representing Hazaras and Ismailis.

Abdul Rashid Dostum is one of Afghanistan's most capable survivors. He remains the warlord commander of the ethnic Uzbek Jowzjani militia, the guys with the baggy pants. Remember how the communist government of Najibullah trusted him with their security during my visit, in the final months of the regime? Well, he soon realized which way the winds were blowing, cut a deal with Ahmed Shah Massoud and betrayed the hand that had fed him for 12 years. He later fought the Taliban, and was one the first warlords to join the US fight against the Taliban after 9/11. Readers may recall him as the alleged author of two serious massacres during the US invasion. He allegedly put hundreds of Taliban prisoners into shipping containers to bake alive. He also brutally suppressed an uprising of Taliban prisoners at a fortress near Mazar-i-Sharif, after the prisoners killed CIA agent, Mike Spann, the first US fatality in Afghanistan. I had the distinctly uncomfortable experience of meeting and sitting next to one of his sons at a conference in Washington in 2018, not long after his father allegedly ordered the kidnapping and rape of a cabinet minister in the Kabul government—a government he allegedly still supported. Despite all that, Dostum remained a viable player in Afghanistan. It's as if our ideas of democracy are nonsense, and what matters in Afghanistan are these networks of local power. Like me, it seems, the world was just bumbling through the Hindu Kush.

A Note on Sources and
Methods and Memory

Everything in this book happened. To me. Or was witnessed by me. I have done everything possible to ensure that it's truthful. I know memory can play tricks, so, dear reader, you deserve a quick note about how I was able to recall dates and events from decades ago. I confess that I was surprised, more than once, when confronted with evidence that contradicted my recall. But overall, as I've researched and fact-checked, I've been pleasantly surprised by how accurate my recollections have been.

In terms of evidence, I have few contemporary documents, but I have tried to extrapolate every detail possible from every passport stamp and such.

I wrote copious notes on the flight home, but have not been able to locate them, having bounced around the continents of the world since then. Periodically, in the intervening years, I have jotted down scenes and dialogue, for myself, or in letters and emails.

But my mainstay has been a set of 90 photos, with notes on the back written as soon as they were developed. That has helped immensely with names and titles and places, and in correcting the imagery in my head. I still have the negatives, and they are numbered, which has been helpful in correcting the sequence of events.

I have also tracked down and spoken with a couple of the principals, and other people who were in Afghanistan at that time. My thanks go particularly to David Hewitson, Alex Shaw and of course, Chris Bowers. But those conversations only helped with a few details, and in corroborating or correcting broad impressions. This one trip—which was so significant for me—was just a single episode in long deployments in multiple hostile environments for these gents.

I was also able to use the power of the Internet to geo-locate some images, and to find out what happened to other principals, in particular the two Russian prisoners of war that I met.

But for the most part, I've had to rely on my own memory. I have told many of these stories many times to friends who would listen, especially in the late 1990s and early 2000s, when the nightmares were at their worst. So the gist of events and impressions is easy to recall. I'm sad that a few details have started to fade away over time. But the core images and dialogues are seared into my consciousness. Ask anyone who's been in a traumatic situation. Time slows down and events get encoded deep in your brain.

It's possible that mistakes remain, but I have not intentionally made anything up, or distorted anything. I've built a career and a reputation as a seeker after truth. What I have written here is my story as I honestly recall it. I have tried to verify and corroborate details where possible with evidence. Where doubt remains, I have mentioned it.

Writing this all down has sometimes been hard, especially reliving some of the awfulness. But I have had a fine old time analyzing each situation, and researching things like the weapons, tactics, personalities and politics of the time. I have learned a lot. I have learned that I was needlessly afraid of some things, and oblivious to other dangers.

The whole process has also been incredibly therapeutic, and for that I am grateful.

Appendices

Appendix 1:
BBC World Service news story on Masum's funeral

MAY 2, 1993 1600 AFGHAN CRASH MEMORIAL Peter Nettleship

HEADLINE: A memorial service has been held in northern Afghanistan for the victims of last week's plane crash, including the BBC journalist, Mohammed Masum

A memorial service has been held at Mazar-i-Sharif in northern Afghanistan for the victims of last week's plane crash. It is now thought more than one hundred people were on board the military plane, which was taking government officials and visitors to anniversary celebrations of the Mujaheddin takeover in the north. (A BBC correspondent who was at the service says the plane broke up completely when it hit a hill in bad weather; there were no identifiable remains, and the victims were buried in a common grave). Among those on board was a BBC journalist, Mohammed Masum, who had sent reports from Kabul for three years, through the Afghan civil war, the Mujahidin takeover of Kabul, and the subsequent bitter internecine fighting. BBC correspondents who have been based during that time have paid tribute to Masum's courage, dedication and bravery in passing on news from the country to the outside world.

Appendix 2:
Despatch from BBC Kabul correspondent, Susannah Price

MAY 2, 1993 PRICE AFGHAN JOURNALIST TRIBUTE KABUL

CUE: Reports from northern Afghanistan have confirmed that BBC journalist Mohammed Masum was killed in a plane crash on Tuesday evening. It is thought that more than a hundred people were on the military plane going from Kabul to the city of Mazar-i-Sharif and there were no survivors. Masum, who was 35, had worked for the BBC for three years, first as a translator, and more recently as a reporter for the Persian and Pashto sections. Suzie Price, who worked with him in Kabul for the past year, looks back at the time they spent together.

"Masum was much than a dedicated journalist working for the BBC. He was also one of my best friends in Afghanistan. A lot of people felt the same. His natural optimism and easy laugh made him a popular figure in Kabul and in the north where he had many friends. I rarely saw him lose his temper during the frequent times of tension we went through together in the past eleven months. Whether we were interviewing the president or a sobbing man whose family had just been killed, Masum always managed to find the right words. He was a natural choice at press conferences to be the impromptu interpreter for the few Western journalists left in Kabul. Masum took a great pride in his work. Before being employed last year as a full-time stringer for the Persian service, he received a very modest salary for his translation work. Although he could have earned much more working for other journalists, Masum always said he could learn much more and improve his journalism skills with the BBC. Money is not the most important thing, he would say. Less than a week ago, his persistent efforts after a Mujahidin press conference in Persian secured an important interview for the Pashto service. He was willing to work all hours for the BBC, occasionally sleeping at the office and often coming in on Fridays, the usual day off. During the terrible rocket attacks on Kabul, he was always willing to risk his own life to go out and see the destruction. We hid in ditches and under stairs together as shells fell around us and used his car as a makeshift ambulance to take the wounded and dying to hospital. It was typical of Masum that when he heard of a flight last Monday to the city of Mazar-i-Sharif, he dashed home and was ready to go, to cover the anniversary celebrations in the north, in less than an hour. That flight was delayed until Tuesday when it tragically crashed. Masum always dreamed of coming to visit London. He was especially fond of the British sense of humour. When Kabul became dangerous, he went to Pakistan to look into moving his wife and three children there. But he missed Afghanistan too much and came back early. Besides his work as a journalist and translator, Masum practically ran the BBC office, making sure bills were paid, petrol bought for the generator, and telex and telephone lines fixed. He had a great appetite for knowledge, always reading or listening to the BBC, had taught himself English, and was learning French. But he also liked to relax. I remember sitting in the garden last summer eating mulberries, he sighed contentedly and said, 'This is the life.' My lasting image of him was a familiar sight, Masum in his flat cap, tea in hand and a huge smile on his face."

SUZIE PRICE, BBC, KABUL

Appendix 3:
Despatch from former BBC Kabul correspondent, Chris Bowers

MAY 2, 1993 BOWERS AFGHAN PERSONAL TRIBUTE MAZAR-I-SHARIF

CUE: In Afghanistan, the remains of more than 70 people killed in a plane crash, including Mohammed Masum, who worked for the BBC, have been buried near the northern town of Tashkorghan. (*ED: now Kholm or Khulm, in Balkh province, 60 miles east of Mazar.) A group of soldiers from Mazar-i-Sharif combed the hillside where the plane crashed on Tuesday night, and brought the remains, which were unidentifiable, back to Tashkorghan. They were buried in a common grave near to the Bagh-i-Jahan Nama fort, built by Abdur Rahman Khan. Masum's BBC diary and notebook were found at the scene. Our

Central Asia correspondent, Chris Bowers, has been to the crash site in the Kohi Kopak Hills above Tashkorghan. Prior to being based in Tashkent, he reported from Kabul, covering the fall of the city to the Mujahidin one year ago. Chris Bowers worked together with Masum during that time and sent us this personal tribute to him:

"I first met Masum two years ago as I arrived somewhat bewildered at Kabul airport. He asked me how long I would stay. 'About one year,' I replied, and for the first time I heard Masum's characteristic gasp of surprise and cackle of infectious laughter. I took to him immediately and we became friends. My respect for him grew. We were once interviewing an important politician who insisted on using his own interpreter. The interview dragged. The politician refused to reply directly on an important issue. Growing impatient, I told him he was wasting our time and asked bluntly whether he was going to answer or not. The politician's translator balked, not used to young foreigners talking like that to his boss. As he mumbled a round-about, watered-down translation, Masum stepped in, but with far more charm than I could muster. We got our answer. In a conflict, bravery is usually associated with storming machine gun posts and the like. Masum did none of that and was proud of the fact that he'd never killed anyone. But I met few people in Kabul with more steadfast courage than he. Whatever pressure I came under working for the BBC in Kabul, I knew it was only a fraction of what Masum faced. He took it all, and through the darkest time, it was he who kept my spirits up. Above all he was a patriot, fiercely proud of his country. Coming back from a trip to India where he met exiles, he said whatever happens, Afghans should die in Afghanistan. They can kill me if they want, I will never leave, he said. When one controversial leader returned to Kabul, the question on everyone's lips was why had he come back. Masum told me to forget that; I should ask how he'd dared to come back. Instinctively generous and loyal, he looked for the best in people, whoever they were. He had a rare gift for finding common ground and for putting people at their ease. He was tolerant and sincere, but had a sharp eye for hypocrisy and could spot humbug a mile off. I never saw him bitter. I met few in Kabul who felt the destruction of Afghanistan more keenly than he. He was in tears at the ancient site of Hadda near Jalalabad; it didn't matter who had smashed, shelled, and looted it. Few countries have suffered as much destruction as Afghanistan; few have lost so many of its best people; few have been so abandoned by the rest of the world. People are left to pick through the ruins, trying to piece together a life. Work has to be done. Water has to be carried up muddy paths. Life has to go on. The remains, including his, that were gathered from the hillside were buried in one grave after a brief ceremony. Masum now lies together with other Afghans, as perhaps he would have wished. The grave is in a beautiful location next to a fort built by Abdur Rahman Khan for one of his wives. Masum, like millions of other Afghans, lived through the worst of times. I'll remember his honesty, his good spirits, and his goodness. Most of all, I will never forget his dignity. Our thoughts are with his widow and children.

CHRIS BOWERS, BBC, MAZAR-I-SHARIF

Appendix 4:
Into the Valley of Death
By Chris Bowers, for the BBC programme,
"From Our Own Correspondent" (FOOC)
Reproduced with kind permission of the BBC.

KABUL 20th May 1993

An Afghan who worked for the BBC in the capital, Kabul—first as a translator then as a freelance journalist—Mohammed Masum became yet another casualty of the country's grueling civil war. Our Central Asia Correspondent, Chris Bowers, who spent some time reporting events from Afghanistan, went back to the country for the funeral to see how it had changed since he was last there, a year ago.

The former Soviet Union and Afghanistan are joined by the Friendship Bridge, a hugely inappropriate name for a bridge that bore Soviet tanks into Afghanistan and carried them back a decade later. The gap in terms of development looks, at times, like centuries. The railway line from Central Asia stops abruptly on the former Soviet side. The border guards there are faceless, formal and unsmiling, awash in paperwork; it still feels like the Soviet Union. Cross the bridge and you pass from concrete and grass to mud and dust; from a land where much is wasted, to one where nothing is; from where popular culture and history have been wiped away by Soviet rule, to one where the weight of centuries hits you in the face. I felt myself sliding back noiselessly into a gentle world of open friendliness, charm and languid politeness, in a land where the Cold War happened to have deposited—for a reason now forgotten—thousands upon thousands of Kalashnikovs, tanks and mines. It seems that only the military hardware disrupts the ageless patterns of Afghanistan, standing out horribly and cruelly from the dust and wind that has moved gracefully over this land, changing little.

The Afghan border official (the only one in sight) let down the piece of wire strung across the road, beamed and invited us to fill in a form, in the same breath and in the same manner as he asked us to drink some tea with him. We drove on. A man stopped and looked, his shoeless foot poised on his shovel, prodding at the stony ground. Adjusting his turban, he dipped and pushed down again. Just off the road a ten-foot circle of empty shells served as a gravestone. Bundles of dried grass provided a living for a wizened old man crouching over a stick. Another man tried to pull a piece of metal from the burnt-out chassis of a lorry that had already been stripped of every-thing of value. As he tugged, the rest of the twisted metal rocked gently, like a bridge in the wind that linked one patch of desert to another. My driver, a Russian, gripped the steering wheel tighter each time we passed a clump of armed men squatting by the road. Afghanistan is still a dangerous land. Ahead of us still, the snow-capped Hindu Kush mountains.

I was back, but my business was death. More than a million dead in Afghanistan over the last 14 years, but the death of Masum, my colleague and companion for a year, had hit me like a punch in the stomach. They say that death is always as unexpected as a plane falling out of the sky. That was just how it was for Masum. We left the northern Afghan plain, drove off the road and then walked up the mountain into which the over-burdened, badly maintained transport plane had smashed. Fifteen men came with us. They picked up the remains—one small cloth bag each—of more than 70 people. What was left fitted into a wooden trunk the size of the table I am now writing on. By chance, perhaps by providence, I found Masum's BBC diary and bloodstained notebook. More of his paper than of his body had survived the crash.

I went on down to Kabul over the Hindu Kush, by bus this time. The responsibilities of power have done little to mend the divisions and rivalries that bedeviled the Mujahidin while fighting the Red Army. One year after Mujahidin fighters swept into the capital, Kabul Radio can—without a hint of irony—announce proudly that some of the forces loyal to the Prime Minister-designate have agreed not to fight the president's men.

The state in Afghanistan remains untended: that means that the schools in Kabul have been closed for a year; there is no power for half of the time; and planes do not get maintained but still fly—until they crash. That accounted for Masum. Of the rest of the people who worked with me in Kabul, the cook—a kind, gentle man—dons a rifle when he finishes work and, for two hours a night, patrols his district on the lookout for marauders. I didn't dare ask him how often he has to fire his gun. The gardener was kidnapped on the grounds of his ethnic background: he is from a minority group. He says he was beaten up. All I know is that he didn't have grey hair before. The washerwoman has sent her children abroad. The driver left his house because of the shelling. Who knows what has happened to it?

The innocent, medieval charm of Afghanistan wears off when you look inside one of its hospitals or hear the dull thud of artillery exchanges, day and night—as pointless as birds twittering in the morning. Shells, fired with little concern for accuracy, have knocked down trees that, in turn, have fallen on and broken some headstones in the small European cemetery. It marks the graves of 1970s hippies, 1930s philanthropists and 1870s British would-be conquerors.

Afghanistan—one of the most beautiful, proud and heart-wrenching of countries—is still tearing itself apart. A land that for Afghans is sacred—if only, perhaps, because so many dead lie around.

THE END

CPSIA information can be obtained
at www.ICGtesting.com
Printed in the USA
LVHW012014240921
698705LV00006B/45

9 781737 530350